Communications
in Computer and Information Science   1689

Andrzej Dziech · Wim Mees ·
Marcin Niemiec (Eds.)

Multimedia Communications, Services and Security

11th International Conference, MCSS 2022
Kraków, Poland, November 3–4, 2022
Proceedings

Editors
Andrzej Dziech
AGH University of Science and Technology
Kraków, Poland

Wim Mees
Royal Military Academy
Brussels, Belgium

Marcin Niemiec
AGH University of Science and Technology
Kraków, Poland

ISSN 1865-0929 ISSN 1865-0937 (electronic)
Communications in Computer and Information Science
ISBN 978-3-031-20214-8 ISBN 978-3-031-20215-5 (eBook)
https://doi.org/10.1007/978-3-031-20215-5

This Springer imprint is published by the registered company Springer Nature Switzerland AG
The registered company address is: Gewerbestrasse 11, 6330 Cham, Switzerland

Preface

In recent years, multimedia communications, services and cybersecurity have contributed extensively to our life experience and are expected to be among the most important applications in the future. However, multimedia and cybersecurity are still hot topics in modern science and technology. Multimedia communication technology is one of the most diverse and multidisciplinary fields of research. Cybersecurity is crucial for network services and users in cyberspace. The 11th International Conference on Multimedia Communications, Services & Security (MCSS 2022) considers both fields of research.

This year's edition of MCSS was characterized by a diversity of topics that perfectly illustrates the wealth of issues that are positioned at the center of scientific interest of researchers, who have demonstrated their commitment to these areas. Consequently, according to the MCSS conference prerogative, the reader of this proceedings book will find a discussion of the issues belonging to the main topics of the conference such as cybersecurity, multimedia processing, and analysis and systems architectures and designs.

A significant part of this edition of the MCSS conference was dedicated to cybersecurity at the European level - more specifically, to the outcomes of the ECHO EU project - "European network of Cybersecurity centers and competence Hub for innovation and Operations". This H2020 project connects and shares knowledge across multiple domains to develop a common cybersecurity strategy for Europe. The readers of this proceedings book will find some important concepts designed and developed in the ECHO project. A novel multi-sector risk management framework for analysing cybersecurity challenges and opportunities is introduced. Also, the results of research on sector-specific cybersecurity certifications schemes and maritime-specific training delivered over a cyber range federation are presented. The other results focus on e-skills in cybersecurity, artificial intelligence to ensure the cybersecurity of autonomous transport systems in various domains, and the impact of nonbinary input vectors on the security features of tree parity machines.

Additionally, more application-related work was also presented at the conference, including solutions supporting the effective analysis of the security of diagnostic and repair work on industrial devices or a brain-computer interface toolkit. The other papers consider secrecy performance in cooperative satellite networks, attacks detection in the popular signalling system no. 7, different types of technologies for police forces, data selection in big data, and assessing video quality for automatic license plate recognition.

As the Editors, we do hope that every participant of MCSS 2022, as well as other readers of this proceedings book, will appreciate the possibility of broadening their knowledge, thanks to the detailed and careful presentation of ideas, methods, and achieved results by their authors.

November 2022

Dziech Andrzej
Mees Wim
Niemiec Marcin

Organization

General Chairs

Andrzej Dziech	AGH University of Science and Technology, Poland
Wim Mees	Royal Military Academy, Belgium
Marcin Niemiec	AGH University of Science and Technology, Poland
Andrzej Czyżewski	Gdansk University of Technology, Poland

Executive Committee

Matteo Merialdo	RHEA Systems, Belgium
Nikolai Stoianov	Bulgarian Defence Institute, Bulgaria
Marton Kis	Semmelweis University Health Service Management Training Center, Hungary

Program Committee

Remigiusz Baran	Kielce University of Technology, Poland
Michael Cooke	National University of Ireland Maynooth, Ireland
Andrzej Czyżewski	Gdansk University of Technology, Poland
Jan Derkacz	AGH University of Science and Technology, Poland
Andrzej Duda	Grenoble Institute of Technology, France
Andrzej Dziech	AGH University of Science and Technology, Poland
Luis Angel Galindo	Telefonica, Spain
Oleg Illiashenko	National Aerospace University (KhAI), Ukraine
Vasilis Katos	Bournemouth University, UK
Vyacheslav Kharchenko	National Aerospace University (KhAI), Ukraine
Marton Kis	Semmelweis University Health Service Management Training Center, Hungary
Chrisitan Kollmitzer	AIT Austrian Institute of Technology, Austria
Paweł Korus	New York University, USA
Bożena Kostek	Gdansk University of Technology, Poland
Anton Kummert	University of Wuppertal, Germany
David Larrabeiti	Universidad Carlos III de Madrid, Spain

Mikołaj Leszczuk	AGH University of Science and Technology, Poland
Suresh Manandhar	University of York, UK
Olaf Manuel Maennel	Tallinn University of Technology, Estonia
Andrzej Matiolałski	AGH University of Science and Technology, Poland
Wim Mees	Royal Military Academy, Belgium
Miralem Mechić	University of Sarajevo, Bosnia and Herzegovina
Matteo Merialdo	RHEA Systems, Belgium
Marcin Niemiec	AGH University of Science and Technology, Poland
Nikolai Stoianov	Bulgarian Defence Institute, Bulgaria
Todor Tagarev	Bulgarian Academy of Sciences, Bulgaria
Theodora Tsikrika	Centre for Research and Technology Hellas (CERTH), Greece
Pavel Varbanov	European Software Institute - Center Eastern Europe (ESI CEE), Bulgaria
Miroslav Vozňák	VSB - Technical University of Ostrava, Czech Republic
Jakob Wassermann	University of Applied Sciences Technikum Wien, Austria

Organization Committee

Remigiusz Baran	Kielce University of Technology, Poland
Piotr Bogacki	AGH University of Science and Technology, Poland
Wojciech Chmiel	AGH University of Science and Technology, Poland
Jan Derkacz	AGH University of Science and Technology, Poland
Andrzej Dziech	AGH University of Science and Technology, Poland
Agnieszka Kleszcz	AGH University of Science and Technology, Poland
Paweł Korus	Center for Cybersecurity, New York University, USA
Mikołaj Leszczuk	AGH University of Science and Technology, Poland
Andrzej Matiolański	AGH University of Science and Technology, Poland
Marcin Niemiec	AGH University of Science and Technology, Poland

Tomasz Ruść   University of Computer Engineering and
                                    Telecommunications, Poland

Contents

Secrecy Performance of Scenario with Multiple Antennas Cooperative
Satellite Networks 1
Nhat-Tien Nguyen, Hong-Nhu Nguyen, and Miroslav Voznak

Attack Detection in SS7 11
Charles Beumier and Thibault Debatty

Sector-Specific Training - A Federated Maritime Scenario 21
*Paloma de La Vallée, Georgios Iosifidis, Andrea Rossi, Marco Dri,
and Wim Mees*

E-Skills in Cybersecurity 36
Harri Ruoslahti and Ilkka Tikanmäki

Multi-sector Risk Management Framework for Analysis Cybersecurity
Challenges and Opportunities 49
*Marcin Niemiec, Salvatore Marco Pappalardo, Maya Bozhilova,
Nikolai Stoianov, Andrzej Dziech, and Burkhard Stiller*

AI Cybersecurity Assurance for Autonomous Transport Systems:
Scenario, Model, and IMECA-Based Analysis 66
*Vyacheslav Kharchenko, Oleg Illiashenko, Herman Fesenko,
and Ievgen Babeshko*

Integration of Image Analysis Component with Industrial Workflow
Management System 80
*Wojciech Chmiel, Stanisław Jędrusik, Piotr Kadłuczka,
Joanna Kwiecień, Zbigniew Mikrut, Dariusz Pałka, and Michał Turek*

Impact of Nonbinary Input Vectors on Security of Tree Parity Machine 94
Miłosz Stypiński and Marcin Niemiec

Approach to Sector-Specific Cybersecurity Schemes: Key Elements
and Security Problem Definition   104
  Consuelo Colabuono, Douglas Wiemer, Maria Vittoria Marabello,
  Domenico Lofù, Marco Pappalardo, Piotr Bogacki, Andrzej Dziech,
  Jan Derkacz, Luis Angel Galindo Sanchez, Ewa Konieczna,
  Maya Bojilova, Giuseppe Chechile, Riccardo Feletto,
  Marco Dri, Massimo Zamagni, Emanuele Sansebastiano,
  Grégory Depaix, Cyril Ceresola, Bernard Opic, Massimo Ravenna,
  Marco Quartullo, Andrea Guarino, Paolo Modica, Raniero Rapone,
  Massimiliano Tarquini, and Stefano Armenia

Technology and Police: A Way to Create Predicting Policing   118
  Abel Gonzalez-Garcia and Luis Angel Galindo Sanchez

BCI: Technologies and Applications Review and Toolkit Proposal   126
  Tânia Rocha, Diana Carvalho, Pedro Letra, Arsénio Reis,
  and João Barroso

Clustering-Based Filtering of Big Data to Improve Forecasting
Effectiveness and Efficiency   144
  Tiago Pinto, Tânia Rocha, Arsénio Reis, and Zita Vale

Method for Assessing Objective Video Quality for Automatic License
Plate Recognition Tasks   153
  Mikołaj Leszczuk, Lucjan Janowski, Jakub Nawała, and Atanas Boev

Author Index   167

Secrecy Performance of Scenario with Multiple Antennas Cooperative Satellite Networks

Nhat-Tien Nguyen[1], Hong-Nhu Nguyen[2(✉)], and Miroslav Voznak[1]

[1] Faculty of Electrical Engineering and Computer Science, VSB - Technical University of Ostrava, 17. listopadu 2172/15, 708 00 Ostrava, Czechia
{nguyen.nhat.tien.st,miroslav.voznak}@vsb.cz

[2] Faculty of Electronics and Telecommunications, Saigon University, Ho Chi Minh City, Vietnam
nhu.nh@sgu.edu.vn

Abstract. The evolution of communication networks has created a huge requirement for massive connectivity, efficient spectral utilization, and high reliability. With the introduction of non-orthogonal Multiple Access (NOMA) technique, most of the user requirements were satisfied. Since NOMA performs the superimposed transmission of user signals in the same resource block, to differentiate these signals, Successive Interference Cancellation (SIC) technique will be used. Till now, most of the research has focused on combining NOMA with key technologies such as Reconfigurable Intelligent Surfaces (RIS), massive Multiple Input Multiple Output (MIMO), millimeter Waves, etc. Whereas, few works have been done on studying the physical layer security of NOMA in direct cooperative satellite networks. In this paper, we study the connection and secrecy performance of such a system in the presence of two legitimate users and one eavesdropper. Closed-form expressions were derived to understand and simulate device performance. To authenticate these expressions, we also performed the Monte-Carlo simulations.

Keywords: Satellite networks · Non-orthogonal multiple access · MIMO

1 Introduction

Radio access networks (RAN) grant permission to the user to access particular resources of the radio spectrum for the purpose of data transmission [1]. With the evolution of communication networks from 1G to 5G, the performing capability of the network has also elevated in terms of connectivity, latency and user data rates. Numerous Internet of Things (IoT) applications have come into existence like smart homes, automated cars, virtual and augmented reality, etc. These services have demanded the requirements of high reliability, low latency, huge connectivity and high data speed [2–4]. Energy limitations are the most significant problem of IoT networks; however, energy harvesting techniques have also been proposed that have contributed to solving this obstacle [20, 21]. Key technologies such as millimeter wave (mmWave) communications, Multiple Input Multiple Output (MIMO), beamforming, and non-orthogonal Multiple Access

© The Author(s), under exclusive license to Springer Nature Switzerland AG 2022
A. Dziech et al. (Eds.): MCSS 2022, CCIS 1689, pp. 1–10, 2022.
https://doi.org/10.1007/978-3-031-20215-5_1

(NOMA) technique were proposed by the International Telecommunication Union (ITU) to support the development of 5G and 6G communication networks. Integrating the NOMA technique with satellite communication networks is said to be a key development for 5G [5–8].

Comparing the performance metrics of NOMA and Orthogonal Multiple Access (OMA) technique, the NOMA has proved to be more efficient than the older technique. NOMA utilizes the same resource block to transmit the data of multiple users [9–12]. All user signals are superimposed, and these signals are differentiated by allocating different power level coefficients to the different users. The allocation of power levels is based on the channel gain of the user. Users with high channel gain will be allotted less power and low channel gain will be allotted with more power. At the receiver, these signals are separated by performing the successive interference cancellation (SIC) technique. The ability of NOMA to perform massive connectivity, acquire less latency and high reliability has made it a novel approach in many other technologies. Very little research has been done on integrating NOMA with terrestrial networks [13, 14]. In [13], the authors conducted a comprehensive study on Cloud RAN technology employed by NOMA networks. In [14], the authors have considered integrating NOMA assisted MIMO technology and NOMA assisted cooperative relay (CR) technology into the terrestrial network applications.

Research works in [15, 16] have mentioned that the problem of security in satellite terrestrial relay networks (STRN) can be approached using Physical Layer Security (PLS). The general concept of PLS is to provide access to the legitimate users while blocking the malicious users and their interception. In [17] and [18], the authors have investigated the secrecy problems in the cognitive SRTN system. In [22], the authors have proposed the cooperative multi-hop transmission protocol (CMT) in the underlay cognitive radio networks and analyze secrecy outage probability (SOP) with the existence of a secondary eavesdropper. Several studies were performed to understand and neutralize the secrecy issues in NOMA networks [19] and [23]. In [19], the authors have studied the application of PLS in NOMA and derived the full analysis of SOP. In [23], a similar system was studied, but in the presence of perfect SIC and imperfect SIC in both the power domain NOMA and code domain NOMA was studied. Asymptotic mathematical expressions were derived to analyze the performance of the system.

To the best of our knowledge, a few paper has considered secure performance of STRN, this motivates us to study secure STRN relying on multiple antennas.

2 System Model

In this paper, we assume a NOMA cooperative satellite network. We assume a satellite (S), two destinations $D_i (i \in \{1, 2\})$, and an eavesdropper (E) as shown in Fig. 1. Moreover, (S) is equipped with M antennas. In addition, we denote $\mathbf{h}_i$ as the $M \times 1$ Shadowed-Rician channel vector form of S to D_i and $\mathbf{h}_E$ is the $M \times 1$ Shadowed-Rician channel vector form of (S) to E.

Moreover, (S) sends the signal $s = \sqrt{(a_1)}x_1 + \sqrt{(a_2)}x_2$, where a_1, a_2 are the power allocation coefficient and x_1, x_2 are the message of D_1, D_2. Therefore, the received signal

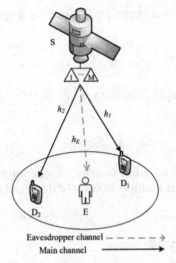

Fig. 1. System model of secure STRN relying on cooperative NOMA.

from S to D_i is given by

$$y_{D_i} = \mathbf{h}_i^\dagger \mathbf{w}_i \left(\sqrt{P_S} \left(\sqrt{a_1} x_1 + \sqrt{a_2} x_2 \right) \right) + v_i \tag{1}$$

where P_S denotes the power transmit at S, a_1 and a_2 are the power allocation coefficient, $(.)^\dagger$ is the conjugate transpose, $v_i \sim CN(0, \sigma_i^2)$ denotes the additive white Gaussian noise (AWGN), $\mathbf{w}_i$ is the $M \times 1$ transmit weight vector and $\mathbf{w}_i = \frac{\mathbf{h}_i}{\|\mathbf{h}_i\|_F}$ as [28], in which $\|\cdot\|_F$ is Frobenius norm.

Next, D_2 is decoded with the signal x_2 and the signal-to-interference-plus-noise-ratio (SINR) is given by

$$\gamma_{D_2, x_2} = \frac{P_S a_2 \|\mathbf{h}_2\|_F^2}{P_S a_1 \|\mathbf{h}_2\|_F^2 + \sigma_2^2} = \frac{\eta_2 a_2}{\eta_2 a_1 + 1} \tag{2}$$

where $\eta_S = \frac{P_S}{\sigma_i^2}$ is the transmitted signal-to-noise ratio (SNR), $\eta_i = \eta_S \|\mathbf{h}_i\|_F^2$. Then, D_1 is decoded with the signal x_1 and the SINR is given by.

$$\gamma_{D_1, x_1} = \frac{P_S a_2 \|\mathbf{h}_1\|_F^2}{P_S a_1 \|\mathbf{h}_1\|_F^2 + \sigma_1^2} = \frac{\eta_1 a_2}{\eta_1 a_1 + 1} \tag{3}$$

with NOMA protocol in [24], by applying SIC to decode its own signal x_1 at D_1, the SNR is given by

$$\gamma_{D_1, x_1} = \eta_1 a_1 \tag{4}$$

Meanwhile, the received signal at E is given by

$$y_E = \mathbf{h}_E \mathbf{w}_E^H \left(\sqrt{P_S} \left(\sqrt{a_1} x_1 + \sqrt{a_2} x_2 \right) \right) + v_E \tag{5}$$

where $v_E \sim (CN, \sigma_E^2)$ Then the SINR of E to detect the signal x_2 of D_2 is given by [25]

$$\gamma_{E,x_2} = \frac{P_S a_2 \|\mathbf{h}_E\|_F^2}{P_S a_1 \|\mathbf{h}_E\|_F^2 + \sigma_E^2} = \frac{\eta_E a_2}{\eta_E a_1 + 1} \tag{6}$$

where $\eta_S = \frac{P_S}{\sigma_E^2}$, $\eta_E = \eta_S \|\mathbf{h}_E\|_F^2$. Similar to D_1, the SINR of E to detect the signal x_1 of D_1 is given by

$$\gamma_{E,x_1} = \eta_E a_1 \tag{7}$$

In the next section, we intend to examine two performance metrics to highlight advances of Non-Orthogonal Multiple Access (NOMA) and multiple antennas scheme to the considered system.

3 Performance Analysis

In this section, we analyze the connection outage probability (COP) and secrecy outage probability (SOP) of D_i. First, the probability density function (PDF) of the channel coefficient h_z^j with $z \in \{1, 2, E\}$ is given by [26]

$$f_{|h_z^j|^2}(\gamma) = \alpha_z e_1^{-\beta_z \gamma} F_1(m_z; 1; \delta_z \gamma), \quad \gamma > 0, \tag{8}$$

where $\alpha_z = \frac{1}{2b_z} \left(\frac{2b_z m_z}{2b_z m_z + \Omega_z} \right)^{m_z}$, $\delta_z = \frac{\Omega_z}{2b_z(2b_z m_z + \Omega_z)}$, m_z is the fading severity parameter, Ω_z and $2b_z$ are the average power of LOS and multipath components, respectively, and $_1F_1(., ., .)$ denotes the confluent hypergeometric function of the first kind [29, 9 .201.1]. Based on [27], we can simplify (8) as

$$f_{|h_z^j|^2}(\gamma) = \alpha_z e^{-(\beta_z - \delta_z)\gamma} \sum_{b=0}^{m_z-1} \zeta_z(b)\gamma^b, \tag{9}$$

where $\zeta_z(b) = (-1)^b (1 - m_z)_b \delta^b/(b!)^2$ and $(.)_b$ is the Pochhammer symbol [29]. Thus, with i.i.d. Shadowed-Rician fading, the PDF of η_z can be expressed by

$$f_{\eta_z}(\gamma) = \sum_{b_1=0}^{m_z-1} \cdots \sum_{b_N=0}^{m_z-1} \frac{\Xi(z)}{(\eta_S)^\Lambda} \gamma^{\Lambda-1} e^{-\frac{(\beta_z - \delta_z)}{\eta_S}\gamma}, \tag{10}$$

3.1 COP of D_2

The COP of D_2 is given by [25]

$$P_2^{COP} = \Pr(\gamma_{D_2,x_2} < \varepsilon_2) \tag{11}$$

where $\varepsilon_i = 2^{R_i} - 1$ and R_i denotes the target rate.

Proposition 1: The COP of D_2 can be obtained as

$$P_2^{COP} = \sum_{b_1=0}^{m_2-1} \cdots \sum_{b_N=0}^{m_2-1} \frac{\Xi(2)}{(\beta_2-\delta_2)^\Lambda} \gamma\left(\Lambda, \frac{(\beta_2-\delta_2)\varepsilon_2}{\eta_S(a_2-\varepsilon_2 a_1)}\right) \tag{12}$$

Proof: With help (2), COP of D_2 can be rewritten as

$$P_2^{COP} = \Pr\left(\eta_2 < \frac{\varepsilon_2}{(a_2-\varepsilon_2 a_1)}\right) = \int_0^{\frac{\varepsilon_2}{(a_2-\varepsilon_2 a_1)}} f_{\eta_2}(x)dx \tag{13}$$

Substituting the PDF in (10) into (13), we obtain the following.

$$P_2^{COP} = \sum_{b_1=0}^{m_2-1} \cdots \sum_{b_N=0}^{m_2-1} \frac{\Xi(2)}{(\eta_S)^\Lambda} \int_0^{\frac{\varepsilon_2}{a_2-\varepsilon_2 a_1}} x^{\Lambda-1} e^{-\frac{(\beta_2-\delta_2)}{\eta_S}x} dx \tag{14}$$

Based on [29, 3.351.1], the closed-form of D_2 is given by

$$P_2^{COP} = \sum_{b_1=0}^{m_2-1} \cdots \sum_{b_N=0}^{m_2-1} \frac{\Xi(2)}{(\beta_2-\delta_2)^\Lambda} \gamma\left(\Lambda, \frac{(\beta_2-\delta_2)\varepsilon_2}{\eta_S(a_2-\varepsilon_2 a_1)}\right) \tag{15}$$

where $\gamma(a, b)$ is the upper incomplete gamma functions.
The proof is completed.

3.2   COP of D_1

The COP of D_1 is written as [25]

$$P_1^{COP} = \Pr\left(\gamma_{D_1,x_1} < \varepsilon_1\right) \tag{16}$$

Substituting (4) into (16), (16) can be rewritten as

$$P_1^{COP} = \Pr\left(\eta_1 < \frac{\varepsilon_1}{a_1}\right) = \int_0^{\frac{\varepsilon_1}{a_1}} f_{\eta_1}(x)dx \tag{17}$$

Similar in Proposition 1, the closed-form of COP for D_1 is given by

$$P_1^{COP} = \sum_{b_1=0}^{m_1-1} \cdots \sum_{b_N=0}^{m_1-1} \frac{\Xi(1)}{(\beta_1-\delta_1)^\Lambda} \gamma\left(\Lambda, \frac{(\beta_1-\delta_1)\varepsilon_1}{\eta_S a_1}\right) \tag{18}$$

3.3 SOP of D_2

As the main result is reported in [25], the SOP of D_2 is expressed as

$$P_2^{SOP} = \Pr\left(\gamma_{E \to x_2} > \varepsilon_2^S\right) \tag{19}$$

where $\varepsilon_i^S = 2^{R_i - R_i^S} - 1$ is the secrecy rate of D_i.

Proposition 2: The exact closed-form SOP of D_2 is given by.

$$P_2^{SOP} = \sum_{b_1=0}^{m_E-1} \cdots \sum_{b_N=0}^{m_E-1} \frac{\Xi(2)}{(\beta_E - \delta_E)^\Lambda} \gamma\left(\Lambda, \frac{(\beta_E - \delta_E)\varepsilon_2^S}{\eta_S(a_2 - \varepsilon_2^S a_1)}\right) \tag{20}$$

Proof: By (6), the SOP of D_2 can be rewritten as.

$$P_2^{SOP} = \Pr\left(\eta_E > \frac{\varepsilon_2^S}{a_2 - \varepsilon_2^S a_1}\right) = \int_{\frac{\varepsilon_2^S}{a_2 - \varepsilon_2^S a_1}}^{\infty} f_{\eta_E}(x)dx \tag{21}$$

With the help of the CDF of η_E (10), we can write (21) as

$$P_2^{SOP} = \sum_{b_1=0}^{m_E-1} \cdots \sum_{b_N=0}^{m_E-1} \frac{\Xi(E)}{(\eta_S)^\Lambda} \int_0^{\frac{\varepsilon_2^S}{a_2 - \varepsilon_2^S a_1}} x^{\Lambda-1} e^{-\frac{(\beta_E - \delta_E)}{\eta_S}x} dx \tag{22}$$

Using [29, 3.351.2], the closed-form SOP of D_2 is given by

$$P_2^{SOP} = \sum_{b_1=0}^{m_E-1} \cdots \sum_{b_N=0}^{m_E-1} \frac{\Xi(2)}{(\beta_E - \delta_E)^\Lambda} \Gamma\left(\Lambda, \frac{(\beta_E - \delta_E)\varepsilon_2^S}{\eta_S(a_2 - \varepsilon_2^S a_1)}\right) \tag{23}$$

where $\Gamma(a, b)$ denotes the lower incomplete gamma function.
The proof is completed.

3.4 SOP of D_1

As [25], the SOP of D_1 can be expressed as.

$$P_1^{SOP} = \Pr\left(\gamma_{E \to x_1} < 2^{R_1 - R_1^S} - 1\right) \tag{24}$$

In similar to Proposition 2, the exact closed-form of D_1 is formulated by

$$P_1^{SOP} = \Pr\left(\eta_E > \frac{\varepsilon_1^S}{a_1}\right) = \int_{\frac{\varepsilon_1^S}{a_1}}^{\infty} f_{\eta_E}(x)dx$$

$$= \sum_{b_1=0}^{m_E-1} \cdots \sum_{b_N=0}^{m_E-1} \frac{\Xi(E)}{(\beta_E - \delta_E)^\Lambda} \Gamma\left(\Lambda, \frac{\varepsilon_1^S}{\eta_S a_1}\right) \tag{25}$$

4 Numerical Result And Discussions

In this section, we set $a_2 = 0.8$, $a_1 = 0.2$, $R_2 = 0.5$ $R_1 = 1$, $R_1^S = 0.5$ and $R_2^S = 0.1$. Moreover, we consider the Shadowed-Rician fading parameters for the satellite links is the heavy shadowing with $m_1 = m_2 = m_E = 1$, $b_1 = b_2 = b_E = 0.063$ and $\Omega_1 = \Omega_2 = \Omega_E = 0.0007$.

In Fig. 2, the simulations were performed to COP versus transmit SNR to analyze the connection outage performance of the system by varying the number of antennas at the satellite. As we can observe, the performance of the system has comparatively increased when the number of antennas were increased from 1 to 2.

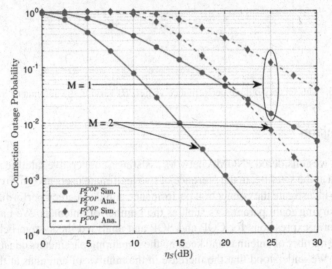

Fig. 2. The connection outage performance vs η_S (dB) varying the antenna of S M.

In Fig. 3, the simulations were performed to SOP versus transmit SNR to analyze the secrecy performance of the system. We can observe that, with the rise in the number of antennas, the SOP of the system shows better performance. We can also observe that increasing a single antenna shows a huge performance gap between the lines. Therefore, we can understand that the number of antennas plays a major role in the efficiency of the system.

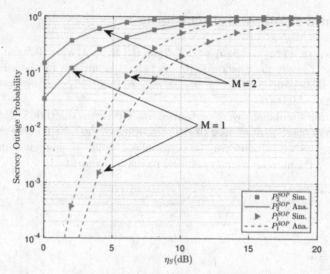

Fig. 3. The secrecy outage performance vs $\eta_S\,(dB)$ varying the antenna of S M.

5 Conclusion

In this paper, we considered a NOMA network assisting a cooperative satellite with antennas equipped at the satellite, in the presence of two legitimate users and an eavesdropper. We aimed to investigate the connection performance and the secrecy performance of the system by varying main parameters such as the number of antennas. We have derived the closed-form expressions for COP and SOP and analysed the system behaviour by changing the number of antennas and keeping the remaining parameters constant for fair comparison. We understood that the increase in the number of antennas at the satellite will help the communication links for efficient data transmission.

Acknowledgment. This research was supported by the Ministry of Education, Youth and Sports of the Czech Republic under the grant SP2022/5 and e-INFRA C.Z. (ID:90140).

References

1. Islam, S., Avazov, N., Dobre, O., Kwak, K.: Power domain non-orthogonal multiple access (NOMA) in 5G systems: potentials and challenges. IEEE Commun. Surv. Tutor. **19**(2), 721–742 (2017)
2. Liu, G., Jiang, D.: 5G: Vision and requirements for mobile communication system towards year 2020. Chinese J. Eng. **2016**, 1–9 (2016)
3. Wang, Y., Ren, B., Sun, S., Kang, S., Yue, X.: Analysis of non-orthogonal multiple access for 5G. China Commun. **2**, 52–66 (2016)
4. Khan, R., Jayakody, D.: An ultra-reliable and lowlatency communications assisted modulation based nonorthogonal multiple access scheme. Phys. Commun. **43**, 101035 (2020)
5. Dai, L., Wang, Z., Yuan, Y.: Non-orthogonal multiple access for 5G: solutions, challenges, opportunities and future research trends. IEEE Commun. Mag. **53**, 74–81 (2015)

6. Zhang, X., et al.: Performance analysis of NOMA-based cooperative spectrum sharing in hybrid satellite-terrestrial networks. IEEE Access **7**, 172321–172329 (2019)

7. Balyan, V., Saini, D.S.: Called elapsed time and reduction in code blocking forWCDMA networks. In: IEEE in Proceedings of International Conference on Software Telecommunication an Computer Networks, SoftCom, pp. 141–245 (2009)

8. Balyan, V., Saini, D.S.: A same rate and pattern recognition search of OVSF code tree for WCDMA networks. IET Commun. **8**(13), 2366–2374 (2014)

9. Do, D.-T., Van Nguyen, M.-S., Voznak, M., Kwasinski, A., de Souza, J.N.: Performance analysis of clustering car-following V2X system with wirelesspower transfer and massive connections. In: IEEE Internet Things J. (2021). https://doi.org/10.1109/JIOT.2021.3070744

10. Do, D.-T., Van Nguyen, M.-S.: Device-to-device transmission modes in NOMA network with and without Wireless Power Transfer. Comput. Commun. **139**, 67–77 (2019)

11. Do, D.-T., Nguyen, M.-S.V., Jameel, F., Jäntti, R., Ansari, I.S.: Performance evaluation of relay-aided CR-NOMA for beyond 5G communications. IEEE Access **8**, 134838–134855 (2020)

12. Do, D.-T., Le, C.-B., Afghah, F.: Enabling full-duplex and energy harvesting in uplink and downlink of small-cell network relying on power domain based multiple access. IEEE Access **8**, 142772–142784 (2020)

13. Ejaz, W., Shama, S., Saadat, S., Naeem, M., Anpalagan, A., Chughtai, N.: A comprehensive survey on resource allocation for CRAN in 5G and beyong networks. J. Nerw. Comput. Appl. **160**, 1–24 (2020)

14. Aldababsa, M., Toka, M., Gokceli, S., Kurt, G., Kucur, O.: A tutorial on nonorthogonal multiple access for 5G and beyond. Wirel. Commun. Mob. Comput. **2018**. 1–24 (2018)

15. Petraki, D.K., Anastasopoulos, M.P., Papavassiliou, S.: Secrecy capacity for satellite networks under rain fading. IEEE Trans. Dependable Secure Comput. **8**(5), 778–783 (2011)

16. Guo, K., An, K., Zhang, B., et al.: Physical layer security for multiuser satellite communication systems with threshold-based scheduling scheme. IEEE Trans. Veh. Technol. **69**(5), 5129–5141 (2020)

17. Li, B., Fei, Z., Xu, X., Chu, Z.: Resource allocations for secure cognitive satellite-terrestrial networks. IEEE Wirel. Commun. Lett. **7**(1), 78–81 (2018)

18. Li, B., Fei, Z., Chu, Z., Zhou, F., Wong, K.K., Xiao, P.: Robust chance-constrained secure transmission for cognitive satellite-terrestrial networks. IEEE Trans. Veh. Technol. **67**(5), 4208–4219 (2018)

19. Chen, J., Yang, L.: Physical layer security for cooperative NOMA systems. IEEE Trans. Veh. Technol. **67**(5), 4645–4649 (2018)

20. Nguyen, T.N., Duy, T.T., Luu, G.T., Tran, P.T., Voznak, M.: Energy harvesting-based spectrum access with incremental cooperation, relay selection and hardware noises. Radioengineering **26**(1), 240–250 (2017)

21. Nguyen, T.N., Tran, M., Nguyen, T.L., Ha, D.H., Voznak, M.: Performance analysis of a user selection protocol in cooperative networks with power splitting protocol-based energy harvesting over Nakagami-m/Rayleigh channels. Electronics **8**(4), 448 (2019)

22. Tran Tin, P., The Hung, D., Nguyen, T.N., Duy, T.T., Voznak, M.: Secrecy performance enhancement for underlay cognitive radio networks employing cooperative multi-hop transmission with and without presence of hardware impairments. Entropy **21**(2), 217 (2019)

23. Yue, X., Liu, Y., Yao, Y., Li, X., Liu, R., Nallanathan, A.: Secure communications in a unified non-orthogonal multiple access framework. IEEE Trans. Wirel. Commun. **19**(3), 2163–2178 (2020)

24. Do, D.-T., Le, A.-T.: NOMA based cognitive relaying: transceiver hardware impairments, relay selection policies and outage performance comparison. Comput. Commun. **146**, 144–154 (2019)

25. Song, Y., Yang, W., Xiang, Z., Wang, B., Cai, Y.: Secure transmission in mmWave NOMA networks with cognitive power allocation. IEEE Access **7**, 76104–76119 (2019)
26. Bhatnagar, M.R., Arti, M.K.: Performance analysis of AF based hybrid satellite-terrestrial cooperative network over generalized fading channels. IEEE Commun. Lett. **17**(10), 1912–1915 (2013)
27. Alfano, G., De Maio, A.: Sum of squared Shadowed-Rice random variables and its application to communication systems performance prediction. IEEE Trans. Wireless Commun. **6**(10), 3540–3545 (2007)
28. Simon, M.K., Alouini, M.-S.: Digital Communications over Fading Channels: A Unified Approach to Performance Analysis. Wiley, Hoboken (2000)
29. Gradshteyn, I.S., Ryzhik, I.M.: Table of Integrals, Series, and Products, 7th edn. Academic, San Diego (2007)

Attack Detection in SS7

Charles Beumier[(✉)] and Thibault Debatty

Royal Military Academy of Belgium, Av. de la Renaissance 30, 1000 Brussels, Belgium
charles.beumier@mil.be

Abstract. Today, more and more interactions rely on smart phones. Their security becomes a real concern to guarantee the protection of identity, life and property. Cybersecurity initiatives regularly emphasize the importance of good practices for passwords, updating patches, encryption or other appropriate defenses. They also announce vulnerabilities discovered in applications. But they rarely warn of the danger of SS7 (Signaling System No. 7), the stack of protocols used between 2G and 3G telecommunications network equipment, including cellular phones. This paper presents on-going research on the detection of SS7 attacks which target the SS7 Mobile Application Protocol (MAP). More specifically, we plan to detect attacks based on so-called *Category 3* MAP messages which are difficult to manage with SS7 firewalls. The method verifies the consistency of the position/speed revealed by the telecommunications equipment involved in SS7 signaling when a subscriber is in outbound roaming situation. In particular, we plan to detect attacks spoofing a SS7 equipment (from anywhere in the world) and injecting *Category 3* MAP messages in order to take control of voice or SMS delivery equipment, which would allow the attacker to intercept calls or SMSs or even to prevent communications.

Keywords: SS7 · GSM · 3G · Vulnerabilities · Attack detection

1 Introduction

The smart phone becomes the essential companion of our daily life. While its use has rarely been questioned due to the ease and multitude of services it offers, its security flaws should not be underestimated. Personal information, activity calendar, navigation history, administrative or financial details are some examples of data shared by applications for which leaks can have significant consequences. From the user's point of view, examples in the media and warnings from security centres regularly remind the importance of appropriate behaviour regarding passwords, firewalls, anti-viruses, suspicious links or attachments, to name a few.

Making calls, texting and accessing the Internet through the telecommunications network require signaling between the telecom nodes. In the case of 2G or 3G networks, the SS7 protocol stack is used. 4G networks rely on DIAMETER, but 2G and 3G technologies are still widely used for backward compatibility with old equipment.

About 10 years ago, several research centres revealed SS7 vulnerabilities. A few public exploits were performed live, demonstrating the ability to track a mobile phone,

A. Dziech et al. (Eds.): MCSS 2022, CCIS 1689, pp. 11–20, 2022.
https://doi.org/10.1007/978-3-031-20215-5_2

listen in on a conversation, or read a short message. In 2017, unscrupulous hackers managed to empty bank accounts [1], after having collected bank credentials by mail phishing and could log in after having recovered the access code sent in a short message (2-Factor Authentication). This real attack probably prompted telecom equipment vendors and operators to set up defence procedures. The Data Protection rules in force since May 2018 in Europe (GDPR) have become another incentive for more security.

Telecommunications security is a concern for every user and every provider. From a national perspective, cybersecurity (including telecom security) has become a new domain for Defence, alongside traditional Land, Air and Naval forces. This was sadly evidenced by cyberattacks just before the start of the Russian-Ukrainian armed conflict.

The Radio laboratory of the Royal Military Academy in Brussels has launched a project on SS7 security which is now hosted by the Cyberlab for reasons of synergy. This project aims to find attacks and vulnerabilities through real SS7 traffic. For this, Belgian operators will provide the data, after having applied an appropriate pseudonymisation and anonymisation procedure to protect the personal data of the subscribers. In the meantime, we have looked for the SS7 details and known flaws and devised a first approach to detecting SS7 attacks that are difficult for SS7 firewalls to handle.

The following section describes SS7 in a minimal way that makes the rest of the paper understandable. Section 3 lists the SS7 threats due to MAP vulnerabilities to show the dangers of telecommunications with SS7. In Sect. 4, we summarize the main defences usually adopted by telecommunications operators. Section 5 describes the goal of the project, explains how the data will be processed and how the first attacks should be detected.

2 Signaling System No. 7 (SS7)

2.1 SS7 Historical Facts

SS7 is the Signaling System No. 7, a protocol stack designed in the 1970s for telecommunications signaling (channel separated from the calls). Its main function was to support the start and termination of calls on landlines, but it was later extended to handle roaming in mobile networks, the seamless handover when phones move, the exchange of short messages, the location tracking (for emergency), the billing and some supplementary services such as call forwarding and calling number display.

At the time SS7 was created, (national) telecom operators owned the network they were using and had no reason to fear attacks. But later, due to the deregulation in the second half of the 90s, the number of providers increased. This trend was reinforced by the use of the Internet Protocol as a signaling medium for telecommunications. The attack surface became considerably larger.

SS7 flaws have been looked for from the beginning of the century. Several vulnerabilities have been presented by research groups in papers and at public events with demonstration since around 2010. They revealed possibilities for eavesdropping of calls, leaking of short messages, location tracking, denial of service and fraud. The situation has improved since the telecommunications industry reacted about 5 years ago so that operators normally put in place firewalls, home routing or install equipment in a better way. They can be helped by the recommendations made on these subjects by GSMA, the

GSM Association whose members are telecommunications equipment vendors, mobile network operators and other telecom actors.

Even though 4G has been available for 10 years now and 5G is just around the corner, 2G and 3G technologies based on SS7 are expected to last another 5–10 years, for backwards compatibility with legacy equipment and older phones. Studying SS7 is still worthy, as companies busy with penetration testing and auditing for telcos attest. For example, P1Security regularly expand its vulnerability database with flaws discovered in newly detected exploits. And in the long term, DIAMETER (replacing SS7 in 4G) would suffer from similar vulnerabilities and would currently be less attacked because SS7 is still offering a sufficient surface.

2.2 Network Components

We present in this subsection the main SS7 components of a 2G/3G network in a very brief way to support our explanations. A more detailed description can be found in [2–4].

A Home Location Register (HLR) is a database that stores the IMSIs (International Mobile Subscriber Identity), telephone number (MSISDN, Mobile Station International Subscriber Directory Number) and subscription details of mobile subscribers. An HLR also keeps a rough last position of all its subscribers to reach them quicker. A Visitor Location Register (VLR) keeps a copy of the subscription details of subscribers geographically located within its area (connected to one of its associated antennas). This significantly reduces request traffic to the HLR. A Mobile Switching Centre routes calls and SMSs to the intended recipient. An MSC is usually physically located with a VLR.

The exchange of information between these network nodes is handled by the SS7 protocol stack. At the highest level, the Mobile Application Part makes it possible to send requests or responses, with nearly 80 operations in the field of mobility management, short message, authentication, calls, supplementary services, etc. A dialogue is established between the nodes thanks to the Transaction Capability Application Part. A transaction ID is created for this dialogue to identify this exchange between these network nodes because many dialogues may exist simultaneously. At a lower level, the Signaling Connection Control Part routes a message towards a node thanks to its Global Title (often similar to a phone number) or to a Point Code and Subsystem Number (SSN). The Global Title is translated into a point code and SSN, so that the low level MTP (Mobile Transfer Part) can be used to route the message.

3 SS7/MAP Threats

This section lists the various threats due to SS7 MAP layer vulnerabilities. The examples are briefly presented here as they are detailed in other publications (see [4–6]). Refer to [7] for a report on monitoring real networks during 2015–2017.

3.1 Location Tracking

Several MAP functions return the MSC to which a phone is currently attached to receive calls and SMSs (e.g. SendRoutingInfo, SendRoutingInfoForShortMessage). A MSC covers a geographical area and leaks an approximate position of the phone (a city or part of a small country). The functions ProvideSubscriberInfo and AnyTimeInterrogation return the MSC but also the cellID which is an identifier for a smaller area (an antenna) which discloses the position with more precision.

The ability to obtain location information for a specific phone number or IMSI has led to a commercial (fraudulent) activity.

3.2 SMS Interception

In SS7, an SMS is sent in two stages, first from the sender to the SMS centre (SMSC) and later, when possible, from the SMSC to the recipient. The two related MAP operations are MO_forwardSM (Mobile Originated) and MT_forwardSM (Mobile Terminated).

A possible exploit for SMS interception takes place in two phases, respectively represented in green and blue in Fig. 1. In a preparation phase, the attacker first pretends to be an SMSC (spoofing is possible since SS7 does not authenticate equipment) to send a MAP SendRoutingInfoForShortMessage (SRI_SM) message to request the IMSI and the serving MSC of a victim (X) identified by his phone number (MSISDN). The attacker then sends a MAP UpdateLocation request to the HLR to become the current Mobile Switch Centre (MSC') which will receive calls and SMSs sent to X.

In the execution phase, once an SMS is sent to victim X, the SMS is first stored in the SMSC attached to the sender and the MSC and IMSI of the recipient (victim) are requested from his HLR through an SRI_SM call. The HLR returns MSC' which was set by the attacker. The SMSC will send the SMS when possible to MSC' controlled by the attacker who can then read it, copy it and possibly send it to the intended recipient.

The importance of this attack, in frequency and in consequences (see [8]), led the GSM industry to set up a defence called SMS home routing, presented in Sect. 4.2.

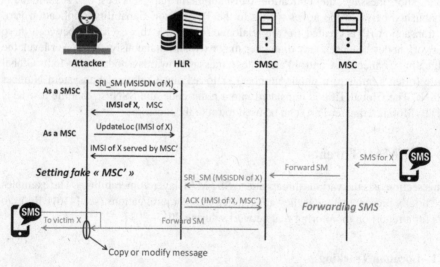

Fig. 1. SMS interception thanks to MAP_SRI_SM and MAP_UL messages.

3.3 Call Eavesdropping

Several options are available to an attacker to spy on a call using SS7/MAP. For example, he can call the RegisterSS MAP function (impersonating an HLR) to set up call forwarding to a number under his control. The interested reader can consult references [4, 5] for more information.

3.4 Denial of Service

An attacker can prevent a subscriber from using certain services (e.g. calling, sending or receiving SMS) thanks to the MAP functions InsertSubscriberData and Delete-SubscriberData which can manipulate subscription details. The CancelLocation MAP function can achieve the same results since the phone is then out of connection.

3.5 Fraud

An example of fraud uses the MAP RegisterSS operation to set up call forwarding to a premium rate number. The money will probably be collected before the subscriber notices.

Another famous example involves an organised theft of bank accounts in Germany in 2017 [1]. The thieves first collected the bank and telephone identifiers by phishing mails. Then they obtained the access codes of 2FactorAuthentication (2FA) by SMS interception.

Since these threats or exploits were demonstrated, a response from the equipment vendors and operators has been given, although it has taken some time. The adoption of GDPR in 2018 certainly reinforced the effort. Some common defence scenarios are (should be) implemented by MNOs, as discussed in the next section. Subscriber action is limited.

4 Common Defences

Subscribers have little ability to defend themselves against telecom attacks. They depend on the technology deployed by operators and can be attacked by fake antennas (called *IMSI catchers* [9]). Sometimes when there is a suspicious situation (e.g. a phone not working due to DoS), the subscriber can power off and restart the phone to force a new authentication and location, if he is aware.. On the contrary, the GSMA association organizes working groups on hot topics in telecommunications and issues recommendations to the industry and operators. Some of the recommendations relate to the security of telecom networks through specific equipment and installations. A few of them are presented in this section.

4.1 Encryption

Encryption is probably the simplest action an operator can take to secure its network against eavesdropping of calls. In SS7, encryption is performed by the so-called A5 algorithm. In 2G, 3 algorithms have been provided, respectively A5/1, A5/2, and A5/3. A5/0 corresponds to 'No encryption'.

GSM A5/3 is the recommended option. GSM A5/2 seemed weak and was abolished by GSMA in 2006. A5/1 could be broken thanks to pre-computed rainbow tables [9]. Although it is advisable to select some encryption rather than none, A5/0 was often used, probably due to operator negligence, when data protection was less of a concern than it is today. Weak encryption is compounded by the fact that a user is unaware of the operator's encryption choice and can have a false sense of protection.

In this regard, the GSMMAP project [10] of the Security Research Lab deserves a little description. It was launched to assess operators regarding the possibility of performing certain attacks like tracking, listening to calls and reading SMSs. It is based on participating subscribers, who must have a suitable phone (limited list) and who will be hacked by the research group. Hacking success rates for each type of attack are evaluated for each operator and reports are automatically generated for each country with sufficient participation.

Encryption, although not directly related to the topic of this paper focused on attacks by SS7 MAP messages, has shown weaknesses that can be exploited for these attacks. Decryption can indeed be used to collect IMSI needed for most MAP messages. A simple defence is to choose secure encryption (A5/3).

4.2 SMS Home Routing

SMS Home routing is a defence procedure developed to reduce location or IMSI leaks as a result of the specific SS7 MAP request SRI_SM used to send SMSs. As presented in Sect. 3.2, MSC and IMSI can help intercept SMSs by an attacker who only needs to know the phone number (MSISDN) and have access to SS7. Much more, the MSC reveals an approximate location of the subscriber's phone and the IMSI is the identifier so valuable to attackers as it is required by many MAP operations.

SMS Home routing uses an SMS Home Router so that the MSC serving the SMS recipient does not have to be disclosed. This MSC is transmitted from the HLR to the SMS Home Router instead of the SMSC. Once the SMS can be sent, the SMSC contacts the Home Router which knows which MSC serves the recipient.

In Fig. 2, the changes to SMS delivery due to the introduction of the SMS Home Router are shown in red. They are mainly the non-disclosure of the MSC to which the recipient MS2 is attached, and the delivery of the SMS taken care of by the SMS Home Router which has learned directly from the HLR of MS2 (Network B) which MSC to use.

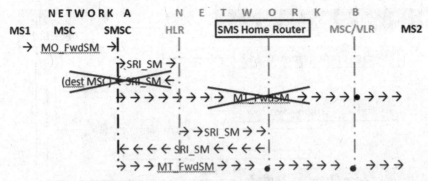

Fig. 2. SMS Home Router and changes to MAP messages.

4.3 SS7 Firewall

A SS7 firewall is a major defence advised by GSMA. Recommendations are given in document FS.11 [11], unfortunately only accessible to GSMA members.

In the recommendations, a distinction is made for the 3 categories of MAP messages. *Category 1* is for MAP messages that should only be received within the home network. A *Category 2* message should only be requested by the home network of a phone roaming outside this home ('roaming in' in the network to be protected). Both are quite easily handled by a rule in a firewall.

Category 3 messages are more difficult to manage because they relate to a phone roaming out of its home network (the network to be protected). The validity of the messages can be based on the plausibility of the phone movement. If the movement is unrealistic (e.g. too fast), it is probably not coming from the phone. This verification needs to keep track of each phone's last location, which is not easily implemented in a firewall. This is the type of anomaly detection we want to implement to improve protection.

5 Planned Implementation

We are targeting the surveillance of GSMA *Category 3* MAP messages as they are not easily addressed by SS7 Firewalls. As Ullah in [4], we will first consider MAP UpdateLocation messages which represent a large part of SS7 traffic and which are implicated in several known threats (e.g. Denial of Service and SMS interception). Other message types will be analysed later with the hope to discover new vulnerabilities and attacks.

5.1 Overall Picture

The implementation of the attack detection using MAP *Category 3* will follow the scheme in Fig. 3.

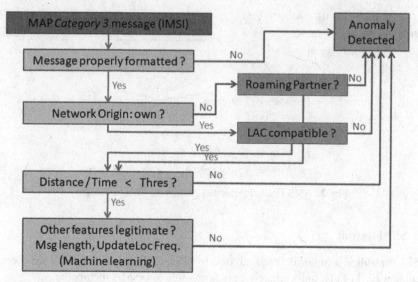

Fig. 3. Scheme for the detection of attacks based on MAP *Category 3* messages.

In this scheme, MAP *Category 3* messages that do not follow the proper format are ignored. The operator origin of the request is then checked to ensure that it is either a local or roaming partner. For valid messages, the mobile location LAC (Location Area Code, covering several antennas), if available, is checked against the current MSC. The known location (LAC or MSC) must be stored and examined over time to verify that it represents a plausible motion pattern in terms of position and travelling speed. And finally, for the remaining valid MAP *Category 3* messages, other features are analyzed by machine learning to look for anomalies.

We will not have any ground truth to guide the research, but we will inspect the distribution of message features to find atypical ones, in an unsupervised way.

5.2 Needed Data

In the targeted passive analysis, there is no need for real-time capture or for access to the SS7 network to inject messages, which simplifies the constraints on data acquisition. SS7 traffic will be acquired from a real network for a long enough period (at least two weeks) to increase the chance of having attacks in number and in complexity (those deployed in several days).

The identifiers contained in MAP messages represent a danger to the privacy of mobile subscribers. This sensitive aspect of mobile data has been reinforced in Europe since the adoption of GDPR. Identifiers such as the IMSI and MSISDN will be pseudonymised with pseudo random values to hide the actual identifiers but retain their uniqueness to allow linking of messages on a subscriber basis. Other message attributes can lead to re-identification: the IMEI (International Mobile Equipment Identity) and the CellID (antenna identifier, leak of a geographical position) will be replaced by 0 values to avoid cross-referencing with other databases.

Finally, the approximate location of a given IMSI revealed by the current serving MSC and possibly by the LAC, is necessary for this research and represents a limited danger for subscribers. It is clear that, in addition to pseudonymisation and anonymisation the data will also be protected by the data server itself, located in premises with access control, in a locked room, not connected to internet and logging any access normally restricted to the researcher and his director.

After verifying the format, network origin, LAC and motion consistency, other message attributes (e.g. message length, Point Codes, frequency or distribution of MAP messages) also merit analysis. We are interested a priori in all available attributes.

5.3 Processing

First, all the messages with an appropriate 'opcode' (e.g. '2' for MAP UpdateLocation) have to be extracted from the SS7 traffic. The format of these messages has to be checked, looking for the existence of the mandatory parameters and their value.

The typical mandatory fields of the MAP messages concern the Global Title of the intervening equipment (e.g. MSC/VLR, HLR) and the IMSI of the subscriber. The time attribute is of course of prime importance for the plausibility test on the subscriber's motion speed.

The first five digits of a subscriber's IMSI reveal the MCC (country, 3-digit) and MNC (operator, 2-digit) of the operator ('home'). A MSC/VLR or HLR is given in the form of a Global Title that also indicates the country and the operator. This helps to check whether the current MSC operator has a roaming agreement with the home of the IMSI. From the storage of the MSC and the timestamp of MAP requests, it is possible to check whether the speed of a given IMSI is realistic. This verification can be more accurate if the LAC is available.

Finally, the remaining features not used so far can be collected for all acceptable MAP messages considered (no anomaly found in the previous checks). We can then apply an unsupervised learning method (clustering) on these features to highlight atypical messages which are anomalies not detected by the previous steps. Our intention is to combine the evidence extracted from different features thanks to the MARk framework [12] developed in our department. By analysing the node origin in the population of detected abnormal MAP *Category 3* messages, we will derive the operators or countries most apparent in those suspicious messages or possibly detect malfunctioning nodes.

6 Conclusions

The security of our identity, life and assets can be compromised by our smartphones. A lesser-known component is at risk: the SS7 protocol stack of 2G and 3G telecom networks.

We have presented an approach to detect suspicious SS7 MAP *Category 3* messages that may be involved in SMS interception and Denial of Service attacks in the case of UpdateLocation. *Category 3* messages require a stateful approach: the position and time indicated in the messages must be stored with the concerned IMSI, so that the speed can be checked to detect suspicious movements revealing a potential attack. The other message attributes will also help finding anomalies. The corresponding messages can then be analyzed to highlight suspicious countries, operators or nodes.

We are looking forward to receiving real network data to test our framework and approach. As mentioned, SS7 information contains personal information of subscriber, so the data exchange is subject to protection rules that slowed down the process.

References

1. Khandelwal, S.: Real-world SS7 attack – hackers are stealing money from bank accounts. In: The Hacker News, 4 May 2017. Accessed 25 Aug 2022
2. Dryburgh, L., Hewett, J.: Signaling System No. 7 (SS7/C7): Protocol, Architecture and Services. Cisco Press (2005)
3. Sauter, M.: From GSM to LTE: An Introduction to Mobile Networks and Mobile Broadband. Wiley, Hoboken (2011)
4. Ullah, K., Rashid, I., Afzal, H., Iqbal, W., Bangash, Y., Abbas, H.: SS7 vulnerabilities - a survey & implementation of machine learning vs rule based filtering for detection of SS7 network attacks. IEEE Commun. Surv. Tutor. **22**, 1337–1371 (2020)
5. Mourad, H.: The fall of SS7 – How can the critical security controls help? https://www. sans.org/reading-room/whitepapers/critical/fall-ss7--critical-security-controls-help-36225. Accessed 25 Aug 2022
6. Jensen, K., Nguyen, H.T., Do, T.V., Årnes, A.: A big data analytics approach to combat telecommunication vulnerabilities. Clust. Comput. **20**(3), 2363–2374 (2017). https://doi.org/10.1007/s10586-017-0811-x
7. Positive Technologies: SS7 Vulnerabilities and Attack Exposure Report 2018. https://www.gsma.com/membership/wp-content/uploads/2018/07/SS7_Vulnerability_2017_A4.ENG_.0003.03.pdf. Accessed 25 Aug 2022
8. Beumier, C.: SMS-based 2FA authentication is insecure. https://cylab.be/blog/171/sms-based-2-factor-authentication-is-insecure. Accessed 25 Aug 2022
9. Dabrowski, A., Pianta, N., Klepp, T., Mulazzani, M., Weippl, E.: IMSI-catch me if you can. In: ACSAC 2014 (2014)
10. GSMMap. https://gsmmap.org/
11. FS11: SS7 Interconnect Security Monitoring and Firewall Guidelines
12. Nikolov, G., Debatty, T., Mees, W.: Evaluation of a multi-agent anomaly-based advanced persistent threat detection framework. In: 12th International Conference on Evolving Internet (INTERNET 2020) (2020)

Sector-Specific Training - A Federated Maritime Scenario

Paloma de La Vallée[1]([✉])(iD), Georgios Iosifidis[2], Andrea Rossi[3], Marco Dri[4], and Wim Mees[1](iD)

[1] Royal Military Academy, Brussels, Belgium
p.delavallee@cylab.be
[2] RHEA Group, Brussels, Belgium
[3] RHEA Group, Rome, Italy
[4] Fincantieri, Trieste, Italy
http://www.cylab.be

Abstract. The infrastructure in the maritime sector has evolved to integrate more and more connected systems. The maritime environment very much relies on modern technology to aid and optimize the daily operations of ships and harbour processes alike. The cyber protection of these systems is essential to prevent the disruption of their activity. While Security Operation Centre teams usually are aided in their tasks by Intrusion Detection Systems, the actual response to cyber attacks remains very much a human activity. In that regard, complex and realistic hands-on training is an excellent way to bolster the efficiency of the defensive actions; this type of exercise is usually performed on a cyber range. In that context, a federation of cyber range allows to generate more elaborate sector-specific scenarios. This paper presents a maritime-specific training delivered over a cyber range federation. The sector-specific aspects, as well as the technical issues of the federation, are discussed.

Keywords: Maritime · Training · Cyber range federation

1 Introduction

Across all sectors, corporate information networks and systems increase in complexity and interconnectivity. The effort required to monitor the security of such systems escalates with the growth of their attack surface. Each year, various reports detail the extend of the cyber-threat defenders have to face [1,2]. While known techniques are still being actively used in different contexts, malicious actors develop new attack with an unfailing regularity. Organizations are under constant pressure to detect intrusions and attacks in a timely manner, while threat- and defense-actors are constantly trying to outmanoeuvre each other.

The Intrusion Detection Systems (IDSes) and other monitoring tools gain in sophistication and efficiency, strongly supporting the Security Operation Centre (SOC) teams in their vigilance. However, the management of threats and

A. Dziech et al. (Eds.): MCSS 2022, CCIS 1689, pp. 21–35, 2022.
https://doi.org/10.1007/978-3-031-20215-5_3

intrusions still require knowledge and expertise. While automated systems can gather, sort and present pertinent information, the actual response to attacks is a delicate task that still requires human supervision. Detecting suspicious incidents and responding to them appropriately, requires a very specific set of knowledge, skills, and abilities (KSA). Developing the cyber-related KSA that are required for each role in the organization, especially for cybersecurity related roles, typically requires hands-on training on a cyber range to improve the learning performance and enhance Situation Awareness (SA).

Situation awareness is a recognition of the state of the environment and is the basis of decision making. It is an essential element for taking appropriate measures in face of a suspected threat, ongoing attack or confirmed intrusion. Endsley defined situation awareness as "the perception of the elements in the environment within a volume of time and space, the comprehension of their meaning and the projection of their status in the near future" [3]. This definition encompasses three components that are actually three levels of situation awareness: the perception, comprehension and projection [4].

- *Perception* is the lowest level of awareness, it relates to the consciousness, or knowledge of relevant information about the environment. In the context of network management, perception relates to the consciousness of the state of the IT system under supervision; the IDSes are designed to aid this perception by reporting suspicious activities or traces in the network. For instance, the SOC operator could be aware of a connection from a workstation to a suspicious external server.
- *Comprehension* is the ability to integrate the perception into the context of the circumstances, in view of operational goals. It links the different basic elements of the perception into a complete contextual understanding of the present situation. In the instance evoked above, the security operator could understand that the connection might be a trace of an infection of said workstation.
- Finally, the *projection* is the ability to predict events and system states in the near future based on the perception and comprehension. It calls mental models created in past experience or training to foresee what the present situation might entail. Referring again to the instance mentioned earlier, the security operator knows that an infected machine can serve as foothold to progress further into the network; it is a security breach that must be tackled at once to limit its impact.

This shows that situation awareness is the essential basis on which efficient decision making is built. The SA allows evaluating the state of the environment, in its present state and near future. In any situation, choosing the optimal action to take demands additional elements such as the goals, the memory, the mental models, etc. However, adequate decision making very much relies on accurate situation awareness. Fortunately, the ability of an individual to acquire correct SA can be enhanced with trainings. These exercices progressively develop the 'comprehension' and 'projection' components of the SA via the consolidation of various and appropriate mental models that are called from long-term memory to organise information. In particular, repeated exposition to various situations help embody the theoretical knowledge, and practical learning has been demonstrated to bolster the training performance [5].

In order to develop best the situation awareness and help personnel improve the adequate mental models, the training scenarios must ideally be sufficiently realistic, complex and varied. In this context, cyber ranges offer a flexible and safe environment to carry out such trainings. This realisation has raised considerable interest in cyber ranges, leading to developments in various directions as attested by numerous surveys and meta-analyses [6–9].

The European Cyber Security Organisation (ECSO) defines cyber ranges as very versatile simulation environments. "A cyber range is a platform for the development, delivery and use of interactive simulation environments. A simulation environment is a representation of an organisation's Information and Communication Technology (ICT), Operational Technology (OT), mobile and physical systems, applications and infrastructures, including the simulation of attacks, users and their activities and of any other Internet, public or third-party services which the simulated environment may depend upon. A cyber range includes a combination of core technologies for the realisation and use of the simulation environment and of additional components which are, in turn, desirable or required for achieving specific cyber range use cases" [10].

This definition demonstrates that cyber ranges have the necessary characteristics requested from an efficient training environment. They offer the possibility to simulate operational networks where experiments and exercises can be carried out safely and repeatedly. Furthermore, cyber ranges allow to deploy diverse complex realistic scenarios on a single infrastructure, providing the necessary variety of situations to generate a broad set of training experiences. Connecting different ranges into a federation allows to increase the capacity and capabilities or the ranges, but this connection brings a series of technological challenges that must be tackled. This paper presents some maritime aspects of cyber security, and how a sector-specific training involving a federation of ranges could successfully be designed and deployed. To the best of our knowledge, no maritime-specific training over a federation of ranges has been reported yet.

The rest of the paper is organised as follows. The Sect. 2 discuss the flexibility brought about by the federation of cyber ranges. The Sect. 3 presents an overview of the cyber security aspects specific to the maritime sector. The Sect. 4 describes a federated maritime scenario and an associated defensive training. Finally, the Sect. 5 discusses perspectives for future work.

2   The Case for a Federation of Ranges

The above discussion stressed the necessity for the trainings to involve realistic and up-to-date elements. However, this requirement poses a sizeable problem when specific and complex systems are considered. Building a virtualised environment representative of a real-life operational system necessitates to incorporate both specialised and generic elements into the cyber range. This duality poses a challenge to stakeholder wishing to offer appropriate trainings. It is unrealistic for a single training provider to offer a catalogue of services that must encompass both generic and a variety of highly specialised ranges.

The federation of cyber ranges must help overcome that issue, allowing different providers to bundle assets with the aim to generate a more diverse, complex, and possibly specialised set of ranges. These specialised ranges, each with a specific area of expertise, can be federated in a modular manner. The idea has gained traction over the years, and different successful instances of federation are reported, in different use cases [11,12], and the scope of the federations increased to reach the international level [13]. The federation of ranges brings its own set of technical issues, that are the object of active research [14–16].

Notwithstanding the connectivity challenges, the advantages of cyber ranges federations are such that the concept of Market Place is earning attention [17], as a convergence point around cyber ranges where service providers and customers can meet. The ECHO Federated Cyber Range (E-FCR) was designed with this very idea in mind: the E-FCR is a central meeting point where providers can offer various pre-designed services, where customer can browse the offer and where both can negotiate a bespoke arrangement [18,19]. The E-FCR is one of the main outcomes of the ECHO project [20].

3   Cyber Security in the Maritime Sector

The maritime sector is critical to the economy and society and an essential link in the supply chain. Like many other industrialised sectors, the maritime sector also increasingly relies on advanced connected systems [21]. The number, type and connectivity of complex digital systems on modern ships increase over the years: modern ships and ports integrate Information Technology to handle and ease their daily operations. Indeed, the automation and digitalisation of tasks enhances the efficiency of the maritime sector. Consequently, ships are increasingly digitized, not only for the business communications, but also for critical vessel system to sustain navigation, power supply, cargo management, etc. This complexity is illustrated on the Fig. 1 that shows some typical digital systems of a commercial ship.

In this perspective, protecting the integrity of ships digital systems is necessary to ensure the security and safety of crew, ships, cargo and ports. Furthermore, cyber incidents can also lead to accidents having a heavy environmental cost that should be avoided where possible [24–26].

The steady integration of standard IT and specific OT in cyber systems for ships and ports, required for the optimization of regular operations, renders maritime systems vulnerable to various attacks, due to their complex and extended attack surface. Indeed, maritime systems have been successfully attacked in the recent past [23]. The cyber profile of the maritime sector has changed, but while the security of IT systems has been the subject of much research and development, the protection of OT system is less mature. This emphasizes the need for maritime cyber security to be studied in depth and integrated into sectorial practices. As a consequence, a number of organisations have issued guidelines and

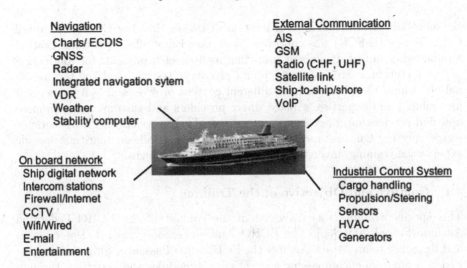

Navigation
Charts/ ECDIS
GNSS
Radar
Integrated navigation sytem
VDR
Weather
Stability computer

External Communication
AIS
GSM
Radio (CHF, UHF)
Satellite link
Ship-to-ship/shore
VoIP

On board network
Ship digital network
Intercom stations
Firewall/Internet
CCTV
Wifi/Wired
E-mail
Entertainment

Industrial Control System
Cargo handling
Propulsion/Steering
Sensors
HVAC
Generators

Fig. 1. Integration of information and operational technology on a ship [22].

rules with respect to the security of assets. ENISA has published guidelines and recommendation specific to the maritime sector [27]. Likewise, the International Maritime Organization also issues guidance documents for the management of cyber risk [28, 29]. The security of ships must be ensured at two different levels: in the construction phase and during daily operations. The structural aspects of security, such as network segmentation, should be addressed in the design phase of the ship. However, in daily operations, the risk management process takes over and relies on the crew for its success [22]. For this reason, raising awareness and training personnel is an integral part of the recommendations issued by overarching organisations of the maritime sector.

As any other sectors, the maritime sector suffers from the general difficulty to find qualified security personnel due to the overall skill gap observed on the market [30, 31]. At the European level, ENISA sees education as the way to overcome the skill gap issue [32]. In line with this effort toward providing adequate education, recent research and initiatives tend to focus on the specific training of maritime personnel. In that context, the cyber ranges are considered an essential part of the solution [33, 34]. In particular, the European H2020 project Cyber-MAR aims at developing maritime-specific cyber ranges, to act as a cost-efficient training solution encompassing the whole logistics value chain [35].

4   Federated Maritime Scenario Training

The need for sector-specific- and in particular maritime-specific training is clearly established. Furthermore, the added-value of a federation of cyber ranges is demonstrated, as far as it can help generate more flexible and diverse simulation environment to develop advanced and representative exercises. It is with the ambition to facilitate such federation of ranges that the ECHO Federated Cyber Range (E-FCR) was conceived, a Market Place offering services centred around cyber ranges. It aims at providing realistic environments for conducting experimentation, exercises, research and prototype testing, enabling the combination of multiple scenarios from different content providers. It is a focus point for training and expertise, a place where providers and customers can propose and find services meeting their expectations. These services can be generic or sector specific. One instance of such services is a hands-on maritime-specific experiential training, involving a federation of cyber ranges.

4.1   Context and Objective of the Training

This specific training was delivered in the context of the ECHO Federated Autumn School 2021 [36]. The ECHO Autumn school, entitled 'Detection of and Response to an Attack Against the ECDIS on a Passenger Ship', was organised as a program encompassing a set of virtual modules and activities, through which the trainees enhance their understanding of the appropriate manner to implement the security controls related to the detection and response to cybersecurity incidents in a ship ICT environment. The program covers best practices and policies to support the overall cybersecurity posture of the ship digital systems; it encompasses theoretical and practical hands-on modules [37].

The experiential module described in this paper aims to train the ICT professionals on how to detect attacks, analyse the issues in the configuration of the ship Electronic Chart Display and Information System (ECDIS) that could lead to the successful attack and restore and secure the ECDIS [37]. Furthermore, the program provides the trainees with exercises handling tools and material to improve the effective reaction to a cyber-incident, including remediation of the affected systems.

The trainees gain a better understanding of attack vectors and the consequences of a security breach. They are guided in the way to gather forensic traces, within the extent permitted by laws and regulations. The restoration operations are explained, as well as the best practices to prevent future breaches.

4.2   The Maritime Scenario

The aim of a Maritime Cyber Range is to provide a virtual environment capable to approximate as much as possible real digital systems present aboard a ship. A sample network infrastructure on a ship will gather some essential elements depicted on the Fig. 2.

The connection to the shore and Internet is provided by a satellite data link: a border router interconnects the internal network to the satellite link.

The ship internal network is organised into different zones, separated by firewalls to control the access of sensitive digital equipment. It should be noted that, on a cruise ship, digital systems must be redundant to guarantee essential ship services in case of fire or flood casualties. For this reason a ship is divided in fire zones: the ship digital systems must be replicated inside at least two different

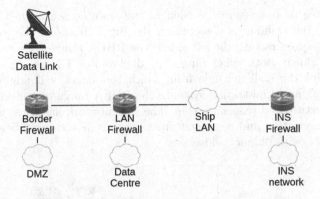

Fig. 2. High level network structure of a modern ship.

fire zones. However, since the redundancy of systems is not reproduced in the federated maritime scenario, this aspect of the network architecture will not be discussed here.

A ship network internal structure will typically encompass a demilitarized (DMZ) zone, a Data Centre, a ship Local Area Network (LAN) and a Integrated Navigation System network.

– The DMZ zone hosts the services exposed to the internet such as an FTP server and Reverse Proxy server.
– The Data Centre is a LAN containing all server equipment; it is designed to contain some equipment for most common ship systems like the Heating, Ventilation, and Air Conditioning (HVAC), etc.
– The 'ship LAN' hosts the servers and workstations offering different services, such as a WIFI access point, IP telephones, workstations for the crew, etc.
– Finally, the Integrated Navigation System (INS) zone gathers the elements pertaining to the Navigation System. It is in charge of providing all the navigation aids needed to safely drive the ship along a route. Navigation data covers:
  • the position, direction and speed of the ship,
  • the external conditions like wind speed, water speed, deep, temperatures etc.,
  • the presence of other ships or obstacles in the surrounding area, thanks to Radar and Automatic Identification System equipment.

The reliability of information from the Navigation System is crucial because it is used by the crew officers to take decisions on the route and the speed of the ship. The Navigation System is by design protected by several levels of firewalls.

The basic structure of these architectural elements are reproduced, if in simplified form, in the maritime training scenario. It should be noted that most of maritime software is proprietary. However, the proprietary software was replaced by an equivalent free or open-source version in the training scenario. The scenario deployed for the training is depicted on the Fig. 3. It shows the federation of two separate cyber ranges: the left side is the RHEA range while the right side is the RMA range. Both cyber ranges are deployed on CITEF [38]. The RMA range contains the Kali machine from which the attack will originate, and a server running an orchestration system. The RHEA range reproduces a typical network structure of a passenger ship. The ship network has three main zones: the server, navigation and passenger areas. Each zone connects its assets via a separate LAN, with distinct addressing.

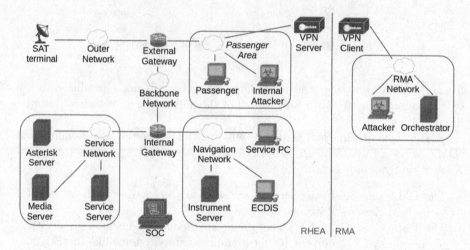

Fig. 3. Network scenario as deployed for the maritime training.

1. The Service Network holds the simulated ship's servers. In particular, the following servers are deployed:
   - A web server (Media Server) that hosts an internal entertainment content website.
   - A multi-purpose server (Service Server) that hosts the Active Directory service (DC role) for the ship's domain, the Mail Server, the DNS Server and the File Server services.
   - An Asterisk Server that hosts the VoIP service.
2. The Navigation Network is a LAN where the ship's navigation system is housed. Specifically:
   - An ECDIS platform (ECDIS), where the ship's electronic charts system is located.
   - An Instrument Server (Server) where the navigational data are generated to simulate the sailing of the ship, this data is fed to the ECDIS system.
   - A Service computer (Service PC) that is used as a gateway for external technical support to gain access to the ship's networks.

3. The Passengers Network is the LAN dedicated to passengers. The ship's passengers can connect to access the internet, and selected services in the Service Network (DNS, Media services).

Two firewalls route and filter the traffic between all the networks; they are interconnected across a backbone network:

1. The Internal Gateway, that connects the Navigation network and the Server network to the backbone network. The gateway firewall has the following configuration:
   - All traffic from the Server or the Navigation Area to any destination is allowed.
   - Connections from the Passenger Area to the Server Area are only allowed if they are http or DNS traffic (ports 80 and 53)
   - All traffic from the Server Area is allowed towards the Navigation Area. (This is an intentional misconfiguration that leads to a vulnerability exploited in the training).
2. The External Gateway, that connects the Passenger Area with the Internet and the backbone network. The gateway firewall has the following configuration:
   - Connections from the Passenger Area to the Server Area are only allowed if they are http or DNS traffic (ports 80 and 53).

Finally, the ship network holds a SOC server, that monitors and logs all the traffic that transits on the networks.

4.3   Technical Aspects of the Federation

Cyber Range inter-connectivity is realized by VPN VM technology. VPN VM allows to interconnect two cyber ranges with client-to-server Layer 3 virtual private network (VPN). In the maritime scenario, the VPN connection is established between two virtual machines developed by RHEA: the VPN software and its configuration are contained within VMs on both client and server-side of this point-to-point connection, as illustrates the Fig. 4.

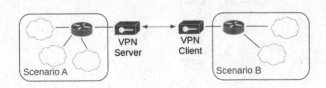

Fig. 4. Federation of two cyber ranges enabled by VPN connection.

The VPN VM technology is agnostic to the virtualization technology used by a cyber range itself. However, it requires certain technical readiness from the cyber range's networking point of view. A VPN tunnel is established between two scenarios running on different cyber ranges. A VM acts as a VPN server in one cyber range scenario while another VM functions as a VPN client in the other cyber range scenario. Virtual Machines running inside Scenario A have network connectivity to Virtual Machines running inside Scenario B at the remote cyber range, and vice versa. The connectivity relies on the proper configuration of the VPN VMs; including network interfaces, routing, VPN protocol and VPN authentication. VPN VMs configuration includes the assignment of specific routes from remote subnets to be visible on both sides.

4.4 The Attacker Perspective

The maritime training focuses on the defensive side, trainees are invited to find forensic traces of a cyber attack on the ship, and take appropriate mitigation actions. The path of the attack designed for the network scenario described above is depicted on the Fig. 5. The attack is structured as follows: a passenger scans the port 80 of the Media Server located in the Server Area, which is accessible to passengers through the firewalls. A vulnerability is found and exploited. Once a foothold is acquired on the Media Server, this server is used to pivot to the Navigation Area, thanks to a misconfiguration of the Internal Gateway. The ECDIS server is successfully attacked, and the console configuration compromised. As a result, the ECDIS is fed corrupted navigation data, which tampers its operations and diverts the ship route. The ECDIS console indicates that the ship sails in Australia, while its actual position is along the west coast of the USA.

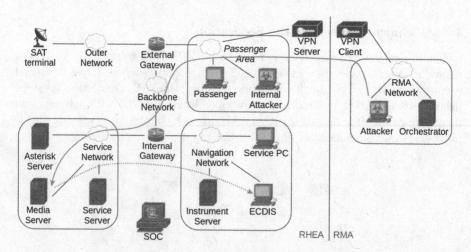

Fig. 5. Representation of the attack path in the maritime scenario.

The attack originates from the Kali machine that is deployed in the RMA range and leverages the underlying VPN connection to the remote cyber range in order to reach the passenger area: from a practical point of view, the attack seems to originate from the passenger area. The attack is carried out in an automated manner, by an orchestration engine deployed on a separate VM of the RMA range. The attack is conceptually organised as an oriented graph of tasks, all tasks being related by parent-child relationships. Children tasks are activated depending on the success or failure of their parents. The orchestrator is responsible to launch the execution of the tasks in a timely manner, and evaluate their success. It communicates with the Kali VM to send instructions and collects tasks outcomes. This orchestration system allows to fully automate the attack, and does not require human intervention once launched[1].

From a technical perspective, for this particular scenario, it is essential that the VPN connection does preserve both the source and destination IP addresses of forwarded packets and that the routing on the respective sides of the federation handles the network addresses harmoniously. Each side of the federation must be aware of the network ranges of the other side, and the routing tables must be configured to forward the packets accordingly via the VPN. There can be no Network Address Translation (NAT) at the boundaries of the cyber ranges nor the scenarios' ones. Indeed, the attacker configures a payload to open a reverse session from the target VM to the attacker's IP address (traffic allowed by the existing firewall rules). If the respective addresses are not preserved, the payload will not be able to connect back to the attacker and the attack will fail. Hence, in the context of such a federation, with a cyber attack executed across the VPN connecting separate cyber-ranges, the VPN cannot execute NAT, the original addresses must be preserved and packets forwarded transparently across the VPN. This in particular means that care must be taken when configuring the ranges that there is no overlap of addressing, nor any ambiguity in the routing of both cyber ranges.

4.5   Training: The Defense Perspective

The maritime scenario was designed to reproduce essential elements of a civilian passenger ship and allows to demonstrate the progress of a cyber attack on the ship's internal network. The scenario is very elaborated and rich; it illustrates and trains many aspects of the defensive posture. The overall aim of the training focuses on the defensive side, and highlights good practices about the defensive actions. The trainees are guided to find forensic traces of the attack. When specific elements of the attack are identified, trainees are invited to suggest corrective and remedy actions. Once normal ship operation is restored, students are expected to consider the network topology, and make suggestions to harden the network against potential future attacks and mitigate threats. This practical training raises awareness of trainees as to different points:

- The general cybersecurity and privacy principles;
- The major cyber threats, vulnerabilities and incidents related to a ship ICT and OT;

---

[1] The automation system is described in an article entitled "Sly, a red teaming orchestration system" accepted for Digilience 2022.

- The incident response lifecycle according to best practices;
- Applying network analysis tools, methods and techniques;
- Identifying and collecting intelligence and forensics Information and analysing a cyber-attack based on collected Information;
- Evaluating and recommending containment actions;
- Prioritizing essential system capabilities or business functions required for partial or full system restoration after a catastrophic failure event;
- Proposing recovery procedures;
- Preparing and communicating cyber-attack related reports;
- Acting within the extent of the laws and regulations.

4.6   Reception from the Audience

This hands-on maritime training was delivered as part of the ECHO Autumn School of November 2021 [36]. The overall School organisation did reflect the implementation of the ECHO cyberskills framework [39]. Beside the training described above, the School also encompassed a number of theoretical sessions delivered via two different channels. Such a mixed delivery is deemed effective for training purposes [40]. On the one hand, a part of the theory was delivered offline via a Moodle platform. A second part was presented to students in the context of a three days live online course. The practical session described in this paper was delivered live, to a group of trainees who were IT personnel operating aboard ships. The general feedback from trainees about the ECHO Federated Autumn School was positive, in particular about the hands-on maritime scenario training. Their comments stressed the added-value of the practical session that exemplified and embodied the theory delivered via the other modules of the School[2].

5   Conclusion and Future Work

This paper describes a maritime sector-specific scenario, as designed for a hands-on training. The maritime scenario incorporates two cyber ranges, interconnected in a federation. It was developed to sustain the delivery of a complex defensive exercise.

The technical challenges of federating cyber ranges were successfully addressed. In particular, the necessity for the VPN to preserve the network address ranges and the routing to be properly configured was successfully met. In this instance, the federation connected the attacker to the target. However, in another situation, the federation could adequately connect two separate ship-specific cyber ranges, with different specialisations, to generate an advanced simulation environment.

The complexity of the network and attack scenarios allowed to touch upon many aspects of defensive actions which were the focus point of the training. The

---

[2] The Autumn School presentation and analysis of its impact will be published in the ECHO deliverable D2.8 in spring 2023.

infection of the ECDIS console was illustrated, and its impact on the navigation system emphasized. The analysis of traffic traces was facilitated by the presence of the SOC server. The repercussions of the misconfiguration of the firewalls and the lag in vulnerability patching were stressed. All defensive actions were contextualised in the general setting of good practices to strengthen the security posture of any system, and a ship in particular.

At present, the maritime aspect of the scenario was reflected in the network topology similar to that of a modern ship, and in the presence of the ECDIS system. In the future, the scenario might be further developed to integrate additional maritime-specific assets holding vulnerabilities susceptible to be the target of cyber attacks. In particular, the attack design was assumed to originate from a passenger hacker. However, it could be envisaged to conceive an insider attack. In such a case, more network areas and hence more assets of the ship could be directly accessible to the attacker. That new perspective would permit to design many different attack paths on basis of a same network topology, illustrating various forensic traces to collect and analyse.

Furthermore, the training scenario in its present state is adapted to a one-on-one setting: each trainee should ideally have access to a specific instance of the scenario, to observe and act on the machines individually. This situation does not scale very well since the scenario makes substantial capacity demands on the virtualisation environment due to its structure complexity. A future version of the training scenario could integrate elements better fitted to be tackled by a group of trainees, gathered in a simulated IT team. The delivery of the training to larger groups would then scale better.

Acknowledgements. This work was supported by the ECHO project which has received funding from the European Union's Horizon 2020 research and innovation program under the grant agreement no 830943.

References

1. NTT: 2021 Global Threat Intelligence Report. Technical report. https://services.global.ntt/en-gb/insights/2021-global-threat-intelligence-report
2. ENISA: ENISA Threat Landscape 2021. Technical report. https://www.enisa.europa.eu/publications/enisa-threat-landscape-2021
3. Endsley, M.: Situation awareness global assessment technique (SAGAT). In: Proceedings of the IEEE 1988 National Aerospace and Electronics Conference, pp. 789–795 (1988)
4. Endsley, M.: Toward a theory of situation awareness in dynamic systems. Hum. Factors **37**(1), 32–64 (1995)
5. Aaltola, K., Taitto, P.: Utilising experiential and organizational learning theories to improve human performance in cyber training. Inf. Secur. **43**(2), 123–133 (2019)
6. Davis, J., Magrath, S.: A survey of cyber ranges and testbeds. Technical Report Defence Science and Technology, Cyber and Electronic Warfare Division, Australia (2013)
7. Darwish, O., Stone, C.M., Karajeh, O., Alsinglawi, B.: Survey of educational cyber ranges. In: Barolli, L., Amato, F., Moscato, F., Enokido, T., Takizawa, M. (eds.)

WAINA 2020. AISC, vol. 1150, pp. 1037–1045. Springer, Cham (2020). https://doi.org/10.1007/978-3-030-44038-1_96

8. Yamin, M.M., Katt, B., Gkioulos, V.: Cyber ranges and security testbeds: Scenarios, functions, tools and architecture. Comput. Secur. **88**, 101636 (2020)

9. Chouliaras, N., Kittes, G., Kantzavelou, I., Maglaras, L., Pantziou, G., Ferrag, M.: Cyber ranges and TestBeds for education, training, and research. Appl. Sci. **11**, 1809 (2021)

10. ECSO, WG5 paper: Understanding Cyber Ranges: From Hype to Reality, March 2020. https://www.ecs-org.eu/documents/uploads/understanding-cyber-ranges-from-hype-to-reality.pdf

11. Ukwandu, E., et al.: A review of cyber-ranges and test-beds: current and future trends. Sensors **20**, 7148 (2020)

12. CyberSec4Europe: Cyber Range Federation - The Real Benefits (2021). https://cybersec4europe.eu/cyber-range-federation-the-real-benefits/

13. EDA: Cyber Ranges Federation Project reaches new milestone (2018). https://eda.europa.eu/news-and-events/news/2018/09/13/cyber-ranges-federation-project-reaches-new-milestone

14. Piispanen J.: Technical specification for federation of cyber ranges. Master thesis, JAMK University of Applied Sciences (2018)

15. Peratikou, A., Louca, C., Shiaeles, S., Stavrou, S.: On federated cyber range network interconnection. In: Ghita, B., Shiaeles, S. (eds.) INC 2020. LNNS, vol. 180, pp. 117–128. Springer, Cham (2021). https://doi.org/10.1007/978-3-030-64758-2_9

16. Nicodème, B.: Federated cyber range challenges. Master thesis, Université Libre de Bruxelles (2020)

17. Graziano, A.: About federation of cyber ranges, market places and technology innovation (2020). https://www.linkedin.com/pulse/federation-cyber-ranges-market-places-technology-almerindo-graziano

18. Varag, C., Cegan, J., Lieskovan, T., Merialdo, M.: The current state of the art and future of European Cyber Range Ecosystem. In: 2021 IEEE International Conference on Cyber Security and Resilience, pp. 390–395 (2021)

19. Oikonomou, N., et al.: ECHO federated cyber range: towards next-generation scalable cyber ranges. In: 2021 IEEE International Conference on Cyber Security and Resilience, pp. 403–408 (2021)

20. European Network of Cybersecurity Centres and Competence Hub for Innovation and Operations (ECHO). https://echonetwork.eu/

21. Fitton, O., Prince, D., Germond, B., Lacy, M.: The future of maritime cyber security. Lancaster University (2015). https://ssg.lancs.ac.uk/wp-content/uploads/oliver-the-maritime.pdf

22. Loomis, W., Singh, V., Kessler, G., Bellekens, X.: Signaling for cooperation on maritime cybersecurity. Atlantic Council, Cyber Statecraft Initiative (2021). https://www.atlanticcouncil.org/in-depth-research-reports/report/cooperation-on-maritime-cybersecurity-a-system-of-systems/

23. Meland, P.H., Bernsmed, K., Wille, E., Rødseth, Ø., Nesheim, D.A.: A retrospective analysis of maritime cyber security incidents. TransNav Int. J. Marine Navig. Saf. Sea Transp. **15**, 519–530 (2021)

24. Teal, J.M., Howarth, R.W.: Oil spill studies: a review of ecological effects. Environ. Manag. **8**, 27–43 (1984)

25. Galieriková, A., Dáivid, A., Materna, M., Mako, P.: Study of maritime accidents with hazardous substances involved: comparison of HNS and oil behaviours in marine environment. Transp. Res. Proc. **55**, 1050–1064 (2021)

26. Deja, A., Ulewicz, R., Kyrychenko, Y.: Analysis and assessment of environmental threats in maritime transport. Transp. Res. Proc. **55**, 1073–1080 (2021)
27. ENISA: Critical Infrastructures and Services - Maritime. https://www.enisa. europa.eu/topics/critical-information-infrastructures-and-services/maritime
28. International Maritime Organization: Maritime cyber risk management in safety management systems (2017). https://wwwcdn.imo.org/localresources/en/ OurWork/Security/Documents/Resolution%20MSC.428(98).pdf
29. BIMCO et al.: Guidelines to cyber security onboard ships (2020). https:// wwwcdn.imo.org/localresources/en/OurWork/Security/Documents/ANNEX %20Guidelines%20on%20Cyber%20Security%20Onboard%20Ships%20v.4.pdf
30. ISSA: The Life and Times of Cybersecurity Professionals 2021 (2021). https:// www.issa.org/cybersecurity-skills-crisis-continues-for-fifth-year-perpetuated-by- lack-of-business-investment/
31. Fortinet: 2022 Cybersecurity Skills Gap (2022). https://www.fortinet.com/ content/dam/fortinet/assets/reports/report-2022-skills-gap-survey.pdf?utm_ source=pr&utm_campaign=report-2022-skills-gap-survey
32. ENISA: Addressing skills shortage and gap through higher education (2021). https://www.enisa.europa.eu/publications/addressing-skills-shortage-and-gap- through-higher-education/@@download/fullReport
33. Tam, K., Moara-Nkwe, K., Jones, K.: The use of cyber ranges in the maritime context: assessing maritime-cyber risks, raising awareness, and providing training. Maritime Technol. Res. **3**(1), 16–30 (2021)
34. Potamos, G., Peratikou, A., Stavrou, S.: Towards a maritime cyber range training environment. In: 2021 IEEE International Conference on Cyber Security and Resilience (CSR), pp. 180–185 (2021)
35. Cyber-Mar: Cyber preparedness actions for a holistic approach and awareness raising in the MARitime logistics supply chain. https://www.cyber-mar.eu/
36. Echo Federated Autumn School. https://echonetwork.eu/echo-federated-autumn- school/
37. Iosifidis, G., Varbanov, P.: Detection of and response to an attack against the ECDIS on a passenger ship. Course Blueprint, ECHO internal deliverable D2.7 - Annex 3 (2021)
38. RHEA group. https://www.rheagroup.com/document/citef-pdf-brochure/
39. Varbanov, P., et al.: ECHO Cyberskill Framework (2021). https://echonetwork. eu/d2-6-hopp/
40. Bertram, V., Plowman, T.: Digital training solutions in the maritime context: options and costs. Maritime Technol. Res. **2**(2), 52–68 (2020)

E-Skills in Cybersecurity

Harri Ruoslahti[1]([⊠]) [iD] and Ilkka Tikanmäki[1,2] [iD]

[1] Laurea University of Applied Sciences, Vanha Maantie 9, 02650 Espoo, Finland
harri.ruoslahti@laurea.fi
[2] National Defence University, Kadettikouluntie, 00800 Helsinki, Finland

Abstract. Today's digital work environments require that organizations increase their cyber resilience. This calls for organizational solutions to find skilled cybersecurity professionals and efficient solutions and procedures that secure digital technologies. Some recent developments deepen the understanding of cybersecurity skills, build skills frameworks, taxonomies and certification systems to base trainings on work-life needs.

This study is part of the project ECHO research activities, and it identifies skills that have been used as base skills to develop the ECHO E-skills and Training Toolkit. This case study collected recruitment advertisements from the web service Monster to understand what the Finnish labor market looks at the most desired e-skills that employers want from their future employees. The results of this study are based on a sample (n = 178) of Finnish job advertisements collected in the summer of 2021. This section looks at the job advertisements both by sector and level of expertise and then discusses the relevant skills categories of Technical, Situation awareness, Problem-solving, and Sector specific e-skills.

The results show that companies are actively looking for Technical e-skills and Problem-solving e-skills. The most sought after Technical e-skills were programming, software (SW) and information technology (IT). The most important Problem-solving e-skills are, according to the results communication, interaction, self-driven, teamwork, and cooperation and collaboration, and situation awareness e-skills were surprisingly very little addressed to.

Keywords: Skills · Recruitment advertisements · Technical e-skills · Problem-solving e-skills · Training

1 Introduction

Today's digital work environments require that organizations increase their cyber resilience [1, 2], which calls for organizational solutions to find skilled cybersecurity professionals [3]. As there is a high need for Information Technology (IT) professionals [4], and efficient solutions and procedures that secure digital technologies [5].

Some recent studies have worked to deepen the understanding of cybersecurity skills by e.g., building skills frameworks, taxonomies and certification systems that support the design of trainings that are based on work-life needs [6–9].

There have been one of several research, development, and innovation (RDI) initiatives on cybersecurity on the European level, such as the European Commission funded

A. Dziech et al. (Eds.): MCSS 2022, CCIS 1689, pp. 36–48, 2022.
https://doi.org/10.1007/978-3-031-20215-5_4

project ECHO (European Network of Cybersecurity Centres for Innovation and Operations) that has, as part of its total effort, developed an E-skills and Training Toolkit. Project ECHO that consists of 30 partners from different sectors (e.g., health, transport, telecom, energy, space, healthcare, defense, civil protection, manufacturing, ICT, education, and research) promotes a European-wide network with methods, and assets that promote information sharing among network partners, with regards to regulatory requirements, [10, 11].

This study serves as part of the prior background research that has made public in academic papers published in relation to ECHO research activities that brings academia, industry, cybersecurity practitioners and end-users together [12]. The skills that have been identified in this study were used as base skills to develop the E-skills and Training Toolkit, where these base skills can be used to identify relevant e-skills and to measure related training and recruitment needs and gaps that may be used to increase organisational cybersecurity.

This paper serves as a potential case study of European recruitment advertisements to deepen understanding of skills acquisition and training in relation to the societal impacts of project ECHO. The skills from the recruitment advertisements analysed in this study were used to create long lists of technical, situation awareness and problem-solving skills that serve as basis in the ECHO E-skills and Training Toolkit.

The research questions of this study are:

– What Technical skills are asked for in European recruitment advertisements?
– What Situation awareness skills are asked for in European recruitment advertisements?
– What Problem-solving skills are asked for in European recruitment advertisements?

2 Literature

Cybersecurity is seen as a multi-disciplinary domain, as it joins elements from mathematics, psychology, engineering, law and computer science, business continuity and other disciplines [3]. Cyberattacks may have varying and serious consequences, and this calls for new techniques to improve organizational resilience in the cyber domain [1, 2], as emerging new technologies radically change the relationships between human and cyber dimensions in many organizations [13].

2.1 Organizational Learning

Knowledge generation and information processing can promote productivity and competitiveness, where ICT acts as a catalyst to increase organizational learning [14], and as ICT has brought new opportunities even for companies with limited resources, to develop skills that enable absorbing state-of-the-art knowledge from external sources [15]. ICT-infrastructures support knowledge sharing in organizations [16], though lack of competences and skills to use ICT can hinder learning to use organizational ICT-tools [17].

Modern participative of ICT and mobile technologies promote the creation of new learning experiences in learning organizations [18]. ICT offers opportunities for strategic learning [19], where even the survival of businesses may depend on its capabilities to implement new ICT solutions and take advantage of the opportunities that they can offer [20].

The perception of ease of usage, and other social factors, influence the acceptance of ICT and mobile technologies in organizations, which directly influences the usage of mobile learning, where mobile devices with graphics and visual applications make them more accessible, which helps learn and renew learning [21]. ICT makes it easier to store and share organizational knowledge [16], and blended learning can improve organizational training and learning performances, and trainee satisfaction [22]. Knowing how to use ICT tools and Knowledge Management (KM) technologies can promote knowledge sharing and transfer within and outside the organization [23].

The level of organizational ICT support influences how motivated organization members are to share knowledge. ICT support eliminates hindrances and provides channels to obtain information [24], and organizations should consider KM when selecting and implementing ICT solutions [25].

2.2 Skills Acquisition

The field of cybersecurity has been under rapid development, and this has challenged the understanding what skills make good cyber experts, and where and how these professionals can become recruited by organizations [3]. Investments in ICT-support and training develop higher competencies in ICT-tools usage [26]. To achieve preparedness and resilience, acquiring cybersecurity skills needs continuous advancement with learning processes that address complex demands of building individual and organizational level capacities with relevant trainings and exercises [27].

Modern ITC tools make it relatively easy to the master the needed technical skills, so the main trait for modern cybersecurity specialists now is flexibility [28], so a promising new source to recruit future cybersecurity experts are people with an aptitude to acquire the new skills that make them likely to succeed in a cybersecurity career [29]. Cybersecurity experts may be recruited from today's IT professionals who can learn the skills needed to solve different cybersecurity issues and have capabilities for continuous learning and skills improvement [30]. Cybersecurity professionals could be recruited from occupations such as electrical, electronics, telecommunications and equipment installers and repairers, geographers, purchasing, sociologists or financial and budget analysts [29].

2.3 Cybersecurity Skills

The cybersecurity domain emphasizes technical and engineering skills [31], though social and organizational aspects are very much needed to successfully perform in everyday digital work-life settings [3].

Besides knowledge and skills of using computer systems, cyber professionals need to be able to use analytical tools, vulnerability analysis, and network scanning [3], but they also need strong skills for situational awareness with continuous risk assessment [32] to successfully maintain security. Problem-solving, communication and collaboration are important non-technical knowledge skills and abilities (KSA) in cybersecurity [33].

Organisational learning can be promoted with ICT technologies, which in turn can have significant impacts in building innovative culture that helps establish competitive advantages [34]. Though ICT does not automatically enhance learning, it can be a means to facilitate skills acquisition, learning and teaching [35], and organizations have to integrate ITC into all of its functions organizational innovation culture, learning, strategy and policies, to have the potential to influence its organizational performance and competitiveness [36].

3   Method

Quantitative research seeks to demonstrate cause-and-effect relationships numerically, most often using statistical methods. Quantitative research describes and interprets phenomena according to the general logic of science [37, 38]. In a quantitative study, such as this study, classification is often used due to the large amount of source material [39] and quantitative findings can be collected for case studies [40, 41]. The basic concepts of quantitative research are the statistical unit and the sample, and the accumulated data are described using scales.

In this case study of the Finnish labour market analysis the most desired e-skills that employers want from their future employees were conducted. To identify relevant skills that are required on the Finnish job market, recruitment advertisements from the web service Monster were collected during the summer of 2021. The sample covered advertisements from the energy, healthcare, and maritime transport sectors, while noting its technology level as cybersecurity, IT professional or information intensive work. The total number of ads analysed were 178. The data collected were stored in a data extraction table (DET) from which more detailed tables were created on separate spreadsheets for each skill category. The DET was specifically designed for this study. It was used to first store data from job postings, and to then to further analyse the collected data by identifying relevant skills and then classifying them into four categories of e-skills: technical, problem-solving, sector-specific, and situational awareness skills.

The columns, presented in Tables 1 and 2, of the DET note the advertisement, its job posting, company, technical level, and sector, which are maritime, healthcare, and energy. Job advertisements that were not clearly in any of the above mentioned three sectors were classified as Other.

Table 1. Data extraction table columns.

Ad no.	Job	Company	Technical level	Maritime	Healthcare	Energy	Other

The Technical level column identified if the company was looking for a cybersecurity specialist, IT professional or a person for information intensive work that is based on constant usage of IT solutions. The three sector columns were further divided in sub-columns that are shown in the table below.

Table 2. Data extraction table sub-columns.

Maritime		Healthcare		Energy	
Manager	Specialist	Manager	Specialist	Manager	Specialist

Each sector specific advertisement, maritime, healthcare and energy were further divided in sub-categories as Manager and Specialist. A manager-level person has subordinates and works on a strategic level. Specialists have expert positions where they work in on a tactical level without subordinates.

4   Results

The results of this study are based on a sample (n = 178) of Finnish job advertisements collected in the summer of 2021. This section looks at the job advertisements both by sector and level of expertise. And then discusses the relevant skills categories of Technical, Situation awareness, Problem-solving, and Sector specific e-skills.

4.1   Job Ads by Sector and Level of Expertise

Of the total sample 123 job advertisements were on the level of Specialist. Figure 1 below shows the distribution of results in relation to Manager or Specialist on each sector. Of the sample of job advertisements, the largest sectors were Energy (n = 55) and Healthcare (n = 38), while there were significantly few on the Maritime sector (n =

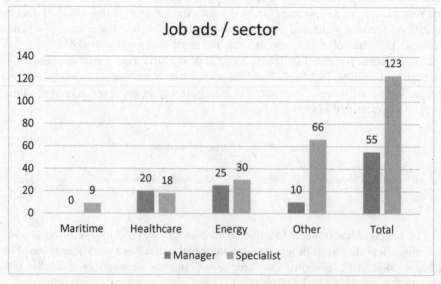

Fig. 1. Results in relation to sector and Manager or Specialist.

9). However, the Other sector had 76 advertisements, and most of these (n = 66) were on the Specialist level. This is over half of all Specialist level jobs advertised.

The categories of Manager and Specialist level jobs were examined against the technical expertise (Cybersecurity, IT Sector, Information intensive). Figure 2 shows, how in the sample, IT sector professionals (n = 96) were the most sought-after workforce, and the advertisements were quite evenly distributed between Specialist (n = 54) and Manager (n = 42). Cybersecurity positions (n = 70) were mostly on the Specialist (n = 59) level. There were relatively few advertisements (n = 12) for information intensive positions in this sample.

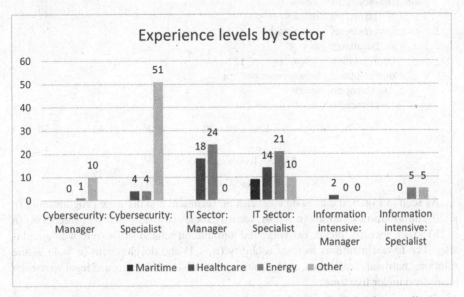

Fig. 2. Manager and Specialist examined against technical level. (Color figure online)

Figure 2 also shows how the technical expertise of Cybersecurity on a Tactical/Specialist level on the Other sector were most sought after (n = 51) in the sample. The sectors that are relevant to project ECHO are seen in blue (Maritime), orange (Healthcare), and grey (Energy). The Energy sector was looking for both Specialists (n = 21) and Managers (n = 24) with IT sector technical expertise. The Healthcare sector was also mainly looking IT sector technical expertise on a Specialist (n = 14) and Manager (n = 18) level. The Maritime sector focused on Expert level IT sector technical expertise.

4.2 Technical E-Skills

Technical skills were listed in the sample job advertisements. The sample yielded a long list of 199 technical skills, abilities, or experience that the job market was asking for. In this context they are referred to as Technical e-skills. To make better sense of these and to enable practical choices, they were classified into 18 categories (Fig. 3).

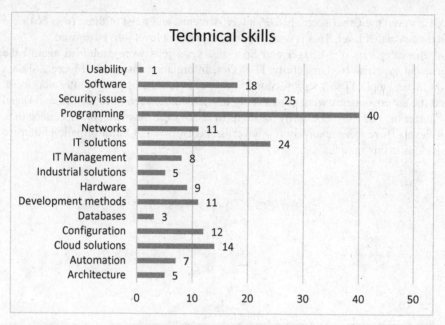

Fig. 3. Technical e-skills.

As seen in Fig. 3, the largest categories of Technical e-skills were programming (n = 40), information solutions (n = 24), security issues (n = 25), and software (SW) (n = 18). Also, security, cloud, network, and automation related skills were well sought-after. The fewest mentions were of usability (n = 1) and development (n = 1), while solutions, hardware, databases, configuration, methods, architecture, and legal were each mentioned under five times.

4.3 Situation Awareness E-Skill

Situational awareness skills, abilities and knowledge were visible in 26 of the sample of job applications. In this context they are referred to as Situation awareness e-skills. Situation awareness e-skills were consolidated into seven categories (Fig. 4). Though there was quite an even distribution between the categories there were only 10 mentions of them, four of which were only mentioned once. Work under pressure, Security framework and tools, and Critical configurations had two mentions each.

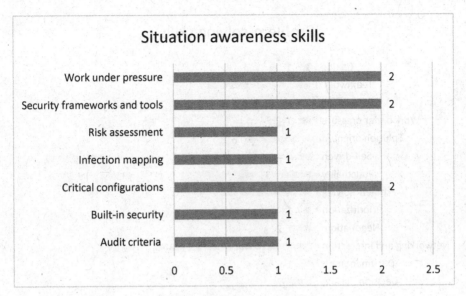

Fig. 4. Situation awareness skills.

As seen in Fig. 4, experience in cybersecurity seems to be seen as being the single most important Situation awareness e-skill. However, it is noteworthy that the relatively low number of mentions (n = 10) of Situation awareness e-skills would indicate that these are not sought-after. Recruiting organizations may not themselves be aware of the importance of building situation awareness, or they see that an adequate level of technical e-skills (n = 199) be enough to also cover this aspect.

4.4 Problem-Solving E-Skills

The sample of advertisements yielded 107 problem solving related skills, abilities, or knowledge that the Finnish job market required. In this context they are referred to as Problem solving e-skills. These were first unified into 24 categories of Problem solving, which were then re-worked into the 15 categories of e-skills that are listed in Fig. 5.

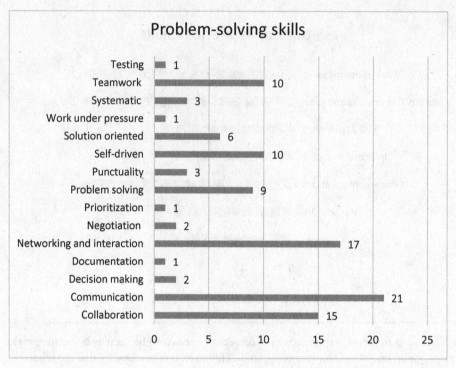

Fig. 5. Problem-solving skills.

As seen in Fig. 5, Communication (n = 21), Networking and Interaction (n = 17), Collaboration (n = 15), and Teamwork (n = 10) come to the forefront. It seems that recruiting organizations see these communication and collaboration related skills as being core to problem-solving. The term 'Problem-solving' was directly mentioned in seven advertisements. There were 8 categories of Problem-solving e-skills that were mentioned only between one and three times This could connote that problem-solving related are recognized as being important but, besides communication and collaboration related skills, they are less generalized.

4.5 Business Administration E-Skills

The relevant skills, abilities, or knowledge that were not deemed as Technical, Situation awareness or Problem-solving e-skills were classified as being Sector specific. These became classified in 12 categories. After this categorization the decision was made to re-name these as Business administration e-skills (Fig. 6).

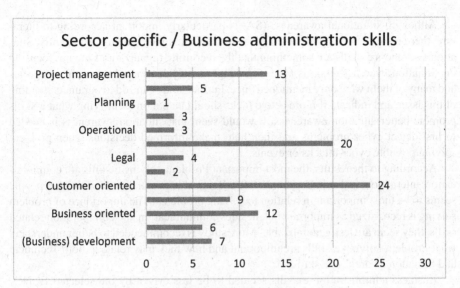

Fig. 6. Sector specific/Business administration skills.

Of the Business administration e-skills Customer oriented (n = 24) and management (n = 20) were the most common skills in the sample of job postings. Project management (n = 13) and business orientated (n = 12) were also common skills that were sought-after in this sample of Finnish job advertisements. Interestingly planning was only mentioned once. Data protection and privacy (n = 2) and organizational skills (n = 3) also had relatively few mentions.

5 Conclusions

Since the sample only included one summer period, further research is recommended to better understand what e-skills are valuable for the recruiting organizations. Also, this study is only limited to one job market (Finland). It is recommended that similar data be gathered also from other EU and relevant non-EU countries. This research should be periodically duplicated, if not done in real-time by using Big Data, AI and other modern possibilities. Organizations in this sample were most actively looking for Technical e-skills and Problem-solving e-skills.

The most sought after Technical e-skills were programming, software (SW) and information technology (IT). This could indicate that not only recruitment, but also education and training should put strong foci on these e-skills. Overall, it seemed to be quite to the recruiting organizations what Technical e-skills they are after. Periodically duplicated studies on different markets could contribute to theory by adding to the overall body of knowledge. On a practical level it could help focus organizations recruitment and training efforts and provide education and training providers with an on-time understanding of what is needed on the modern job markets across Europe.

Although, situational awareness (SA) is particularly important according to literature, there were surprisingly few job advertisements that indicate this. Apparently, Situation awareness e-skills are something that the recruiting organizations are not focusing on. Situation awareness e-skills were surprisingly evenly distributed across the categories and many of them were only mentioned once. Further study can add to our understanding of this issue and indicate if more active focus should be put on identifying what e-skills promote better situation awareness. It would seem that situation awareness is needed to first detect cyber problems and then help make informed decisions when problem solving possible cyber-attacks or events.

According to the results, the most important Problem-solving e-skills are communication, interaction, and collaboration related. Being able to collaborate with other people seems to be most important in relation to solving problems. The importance of problem solving is recognized as important but, besides communication and collaboration related skills, they seem are less generalizable. More study is recommended to better understand what Problem-solving e-skills are important and how they may relate to both Technical and Situation awareness e-skills.

Business administration e-skills seemed to be less driven by the selected ECHO-sectors of energy, healthcare and maritime than expected. Business administration e-skills seem more general in nature, with focus on business and customer orientation and both management and project management and seem to be common for jobs in any specific sector.

Organizations use many terms to describe some of the same e-skills (skills, knowledge, and abilities), or they use the same terminology to describe the same e-skills. Consolidating these into categories is not an easy task, and this will need further work and study. Further work is recommended to build relevant measures for Technical, Situation awareness and Problem-solving e-skills. Such measures could provide very practical contribution for organizations in recruitment, education and training, as well as organizational leaning and development. These measures could contribute to science if used to cumulate larger sets of data that can be analyzed to deepen our understanding of e-skills and the changes in e-skills needs.

Acknowledgements. This work was supported by the ECHO project, which has received funding from the European Union's Horizon 2020 research and innovation programme under the grant agreement no. 830943. This case is presented in the ECHO deliverable D9.15 Case Studies. The European Commission funded cyber pilot projects, such as European network of Cybersecurity centres and competence Hub for in-novation and Operations (ECHO), bring opportunities for researchers to conduct experiments and gather empirical data to study these aspects from different perspectives.

References

1. Aaltola, K., Taitto, P.: Utilising experiential and organizational learning theories to improve human performance in cyber training. ISIJ. **43**, 123–133 (2019). https://doi.org/10.11610/isij.4311
2. Ruoslahti, H.: Business continuity for critical infrastructure operators. Ann. Disast. Risk Sci.: ADRS **3** (2020)

3. Dawson, J., Thomson, R.: The future cybersecurity workforce: going beyond technical skills for successful cyber performance. Front. Psychol. **9**, 12 (2018). https://doi.org/10.3389/fpsyg.2018.00744

4. Crumpler, W., Lewis, J.A.: The cybersecurity workforce gap. Center for Strategic and International Studies (CSIS) Washington, DC, USA (2019)

5. Soni, S., Bhushan, B.: Use of machine learning algorithms for designing efficient cyber security solutions. Presented at the 2nd International Conference on Intelligent Computing, Instrumentation and Control Technologies (ICICICT), Kannur, India (2019)

6. Aaltola, K., Ruoslahti, H., Heinonen, J.: Cyber Range (CR) capabilities, interactions and features in acquisition of cyber skills by experts – empirical study. Presented at the, Chester, UK

7. Carlton, M., Levy, Y., Ramim, M.: Mitigating cyber attacks through the measurement of non-IT professionals' cybersecurity skills. Inf. Comput. Secur. **27**, 101–121 (2019). https://doi.org/10.1108/ICS-11-2016-0088

8. Furnell, S., Fischer, P., Finch, A.: Can't get the staff? The growing need for cyber-security skills. Comput. Fraud Secur. **2017**, 5–10 (2017). https://doi.org/10.1016/S1361-3723(17)30013-1

9. Levy, Y.: A case study of management skills comparison in online and on-campus MBA programs. Int. J. Inf. Commun. Technol. Educ. **1**, 1–20 (2005)

10. Oikonomou, N., et al.: ECHO federated cyber range: towards next-generation scalable cyber ranges. In: 2021 IEEE International Conference on Cyber Security and Resilience (CSR), pp. 403–408 (2021)

11. Rajamäki, J., Katos, V.: Information sharing models for early warning systems of cybersecurity intelligence. Inf. Secur.: Int. J. **46**, 198–214 (2020)

12. Yanakiev, Y.: A governance model of a collaborative networked organization for cybersecurity research. Inf. Secur.: Int. J. **46**, 79–98 (2020). https://doi.org/10.11610/isij.4606

13. Aaltola, K.: Empirical study on cyber range capabilities, interactions and learning features. In: Tagarev, T., Atanassov, K.T., Kharchenko, V., Kacprzyk, J. (eds.) Digital Transformation, Cyber Security and Resilience of Modern Societies. SBD, vol. 84, pp. 413–428. Springer, Cham (2021). https://doi.org/10.1007/978-3-030-65722-2_26

14. Hortovanyi, L., Ferincz, A.: The impact of ICT on learning on-the-job. Learn. Organ. **22**, 2–13 (2015). https://doi.org/10.1108/TLO-06-2014-0032

15. Cupiał, M., Szeląg-Sikora, A., Sikora, J., Rorat, J., Niemiec, M.: Information technology tools in corporate knowledge management. Ekon. Prawo. Econ. Law **17**, 5–15 (2018)

16. Siddiqui, S.H., Rasheed, R., Nawaz, S., Abbas, M.: Knowledge sharing and innovation capabilities: the moderating role of organizational learning. Pak. J. Commer. Soc. Sci. (PJCSS) **13**, 455–486 (2019)

17. Yau, H.K., Cheng, A.L.F.: Factors hindering the learning of ICT: an empirical study in transport sector. Knowl. Process. Manag. **18**, 220–229 (2011). https://doi.org/10.1002/kpm.382

18. Im, T., Porumbescu, G., Lee, H.: ICT as a buffer to change. Public Perform. Manag. Rev. **36**, 436–455 (2013). https://doi.org/10.2753/PMR1530-9576360303

19. Lopez-Nicolas, C., Soto-Acosta, P.: Analyzing ICT adoption and use effects on knowledge creation: An empirical investigation in SMEs. Int. J. Inf. Manage. **30**, 521–528 (2010). https://doi.org/10.1016/j.ijinfomgt.2010.03.004

20. Hernández, B., Jiménez, J., Martín, M.J.: Customer behavior in electronic commerce: the moderating effect of e-purchasing experience. J. Bus. Res. **63**, 964–971 (2010). https://doi.org/10.1016/j.jbusres.2009.01.019

21. Turi, J.A., Javed, Y., Bashir, S., Khaskhelly, F.Z., Shaikh, S., Toheed, H.: Impact of organizational learning factors on organizational learning effectiveness through mobile technology. Qual.-Access Succsess **20**, 114–119 (2019)

22. Isidro-Filho, A., Guimarães, T.D.A., Perin, M.G., Leung, R.C.: Workplace learning strategies and professional competencies in innovation contexts in Brazilian hospitals. BAR Braz. Adm. Rev. **10**, 121–134 (2013). https://doi.org/10.1590/S1807-76922013000200002
23. Conkova, M.: Analysis of perceptions of conventional and E-learning education in corporate training. JOC. **5**, 73–97 (2013). https://doi.org/10.7441/joc.2013.04.05
24. Rahman, S., Islam, M.Z., Abdullah, A.D.A.: Understanding factors affecting knowledge sharing: a proposed framework for Bangladesh's business organizations. J. Sci. Technol. Policy Manag. **8**, 275–298 (2017). https://doi.org/10.1108/JSTPM-02-2017-0004
25. Perez-Soltero, A., Moreno, F.J.L., Barcelo-Valenzuela, M., Gamiño, J.A.L.: An approach based on knowledge management for the use of ICTs in Mexican SMEs. IUP J. Knowl. Manag. **15**, 7–23 (2017)
26. Salleh, K., Chong, S., Ahmad, S., Ikhsan, S.: Learning and knowledge transfer performance among public sector accountants: an empirical survey. Knowl. Manag. Res. Pract. **10**, 164–174 (2012)
27. Nevmerzhitskaya, J., Norvanto, E., Virag, C.: High impact cybersecurity capacity building. eLearn. Softw. Educ. **2**, 306–312 (2019)
28. Skorenkyy, Y., Kozak, R., Zagorodna, N., Kramar, O., Baran, I.: Use of augmented reality-enabled prototyping of cyber-physical systems for improving cyber-security education. J. Phys: Conf. Ser. **1840**, 012026 (2021)
29. Neal, J., Facteau, J., O'Connell, B.: To find cybersecurity talent, poach from other – ProQuest. https://www.proquest.com/docview/2555709888?accountid=12003.&forcedol=true&forcedol=true
30. Rotim, S.T., Komnenić, V.: Cybersecurity Talent Shortage. Ann. Disast. Risk Sci. **3** (2020). https://doi.org/10.51381/adrs.v3i2.26
31. Gates, A., Salamah, S., Longpre, L.: Roadmap for graduating students with expertise in the analysis and development of secure cyber-systems. The University of Texas at El Paso, El Paso (2014)
32. Jajodia, S., Noel, S.: Topological vulnerability analysis. In: Jajodia, S., Liu, P., Swarup, V., Wang, C. (eds.) Cyber situational awareness. Advances in Information Security, vol. 46, pp. 139–154. Springer, Boston (2010). https://doi.org/10.1007/978-1-4419-0140-8_7
33. Sussman, L.L.: Exploring the value of non-technical knowledge, skills, and abilities (KSAs) to cybersecurity hiring managers. J. High. Educ. Theory Pract. **21**, 19 (2021)
34. Ruoslahti, H., Trent, A.: Organizational learning in the academic literature–systematic literature review. Inf. Secur.: Int. J. **46**, 65–78 (2020)
35. Marwan, A.: Empowering English through project-based learning with ICT. TOJET **14**, 28–37 (2015)
36. Tworek, K., Walecka-Jankowska, K., Zgrzywa-Ziemak, A.: Information technology reliability in shaping organizational innovativeness of SMEs. Organizacija **52**, 143–154 (2019)
37. Hirsjärvi, S., Remes, P., Sajavaara, P.: Tutki ja kirjoita. Bookwell Oy, Porvoo (1997)
38. Metteri, J.: Kvantitatiiviset tutkimusmenetelmät operaatiotaidon ja taktiikan tutkimuksessa. Maanpuolustuskorkeakoulu (2006)
39. van Aken, J.E.: Management research based on the paradigm of the design sciences: the quest for field-tested and grounded technological rules. J. Manage. Stud. **41**, 219–246 (2004)
40. Benbasat, I., Goldstein, D.K., Mead, M.: The case research strategy in studies of information systems. MIS Q. **11**, 369–386 (1987). https://doi.org/10.2307/248684
41. Eisenhardt, K.M.: Building theories from case study research. AMR **14**, 532–550 (1989). https://doi.org/10.5465/amr.1989.4308385

Multi-sector Risk Management Framework for Analysis Cybersecurity Challenges and Opportunities

Marcin Niemiec[1]([⊠]), Salvatore Marco Pappalardo[2,3], Maya Bozhilova[4],
Nikolai Stoianov[4], Andrzej Dziech[1], and Burkhard Stiller[5]

[1] AGH University of Science and Technology, Mickiewicza 30, 30-059 Krakow, Poland
{niemiec,dziech}@agh.edu.pl
[2] CIRM, Viale Ortles 22, Milan, Italy
marco.pappalardo@softwareengineering.it
[3] Software Engineering Italia S.r.l., Piazza Abramo Lincoln 7, Catania, Italy
[4] Bulgarian Defence Institute, Sofia, Bulgaria
{m.bozhilova,n.stoianov}@di.mod.bg
[5] Communication Systems Group CSG, Department of Informatics IfI, University of Zurich
UZH, Binzmühlestrasse 14, 8050 Zürich, Switzerland
stiller@ifi.uzh.ch

Abstract. This paper describes an approach to analyse transversal and inter-sectoral cybersecurity challenges and opportunities: dedicated risk assessment and management framework, which can be used to develop cybersecurity technology roadmaps. This multi-sector assessment framework is able to prioritise and evaluate cybersecurity risks in trans-sectoral and inter-sectoral contexts as well as supports proper resource allocations and mitigation actions. To achieve this goal, the analysis of known risk management and risk assessment frameworks was performed, and results are presented in this paper. Also, an overview on transversal, inter-sectoral and multi-sectoral technological challenges and opportunities is provided. The result of this analysis is an architecture of the ECHO Multi-sector Assessment Framework, which was described in detail, including identified and analysed transversal aspects, multi-sector dependencies, and technological challenges and opportunities determine the input data for the framework. This solution is applicable in many sectors, such as energy, healthcare, maritime transportation, or defence, however it can also be extended to others. The architecture of the framework proposed supports the design of cybersecurity technology roadmap and the definition of governance models.

Keywords: Cybersecurity · Threats · Risk assessment · Challenges and opportunities

1 Introduction

Ensuring cybersecurity is becoming more difficult in every next year, since new attacks exploiting new vulnerabilities are carried out, while regulatory institutions and

A. Dziech et al. (Eds.): MCSS 2022, CCIS 1689, pp. 49–65, 2022.
https://doi.org/10.1007/978-3-031-20215-5_5

researchers change and improve rules (such as regulations or standards). However, society needs to be prepared to face new cybersecurity challenges. At a national level recognised needs and challenges for personal data protection, organisational and corporate cybersecurity, and a national cybersecurity system exist. Unfortunately, threats in cyberspace are not limited to one country or sector. They cross borders and could have devastating consequences at a regional or European level. The European Union recognised increasing threats and challenges by cyberattacks as well as opportunities and advantages in the new information age. Therefore, in 2019 four pilot projects (ECHO, CONCORDIA, SPARTA, and CyberSec4Europe) to establish a European Cybersecurity Competence Network were started [1].

This paper describes a multi-sector the risk management framework, which was proposed and currently developing by the WP2 group of ECHO project. At the beginning the analysis of risk assessment and management frameworks is presented. Also, multi-sector-specific cybersecurity frameworks are described, taking into account four sectors: healthcare, energy, maritime, and defence. Then, an overview on cybersecurity challenges and opportunities is provided. As a result of the analysis conducted, the architecture of the ECHO multi-sector risk assessment framework is derived. Thus, this paper extends the idea of the risk assessment framework introduced in [2] and describes the major updates of this solution. First, the logical model of the designed framework is described, and second, the paper considers new cybersecurity challenges and opportunities as well as sector-specific cybersecurity frameworks.

2   Risk Assessment and Management

Risk is defined as a threat exploiting a system's weakness and causing an adverse effect [3]. The two main factors of risk include impact (the degree of harm caused by the threat) and the likelihood of this threat. This approach to cybersecurity can support entities in making decisions associated with the security and operational stability of IT environment. Therefore, this overall process is called risk management. Risk assessment – the crucial stage of the risk management lifecycle – performs an assessment of threats in a measurable way and identifies cost-effective actions.

The risk assessment process describes the overall process including three main activities: identify hazards and risk factors that have the potential to cause harm (risk identification), analyse and evaluate the risk associated with that hazard (risk analysis and risk evaluation), and determine appropriate solutions to eliminate the hazard or control the risk if the hazard cannot be eliminated (risk control). However, different standards can describe and approach this process in different ways. Therefore, the basic risk assessment frameworks and methodologies are overviewed in the following and comprehensively analysed to derive a broadly applicable multi-sector assessment framework [4].

Five selected frameworks were analysed by the authors in [2]: ISO 31000, TOGAF, SP800-30, MEHARI, and MAGERIT. ISO 31000 [5] is the international standard that provides a common approach to the management of any type of risk (from strategic to operational risks) and a model, which can be integrated into the business management system. The TOGAF standard [6] is a framework for enterprise architectures which defines risk management as a technique used to manage risk during an architecture transformation project. SP 800-30 [7] was introduced by National Institute of Standards and Technology and provides guidance for carrying out the risk management process It focuses on the risk assessment component, providing a detailed step-by-step process for organisations. MEHARI [8] is a European open-source risk assessment methodology (provided under a Creative Commons License), fully compatible with ISO 27001 and part of the ENISA suggested risk assessment methodologies, including multiple guidelines and manuals. MAGERIT [9] is also an open-source methodology for risk analysis and management, developed in 1997 by the Spanish Ministry of Public Administration.

OCTAVE [10, 11] defines another framework and was proposed by the Software Engineering Institute at Carnegie Mellon University with cooperation with the Telemedicine and Advanced Technology Research Center in 1999. The OCTAVE methodology addressed the security compliance challenges and was defined by a method implementation guide and training. This approach is performed in a series of workshops carried out and eased by an interdisciplinary analysis team composed by people coming from the business units of the organization and members of the IT staff. OCTAVE addresses large organizations (300 employees or more), which are organised in a multilevel hierarchy, maintain their own computing infrastructure, and show the ability to run vulnerability evaluation tools and interpret respective results of vulnerability evaluations. This framework is based on three phases, which allow the organization to identify and evaluate information security risks: build asset-based threat profiles and requirements (phase 1), identify and assess infrastructure vulnerabilities (phase 2), and develop security strategy and risk mitigation plans (phase 3). OCTAVE provides an assessment framework based on the evaluation of organisational risks and focused on strategic, real and practical issues that can be adapted to the most part of the organizations.

3   Sector-Specific Cybersecurity Frameworks

The main goal of a risk assessment framework is to serve as an approach for prioritising risks posed to an organization, thus, enabling a sound decision making in terms of allocation of resources. A new risk assessment framework should support the evaluation of the cyber incident risk in the domains selected. This will be done in a comprehensive way, tackling the vertical and horizontal dimensions of the domains:

- vertical analysis, by zooming in on each specific domain; and
- horizontal analysis, by looking at the transversal/intersectoral aspects, i.e., covering more than one domain.

This two-dimensional analysis will track the route to innovate activities and identify and isolate transversal, inter-sectoral, and multi-sectoral elements. The horizontal analysis is a key added value in today's interconnected and interdependent world. It is also a core part of the vision of the ECHO project: deliver an EU trans-sectoral and inter-sectoral cybersecurity concept and marketplace.

For each domain (vertical path) a specific analysis had been performed to investigate how the ECHO-domains apply the risk frameworks to their key business processes in the light of well-known domain-related storylines. This analysis led to a clear assessment of what the needs and the basic requirements are for a modern risk assessment framework for specific domains. The identified gaps between target security and current security levels will represent a clear qualitative metric to understand what is missing in the current solutions.

The horizontal analysis followed a different path, as it first defined what is intended by transversal and inter-sectoral risk assessment. Then, it assessed existing risk assessment frameworks in order to verify whether they do cover by design transversal and inter-sectoral risk assessment and also to identify key trans-sectoral and inter-sectoral business processes and security challenges (and how storylines cover these).

Every issue referred as 'sectoral' can be considered to be related to either the sector meant in Directive 2008/114/EC (e.g., energy), or as a 'sub-sector' (e.g., electricity, as for the "infrastructures and facilities for generation and transmission of electricity in respect of supply electricity") [12]. The term 'cross-sectoral' (or 'inter-sectoral') refers to the choices in terms of resource allocation, considering cross-sector results due to the interdependencies including systems and infrastructures, as in the case of telecommunications and electricity distribution, financial services, and digital infrastructures. Interdependences occurring among a minimum of three or more sectors and possible cascading effects due to the cyberattack are referred to as 'multi-sectoral'. In a different perspective, they can include precise measures in order to decrease cyber risks, as in the case of the institutionalization of a relevant and accredited training program including cybersecurity (necessaries) capabilities (as follows, meant as 'transversal').

3.1 Healthcare

As the healthcare sector continues to offer life-critical services, while improving treatment and care by involving new technologies, cyber threats can have critical impact on people's life. In the last 5 years, more than 125 million people were affected by cyberattacks in the Healthcare sector. In this domain, cyberattacks are especially worrying, because they can directly threaten not just the security of medical systems and information, but also the health and safety of the patients. Innovation in health information technology is surely one of the main achievements in addressing clinical problems considered unresolved until recently, but the technology itself is an added value only if it is secure.

Another element highlighted by reports is that the healthcare industry is behind other industries in protecting its infrastructure and digital health information. Despite the huge yearly general investments by both public and private Health Service actors, cybersecurity is not yet seen as important as it should be. A cyberattack can void important investments, reducing the availability of key services.

Health organizations are now addressing the need to provide reassurance to patients and, in general, to healthcare players that their internal processes, infrastructures, and medical devices are under an efficient supervision and protected by adequate security measures. From this growing awareness, surely more evident in the USA than in Europe, comes a correspondingly increasing demand to comply with security by adopting recognised cybersecurity frameworks (CSF) and standards.

As also reported in 2018 by the Healthcare Information and Management Systems Society – North America (HIMSS) [13], most popular cybersecurity frameworks in the American health sector are described below.

- The (American) National Institute of Standards and Technology (NIST) has developed its general- purpose Cyber Security Framework [14], today adopted worldwide to improve the management of cybersecurity risk, proactively addressing active and emerging threats. Born to reinforce the resilience of Critical Infrastructure (2014), it is nowadays the most adopted CSF also in the Healthcare sector.
- ISO standards (International Organization for Standardization), a non-governmental organization that publishes standards to facilitate world trade, are well used. Along with the International Electrotechnical Commission (IEC), ISO maintains a series of standards for creating and maintaining an Information Security Management System (ISMS), known as ISO/IEC 27000 – or simply "the ISO", actually comprising of dozens of related standards (such as ISO/IEC 27001, 27002, or 27003). The requirements for information (cyber)security are listed under ISO/IEC 27001 ISMS (2013) [15].
- A large group of HC organizations follows the CSF maintained by the Health Information Trust Alliance (HITRUST) [16], a private organization led by representatives from some of the biggest names in healthcare. The organization maintains the Common Security Framework, a comprehensive and flexible framework for healthcare organizations of any size tailored on security control requirements and various US federal and state regulations along with standards and frameworks, such as HIPAA, ISO, COBIT, and NIST. It is a certifiable framework using the ISO/IEC 27001:2005 ISMS as its foundation, primarily with the objective of supporting non-US organizations, even if it is not a standard for the HC domain.
- Others are following the Critical Security Controls by the Centre for Internet Security (CIS), a non-profit organization maintaining the 20 Critical Security Controls (CSC, formerly the CIS 20) [17]. The CSC is a list of cybersecurity practices intended to stop the most common attacks. The controls, listed in order of priority starting with the most important, are not intended to provide a complete CSF. The CIS 20 are often used alongside other frameworks, such as NIST's.
- Today, hospitals and insurance companies are joining other organisations in adopting COBIT [18] that has become an integrator for IT best practices by harmonizing other standards. The framework, created by the non-profit organization ISACA (Information Systems Audit and Control Association), further allows entities covered to optimize resources, while mitigating risks. COBIT is focused on efficiency and effectiveness of IT environment, rather than information security linked to business issues. However, the framework is used to implement practices provided by other information security standards such as the NIST CSF and ISO27001.

3.2 Energy

It is a well-known fact that the energy sector requires specific considerations in terms of cybersecurity and that, among critical infrastructures, it is the one requiring resilience. Real-time requirements simply cannot be addressed by standard cybersecurity solutions, like authentication or encryption. Cascading effects can trigger blackouts in other sectors and countries. A technology mix creates risks from legacy components designed, when cybersecurity was not a concern, and from new Internet-of-Things (IoT) devices, not designed with cybersecurity in mind.

A smart meter is an electronic device recording consumption of electric energy and sets up a two-way communication channel to deliver information to and from the supplier for monitoring, messaging, and billing. Smart meters can vehiculate cyberattacks or be used to interfere on the consumption measurement.

The European Parliament and Council Directive (EU) 2016/1148 of 6 July 2016 (also known as NIS Directive [19]) requires all member states to analyse cyberrisks by evaluating the governance of IT security of Critical Infrastructures, especially the energy sector. Each nation of the EU has acted in this regard by supplying the owners of critical infrastructures of the energy sector with reference analysis models. Most of these models and methodologies for Risk Assessment (RA) are based on existing security frameworks and standards. The following list of cybersecurity frameworks and Risk Assessment/Management methodologies include the most used ones in the energy domain: MEHARI, MAGERIT, IEC/ISO 31000, NIST CSF, ISO 27001, COBIT, and OCTAVE. OCTAVE had been one of the most complete methodology for a risk assessment of IT systems, thus, some organisations in the energy domain adopted it even, although it was not conceived for industrial systems. However, its results may be less accurate compared to the ones produced by other methods, when analysing impact, vulnerabilities, and consequences.

3.3 Maritime

The maritime transport industry is increasingly using information and operational technology systems that depend on digitization, integration, automation, and network-based systems. This reliance has created an increasing need for cyberrisk management in the shipping industry. The impact emerging from cyberrisk threats are underestimated, because they are not widely spread and occur rarely. Increasing awareness obviously is the first necessary step to assess and mitigate cyberrisks as well as to think about it as a concrete treat, because of the high level of impact a single violation of security can cause. This can be intended not only as loss of money, but also as causing environmental issues, loss of human lives.

Recently, the International Maritime Organization (IMO) has published "Guidelines on high-level recommendations on maritime cyber risk management" [20]. By January 1, 2021, vessel owners and operators must have incorporated measures to manage cyberrisk into their existing risk management processes, which have traditionally focused on the physical risks to safe shipping operations.

For cybersecurity risk management, IMO proposes a framework based on five functional elements, which are not sequential, but all should be concurrent and continuous in practice and are to be incorporated in a risk management: identify, protect, detect, respond, recover. The approach to cyberrisk management described herein provides the basis for understanding and managing of cyberrisks, thus, enabling a risk management approach to address cyberthreats and vulnerabilities.

ISO/IEC 27001 is the most applicable standards for network and information systems security in the maritime domain and is divided into ten clauses, which support the implementation and maintenance of an ISMS, and an Annex A defining in detail all controls to be used for the main clauses of the standard. A risk assessment process in the maritime domain is necessary for what concerns the cybersecurity of the technological system in an industrial ship.

The top-down approach proposed by the ISO 27000 framework outlines requirements for Information Security Management Systems and gives organizations a guidance on how to establish, implement, maintain, and continually improve an ISMS. In this case the focus is on main critical systems and implements specific controls in order to mitigate cyberrisk related to the critical aspects of the ship (e.g., navigation or safety system). ISO also offers an approach, less technical, though, and related to NIST, but it could be far from the real case scenario of a ship.

The TOGAF standard is widely adopted, even being an enterprise architecture methodology, and considers a high-level approach to manage an enterprise architecture, but does not providing an adequate way for managing cyberrisks in a maritime domain, since the shipping industry meets very strict regulations.

3.4 Defence

The technological progress characterizing the digital era has long reached a high level of pervasiveness, clearly perceivable by industrialized nations and by users of Information and Communication Technology (ICT) services and tools as well as of the wide and tightly-connected context of IoT. Diffusion of technology, however, brings also a series of challenges that nations are facing. Concepts like "cyber defence" and "cyber resilience" fill agendas of international governments wanting to mitigate risks derived from the inevitable exposure to cyberthreats.

Several European countries have been following this trend and participate in international civil and military exercises, like the biennial exercise Cyber Europe, an important European cyber-themed event planned and conducted by the European Network and Information Security Agency (ENISA). The various Computer Security Incident Response Teams operate in synergy with Ministries of Defence and National Cyber Crime Centres in the management and mitigation of a large-scale cyberattacks (e.g., targeting air traffic control infrastructures).

NATO organizes the Cyber Coalition exercise (in 2018 700 cyber-defenders from 28 nations of the Alliance and 5 partner organizations participated) to consolidate on an international level technical collaboration procedures under the coordination of NATO's Allied Command, in order to defend the "Alliance Cyberspace" and to conduct military operations within and through it.

National cyber defence skills are verified through the NATO Cooperative Cyber Defence Centre of Excellence in Tallinn, Estonia, a true and international think-tank priority, organizing every year the "Crossed Swords" and the "Locked Shields" events. Locked Shields, in particular, determine the most complex exercise (attack and defence in real-time) in the world devoted to the defence of complex virtual systems, such as power plants, communication systems, 4G networks, or drones piloting systems, from over 2,500 attacks. Despite the great interest in cybersecurity depicted above and the work that is being performed behind the scenes in order to innovate risk assessment and cyber governance in the defence sector, the military world is still tightly bound to some of the general-purpose solutions enlisted in the previous subsections and which cannot be further discussed in detail for security reasons.

4   Cybersecurity Challenges and Opportunities

Modern technologies, new services, and changing user requirements raise both challenges and opportunities, especially in cybersecurity. A challenge is defined as an obstacle or hard task related to technological, organisational, economic, societal, or any other dimension that is difficult to mitigate or to overcome. Usually, the challenge is a result of the current status of dimensions under investigation or due to upcoming advancements/changes in respective fields. An opportunity determines the possibility or chance, which occurs because of a favourable combination of circumstances.

4.1   Transversal Challenges and Opportunities

The first group considered includes transversal challenges and opportunities. These factors are universal and multi-factorial. Note that they do not occur in isolation, but interact with others [21].

Some of these transversal factors are concentrated on the human. Among these factors the following ones are distinguished: cognitive, behavioural, social, psychological, affective, and motivational. Another set of examples of human factors are individual differences (i.e., impulsivity of a user) and personality traits, which can impact cybersecurity procedures applied. Other transversal factors are of financial nature. They can be connected with financial limitations influencing infrastructure conditions, staff motivation, or activities like corporate espionage or active attacks (i.e., ransomware or crypto-jacking). An important role is also addressed by privacy – especially related to GDPR (General Data Protection Regulation), i.e., the governance structure for privacy, privacy policy, or data privacy operational procedures. Additionally, political factors are relevant. This group contains geo-political situations, cyber-terrorism, international relations, and activities like fake news or hacktivism, thus, politically motivated cyberattacks are of concern.

Another transversal factor is education and training. For example, employees can receive minimal or partial training in the cybersecurity field (inadequate or outdated training) and sometimes they are not informed about crucial threats. Education and training are important for non-cyber staff. Awareness of basic cybersecurity regulations/policies (i.e., password policy or information security policy) is crucial. Non-IT staff has to be made aware of the fact that cybersecurity is crucial, and they staff needs basic knowledge about the company's security policy. Further details are discussed in [2].

4.2   Inter-sectoral Challenges and Opportunities

Inter-sectoral cyber security challenges and opportunities are based on inter-sectoral dependencies. The inter-sectoral dependency in the context of cybersecurity is defined as a one-directional or bi-directional cyber relation between entities across two or more sectors. The tightness of the dependency of the bi-directional relation could be different in both directions.

The ECHO sectors – healthcare, transportation, energy, and defence are among the top targets of cyber criminals. The inter-sector cybersecurity dependencies, introduce new cybersecurity challenges and open a new way for threats. As a consequence, many cyber incidents are caused by inter-sectoral dependencies, which either propagate across the sectors or have a cascading effect on services, provided by these sectors.

The Inter-sectoral challenges are classified into three main categories [2]: challenges due to common vulnerabilities, challenges due to propagation of cyberattacks in connected ICT systems in different sectors, and challenges due to dependencies of services in two or more sectors. Risk analysis, risk assessment, and risk management of cybersecurity challenges due to inter-sectoral dependencies require to have a measure for the degrees of dependencies of one sector to other sectors and need to be based on an impact evaluation. Due to a lack of a common methodology for assessing inter-sector dependencies in order to conduct cybersecurity risk-based analysis the analysis of inter-sector dependencies between selected sectors (i.e., energy, health care, maritime, defence, and space) are classified by inter-sector challenges in the three of the categories mentioned above.

The first category determines a group of challenges due to common vulnerabilities. These common vulnerabilities could lead to the disruption of services in two or more sectors at almost the same time. This occurs when a cyberattack is widespread and ICT systems of the victim sectors are located in the same geographic area. In this case, the inter-sectoral dependency is not operational but logical (based on the location). Currently, only operational inter-sectoral dependencies are considered. However, dependency based on the location is worth to consider.

The second category is the group of challenges due to the propagation of cyberattacks in connected ICT systems in different sectors. The analysis of inter-dependencies in the selected sectors shows that there are not ICT systems which directly connect components of different sectors. It seems that such a scenario is rather unusual, however is still possible.

The third category is the group of challenges due to dependencies of services in two or more sectors. The ECHO project reports [22, 23] identified dependencies between services in one sector and services in other sectors. Operational dependencies analyzed show that, i.e., one service uses other sectors' services to perform its function. A cyberattack could break such services in one sector, impacting services in another sector using this service, which further impacts other services dependent upon that service. Usually, the risk assessment is conducted at the sectoral level, and inter-sectoral dependencies are not taken into account. However, they should be considered during the risk assessment process, because underestimated inter-sectoral dependencies could mask many risks.

Inter-sector dependencies can be modeled using graphs, which represent the dependency relations of a service in one sector upon services in other sectors. Formally, let $S^i = \{S_1^i, S_2^i, \ldots, S_j^i, \ldots\}$ be sets of services of each selected sectors of interest, where i indicates a given sector. Let S denote the union of the sets S^i, i.e. $S = \cup S^i$, $i = 1$, 2, 3,...,n, where n is a number of considered sectors. Let G^i be sets of graphs, $G^i =$

$\{G_1^i, G_2^i, ..., G_j^i, ...\}, i = 1, 2, 3, ..., n, G_j^k = (N_j^k, E_j^k)$, where $N_j^k = \{S_j^k\} \cup D_j^k$ is a set of nodes (services), $D_j^k \subseteq S \backslash S^k$ and $E_j^k = \{(S_j^k, s) | s \in D_j^k\}$ is a set of edges (inter-sectoral dependencies). Each edge $S_j^k \to S_l^i$, $k \neq i$ is associated with an impact $I_{j,l}^{k,i}$ of service S_l^i on service S_j^k. If S_j^k is independent on other sectors' services, then $N_j^k = S_j^k$, and $E_j^k = \emptyset$. Let R be a function, $R: S \to G = \cup G^i, S_j^k \mapsto G_j^k$, for $k = 1, 2, ..., n$. Function R maps each service in a sector given to its dependency graph.

The edge from node S_j^k to node S_l^i denotes a dependency relation of service S_j in sector k on service S_l in sector i. This relation is quantified using impact $I_{j,l}^{k,i}$. The impact could be assigned using a scale to be chosen, for example from 1 to 5. The resulting risk is due to the respective dependency, which could be derived by multiplying this impact by the likelihood of a disruption of service S_l in sector i. The total dependency risk of service S_j^k will be the sum of all risks obtained based on all elements of the set E_j^k.

The main input to the approach proposed has to be provided by sectoral experts, because they have to identify dependencies and quantify them with respective impacts, when $E_j^k \neq \emptyset$. To manage risks due to inter-sectoral dependencies the approach suggested here can be integrated into the multi-sector assessment framework.

4.3 Technological Challenges and Opportunities

Technological factors determine another important aspect influencing cybersecurity. Besides those previously described factors technological factors are a source of crucial challenges and opportunities. The awareness of technological challenges and opportunities is significant also in the context of cybersecurity. Technology deployed typically involves multiple sectors, thus, the risk of cyberattacks propagates to different domains and end-users. Because modern technologies raise both opportunities and challenges, several technological solutions were taken into account [24].

To analyse technological factors of cybersecurity, the JRC Technical Report 'A Proposal for a European Cybersecurity Taxonomy' was chosen [25]. This taxonomy presents crucial technologies related to the cybersecurity domain, which enhances the development of different sectors (i.e., artificial intelligence, big data, blockchain and distributed ledger technology (DLT), cloud, edge and virtualisation, and critical infrastructure protection). Additionally, research domains are introduced, which represent areas of knowledge related to different cybersecurity facets (i.e., assurance, audit and certification, cryptography and cryptanalysis, data security and privacy, and identity management). These domains represent different areas of knowledge related to cybersecurity and cover technological aspects of cybersecurity. As for technologies, these research domains can be used across multiple sectors, including healthcare, energy, maritime, and defence.

The first research domain is cryptology (cryptography and cryptanalysis), including modern symmetric and asymmetric encryption. The important challenge of symmetric-key cryptography is the secure, light-weight encryption to protect small, inexpensive electronics or low-powered devices with limited resources. The source of many threats is due to the implementation of cryptographic algorithms, since they can work in a different way than standards define them or they may contain backdoors. This challenge concerns also open source applications. Other challenges (but also an opportunity) include post-quantum cryptography, which works on quantum computer-resistant security mechanisms. The importance of this challenge will be increasing, when quantum computers allow for searching the unstructured database using Grover's algorithm and allows to fast integer factorization by means of Shor's algorithm.

The main challenge of asymmetric cryptography involves conditional security of these algorithms. These cryptography algorithms are secure under specific conditions only and are based on the difficulty of specific mathematical problems (e.g., security of ElGamal depends on difficulty of computing discrete logarithms and the security level of RSA algorithm depends on the prime factorization difficulty). Additionally, asymmetric cryptography is characterised by low efficiency, because of longer keys and operations which are not time-effective. Also, the trust on public keys in a network environment is a crucial issue. Thus, related identities determine the practical security of asymmetric cryptography (i.e., user-based trust vs. hierarchical public key infrastructure).

Many technologies are based on the cryptology research domain. The one of them is blockchain, a solution resistant to modifications of data due to one-way hash functions. Therefore, blockchains and distributed ledgers use many devices on a peer-to-peer network to store, replicate, and share digital data. Some approaches build exchanges for cryptocurrencies. Although challenges exist, e.g., low numbers of transactions or high energy consumption, this technology is deployed in many sectors. An example is healthcare, where blockchains and distributed ledgers help to store medical data and to provide secure access for pharmaceutical, research, or insurance companies. Blockchains can also be used to solve problems of drug counterfeiting, connecting patients and medical facilities, and promoting a healthy lifestyle.

Currently, a strong driver in security-related steps is Artificial Intelligence (AI) and detailed Machine Learning (ML). For such system components, the security and accuracy determine a challenge. However, these solutions can be used to detect cyber threats and risk management, authentication, behavioural analysis, and anomaly detection or cryptography purposes (e.g., to establish a secret key using neural cryptography solutions and correct errors in quantum key distribution process). ML-based approaches can be used to estimate risk scores based on behavioural patterns, geolocation, time, and other variables to control access to information systems. Another example includes the fast detection/prevention of malware attacks, including new malware companions.

Big data and its mechanisms generate new possibilities for security solutions, however, they also give rise to opportunities for adversaries to access sensitive and personal information. The volume, speed of data generation, and different types of data form crucial challenges. Cloud-based systems can solve selected problems with processing big data, however, confidentiality or privacy of data sent to the cloud can be compromised. Thus, dishonest cloud data providers can also analyse packets and active connections with users. One of the important challenges with Security-as-a-Service (SecaaS) is the necessity of exposing the customer's security policy to the cloud service provider. Such policies contain confidential information regarding the organisation's infrastructure, vulnerabilities, and threats. However, anonymization mechanisms can be used to protect data privacy (i.e., based on Bloom filters).

The rapid development of quantum technology allows users to improve the security and performance of communication networks. By means of this technology, entirely new ways of problem solving of cybersecurity is possible. For instance, quantum cryptography uncovers passing eavesdroppers in quantum channels and quantum random generators, which are producing truly random sequences for cryptography purposes. Quantum technology is characterized by a very high level of security, however, still many challenges limit the widespread use of such services, since quantum key distribution or quantum computing are not yet fully deployable. The problem with secure and effective mechanisms for the key distillation process during quantum cryptography systems remains as of today, thus, the implementation of quantum solutions in real networks and systems determine the biggest challenge in this domain.

5   Multi-sector Assessment Framework

ECHO's Multi-sector Assessment Framework (ECHO MAF or, in short, E-MAF) provides the analysis of transversal and inter-sectoral challenges and opportunities, supports the development of cybersecurity technology roadmaps, and leverages cyber-risk management fundamentals by having a large multi-domain community. E-MAF refers to the analysis of challenges and opportunities, derived from sector-specific use cases, transversal cybersecurity needs analysis, and development of inter-sector technology roadmaps involving horizontal cybersecurity disciplines.

Since a risk management framework must include a risk assessment, the core of E-MAF contains the cyber risk assessment methodology. There, three important steps take place: (a) risk identification (the process of determining, document and communicating risks that could potentially prevent an organisation or a process from achieving the foreseen objectives), (b) risk analysis (analysis of potential issues which could negatively impact processes or systems), (c) and risk evaluation (a comparison of the results of the risk analysis with the risk evaluation criteria to determine whether the level of cyber-risks is acceptable) in a multi-domain environment. Compared to other CSFs, E-MAF provides risk assessment taking into consideration not only direct effects of cyber incidents, but also indirect consequences between different domain, up to several levels of interaction. The outputs of E-MAF determine the basics for an effective risk management and support decision makers into defining the adequate cyber skills the IT and non-IT staff should have in the target organisation.

5.1   Architecture

Organisations and sectors show unique risks (e.g., different threats, vulnerabilities, risk tolerances) and implementation of practices to achieve positive outcomes. Therefore, E-MAF will not be implemented as a non-customised checklist or a one-size-fits-all approach for all critical infrastructure organisations, but as the overlap of three different complex subsystems in a three-tier architecture comprising:

- ECHO MAF Transversal Foundation Tier (E-MAF TFT), guiding organisations in managing and reducing cybersecurity risks in a way that complements their existing cybersecurity and risk management processes;

- ECHO MAF Multi-sector Implementation Tier (E-MAF MIT), where all multi-sector and inter-sector specific aspects are managed; this tier will support organisations by providing the context on how they view cybersecurity risk management (risks, priorities, budgeting); and
- ECHO MAF Security Alignment Tier (E-MAF SAT), where security controls will be defined and implemented, also specific organisation's alignment to ECHO MIT and TFT will take place by identifying and prioritising opportunities for improving cybersecurity in general and in a use cases-driven manner.

E-MAF requires several inputs: transversal aspects, technological challenges, and opportunities as well as multi-sector dependencies. Output of E-MAF distinguishes sore crucial elements: Governance Model, Inter-sector Technology Roadmaps, Early Warning System (EWS), Federated Cyber Range (FCR).

5.2   Logical Model

E-MAF is composed by different modules, also involved as logical model's elements, and able to include introductive and describing key functions addressed by every component providing coordination and inter-relation [26]. It is fundamental to consider E-MAF objectives together with the arguments to be included during the ECHO's project duration and onward.

One of the main features advertised by E-MAF is referred to the possibility to overcome the risk assessment *per se*, providing solutions and support for risk management decision-making procedures, present in a large amount of frameworks, methodologies, and standards (e.g. ISO27005 [27] and others considered in Sect. 2). Therefore, it is possible to comprehend cyber risks and consider where to endow resources in order to decrease risks. Moreover, the decisions concerning the allocation of resources are considered within organizational aspects, such that E-MAF supports individual organizations and promotes risk management at sectorial, inter- and multi-sectorial, national, and pan-European levels.

E-MAF may be extended and used at the European Union and national levels in order to establish policies and create measures useful for the reduction of the above-mentioned risks, related to projects and the design of crucial services and critical infrastructures. Table 1 details E-MAF's logical model for which rows determine the coverage/scope item along with these 'Risk Assessment' and 'Risk Mitigation' components.

E-MAF covers transversal, sectoral, and cross-sectoral aspects. Data contained in the dark blue spaces (and the 'v' mark) in Table 1 refer to the prototype of E-MAF (Y2, 2021), differently from those included within the light blue ones (and the 'V' mark), which relate to further versions (Y3, 2022). Certain limitations, mainly due to resources and time, are determined in selected cells in the last column of Table 1 (the 'x' mark was used) and these will not be treated within ECHO. Thus, sectoral and organizational figures are considered by the prototype version of E-MAF, others considered as EU/national aims will be handled by future developments. An additional integration of cyber-physical interdependencies will be provided by an E-MAF commitment in coping with cyber threats via the risk assessment processes. Finally, selected aspects, such as industrial accidents, terror attacks, and natural hazards, are not covered by E-MAF.

Table 1. The logical model of E-MAF.

		Issues/Elements	1st Prototype	Final Prototype	Out of Scope
	Coverage/Scope	Organisational	v	V	
		Sectoral	v	V	
		Cross-Sectoral		V	
		Transversal		V	
		EU/National			x
Risk Assessment	Threats	Cyber Threats	v	V	
		Cyber-Physical interdependencies		V	
		Natural hazards, industrial accidents, terrorist attacks			x
	Vulnerabilities	Hardware	v	V	
		Software	v	V	
		Networking		V	
		Organisation		V	
	Impact	Negative consequences	v	V	
		Opportunities/benefits of risk mitigation measures		V	
	Negative Consequences	Direct (physical, loss of information, financial)	v	V	
		Injuries, death, health & safety		V	
		Reputational			x
		Lost opportunities			x
		Social impact			x
	Risk Estimation	Qualitative	v	V	
		Quantitative	v	V	
		Combination of Qualitative & Quantitative		V	
Risk Management	Measures to enhance	Awareness	v	V	
		Protection	v	V	
		Response and recovery			x
		Resilience and adaptiveness			x
		Prevention			x
	Decisions on Measures	Selective	v	V	
		Prioritisation		V	
		Optimisation			x
	Applications	Ad-hoc	v	V	
		Recurring		V	
		Proactive (based on predictive analytics)			x

Vulnerabilities have been considered in terms of hardware- and software-related/networking- and organization- related ones only, the former two in the first prototypes, the latter two in the following ones. Negative consequences are considered, in order to access the impact (first prototypes), including costs/benefits evaluations related to risk mitigation measures (next prototypes). The attention has been directed to negative outcomes only, e.g., information loss, physical damage, or economic loss. Other outcomes and consequences, intended as death, safety issues, and possible injuries, will be included in the subsequent versions. Wasted opportunities, reputational consequences, and social impact are outside the consideration of E-MAF.

Qualitative and quantitative methodologies are both implemented by the risk estimation in E-MAF. Risk mitigation is based mainly of the following three factors:

- measures to enhance, including awareness and protection actions; response and recovery, resilience and adaptiveness as well as prevention actions are not considered;
- decision-making process support depending on measures, which is considered being both selective (1st prototype) and prioritized (the next one); optimization-based approach is out of scope; and
- application of risk mitigation is ad-hoc and recurring, even the option for a proactive approach based on predictive analytics could be enabled.

6 Summary

This paper presented a logical model of a "Multi-Sector Risk Management Framework" architecture, which evaluates and prioritises cybersecurity risks in trans-sectoral and inter-sectoral contexts, and, thus, enables a relevant risk management process. The analysis of existing frameworks identified that current risk assessment frameworks do not take into consideration relations between sectors and are not able to address multi-sector and transversal issues. The new E-MAF proposed is based on a comprehensive study of cybersecurity technological, transversal, and inter-sectoral challenges and opportunities.

Respective technological challenges and opportunities identified as well as multi-sector dependencies and transversal aspects listed now define the relevant input data for the new framework. E-MAF provides a structured method for a multi-dimensional analysis. Its architectural design deploys a three-tier architecture, encompassing (a) a transversal foundation tier, which identifies the transversal and independent cybersecurity challenges and opportunities, (b) a multi-sector implementation tier, which supports organisations by providing contexts on how they view cybersecurity risk management especially with respect to risks, priorities, and budgeting; and (c) a security alignment tier, where ECHO security controls are implemented and a specific organisation's alignment to the previous two layers is taken place by identifying and prioritising opportunities for improving cybersecurity. The logical model of E-MAF coordinates the adoption of a set of key functions to implement related elements and the enables risk assessment and mitigation in the scope of E-MAF, going far beyond several frameworks' and methodologies' scopes currently adopted worldwide.

Acknowledgements. This work has been partially funded by the European Union's Horizon 2020 Research and Innovation Programme, under Grant Agreement no. 830943, the ECHO project and partially by the European Union's Horizon 2020 Research and Innovation Program under Grant Agreement no. 830927, the CONCORDIA project.

The authors would like to thank all our colleagues involved in WP2 of ECHO project who contributed to deliverables D2.1, D2.2, D2.3, D2.4, and D2.5.

References

1. ECHO Project website. https://echonetwork.eu. Accessed 22 Aug 2022
2. Pappalardo, S.M., Niemiec, M., Bozhilova, M., Stoianov, N., Dziech, A., Stiller, B.: Multi-sector assessment framework – a new approach to analyse cybersecurity challenges and opportunities. In: Dziech, A., Mees, W., Czyżewski, A. (eds.) MCSS 2020. CCIS, vol. 1284, pp. 1–15. Springer, Cham (2020). https://doi.org/10.1007/978-3-030-59000-0_1
3. Niemiec, M., Jaglarz, P., Jękot, M., Chołda, P., Boryło, P.: Risk assessment approach o secure northbound interface of SDN networks. In: Proceedings of the International Conference on Computing, Networking and Communications (ICNC 2019), Honolulu, HI, USA (2019)
4. D2.2 ECHO Multi-Sector Assessment Framework, ECHO project consortium (2019)
5. ISO 31000:2018 Risk management—Guidelines. https://www.iso.org/standard/65694.html. Accessed 22 Aug 2022
6. The TOGAF Standard. https://publications.opengroup.org/c182. Accessed 22 Aug 2022
7. NIST Special Publication 800-30 Guide for Conducting Risk Assessments. https://nvlpubs.nist.gov/nistpubs/Legacy/SP/nistspecialpublication800-30r1.pdf. Accessed 22 Aug 2022
8. MEHARI Overview. http://meharipedia.x10host.com/wp/wp-content/uploads/2019/05/MEHARI-Overview-2019.pdf. Accessed 22 Aug 2022
9. MAGERIT v.3: Metodología de Análisis y Gestión de Riesgos de los Sistemas de Información. https://administracionelectronica.gob.es/pae_Home/pae_Documentacion/pae_Metodolog/pae_Magerit.html?idioma=en#.Xl1XC0pCdPY. Accessed 22 Aug 2022
10. Alberts, C.J., Behrens, S.G., Pethia, R.D., Wilson, W.R.: Operationally critical threat, asset, and vulnerability Evaluation^{SM} (OCTAVE^{SM}) framework. https://resources.sei.cmu.edu/library/asset-view.cfm?assetid=13473. Accessed 22 Aug 2022
11. Caralli, R.A., Stevens, J.F., Young, L.R., Wilson, W.R.: Introducing OCTAVE allegro: improving the information security risk assessment process (2007)
12. Council Directive 2008/114/EC of 8 December 2008 on the identification and designation of European critical infrastructures and the assessment of the need to improve their protection, pp. 75–82. http://data.europa.eu/eli/dir/2008/114/oj. Accessed 22 Aug 2022
13. HIMSS Cybersecurity Survey. https://www.himss.org/2018-himss-cybersecurity-survey. Accessed 22 Aug 2022
14. NIST Cyber Security Framework, Framework for Improving Critical Infrastructure Cybersecurity. https://www.nist.gov/cyberframework/framework. Accessed 22 Aug 2022
15. ISO27001:2013. https://www.iso.org/isoiec-27001-information-security.html. Accessed 22 Aug 2022
16. HITRUST Cyber Security Framework. https://hitrustalliance.net/csf-license-agreement. Accessed 22 Aug 2022
17. CIS 20 Controls. https://learn.cisecurity.org/cis-controls-download. Accessed 22 Aug 2022
18. COBIT framework. http://www.isaca.org/cobit/pages/default.aspx. Accessed 22 Aug 2022
19. Directive (EU) 2016/1148 of the European Parliament and of the Council of 6 July 2016 concerning measures for a high common level of security of network and information systems across the Union (2016)
20. Guidelines on high-level recommendations on maritime cyber risk management. https://www.imo.org/en/OurWork/Security/Pages/Cyber-security.aspx. Accessed 22 Aug 2022
21. D2.3 Transversal Cybersecurity Challenges and Opportunities, ECHO project consortium (2019)
22. D2.5 Multi-sector Requirements Definition and Demonstration Cases, ECHO project consortium (2020)
23. D2.1 Sector Scenarios and Use Case Analysis, ECHO project consortium (2019)

24. D2.4 Inter-Sector Technology Challenges and Opportunities, ECHO project consortium (2020)
25. Nai-Fovino, I., et al.: A proposal for a European cybersecurity taxonomy. Publications Office of the European Union (2019)
26. Tagarev, T., Pappalardo, S.M., Stoianov, N.: A logical model for multi-sector cyber risk management. In: Proceedings of the Digital Transformation, Cyber Security and Resilience (DIGILIENCE 2020), Varna, Bulgaria (2020)
27. ISO/IEC 27005:2018. https://www.iso.org/standard/75281.html. Accessed 22 Aug 2022

AI Cybersecurity Assurance for Autonomous Transport Systems: Scenario, Model, and IMECA-Based Analysis

Vyacheslav Kharchenko⑩, Oleg Illiashenko(✉)⑩, Herman Fesenko⑩, and Ievgen Babeshko⑩

Department of Computer Systems, Networks and Cybersecurity, National Aerospace University "KhAI", 17 Chkalova street, Kharkiv 61070, Ukraine
{v.kharchenko,o.illiashenko,h.fesenko,e.babeshko}@csn.khai.edu

Abstract. The paper investigates problems and ways of utilizing Artificial Intelligence (AI) to ensure the cybersecurity of autonomous transport systems (ATSs) in different domains (aviation, space, maritime). A systematic approach to solving problems of analyzing and assuring ATS cybersecurity in conditions of attacks by use of AI means is suggested. This approach is based on: the development of a set of scenarios describing the operation of ATS under cyberattacks and actor activities considering AI contribution to system protection; scenario-based development and analysis of user stories describing different cyber-attacks, their influence, and ways to protect ATs via AI means/platforms; profiling of AI platform requirements by use of characteristics based AI quality model and risk-based assessment of cyberattacks criticality and efficiency of countermeasures, which can be implemented by actors. A modified IMECA technique for risk-based cyber security assessment and choice of countermeasures applied by different actors to minimize the effect of attacks on the system is suggested.

Keywords: Artificial intelligence · Automation transportation systems · Cybersecurity assurance · IMECA

1 Introduction

Nowadays the market for autonomous transport systems (ATS) has been significantly extended. Current research shows that by 2023 it will transform into one that is 60 percent civilian including ground, sea, air, and space transportation and expand to 636 billion euros—more than 40 times its current size. According to industrial and researchers' calculations, autonomous vehicles (AV) will make up 20 percent of the total vehicle market by 2030, and three out of four of them will be used as ground transportation [1].

Cybersecurity ensuring of the ATSs of all types is extremely important since its secureness influences the safety of people (e.g. in an urban area, suburbs, etc.) and the environment as well. Especially cybersecurity should be provided as far as AVs should transmit (store and handle) data between each other thus being the part of constantly changing let's say the system of Internet of Things, considering the massive amount of data, which should be transmitted over this flexible Internet of AVs [2–4].

A promising way to cope with providing the cybersecurity of the ATSs of different types could be the application of artificial intelligence (AI) based approaches and platforms (AIP) [5, 6]. The trustworthiness of the assessing AIP for ATS cybersecurity assurance is a very important metric addressing the high level of the severity of the consequences relevant to accidents with autonomous vehicles of all types. These accidents can be caused by failures and cyber-attacks on ATS assets.

Thus, challengeable questions cover:

a) how AI-based solutions will help to reduce cybersecurity risks and be resistant to cyberattacks;
b) how to assess the trustworthiness and transparency of AI algorithms and means in the point of view ATSs cybersecurity (via systematic vulnerabilities analysis, AI data, models and means security validation);
c) how to develop and implement protection techniques against AI-powered attacks or other intrusions in communications, nodes, and assets of ATSs.

The purpose of the paper is to highlight problems and propose ways of utilizing AI to ensure the cybersecurity of ATS in different domains such as aviation, space, and maritime. The objectives and the structure of the paper are the following:

– to analyze existing challenges and solutions related to AI application for ATS cybersecurity assessment (Sect. 2);
– to suggest a systematic approach to solving problems of analyzing and assuring cybersecurity of ATS in conditions of attacks by use of AI means (Sect. 3);
– to discuss a theoretical-set presentation of scenario determining a structure of user stories that describe different cases (Sect. 4);
– to demonstrate the application of the AI quality model for profiling requirements to AIP ensuring the cyber defense of the system under consideration (Sect. 5);
– to suggest and demonstrate possibilities of a modified IMECA technique for cyber security assessment and risk-based procedure for choice of countermeasures applied by different actors to minimize the effect of attacks on the system (Sect. 6);
– to highlight new research steps (Sect. 7).

2 State of the Art

There are a huge number of publications connected to ATSs cyber security assessment and assurance techniques including decisions based on the application of AI and AIP. They can be divided into the following groups: (a) application of AI for the cyber defense of ATSs and cases dealing with cyber incidents and potential threats to ATS assets [2–13]; (b) methods and techniques of ATS cybersecurity analysis and assurance [14–16]; (c) AI quality models in the context of cyber security assessment assurance [17–21].

AI can be used to provide good cybersecurity practices and decrease the attack surface. On the other hand, well-sponsored hackers, and cyber-gangs can use the same

AI techniques to defeat cyber defense and avoid detection. The level of security threats for the various drone categories was investigated and comprehensive taxonomy of the attacks on the Internet of Drones (IoD) network was given in [2]. The authors also reviewed the recent IoD attack mitigating techniques, presented the performance metrics, highlighted the need for secured IoD architecture, and proposed one.

To identify potential cyber-attacks against systems of an autonomous ship (Engine Automation System, Bridge Automation System, Navigation System, etc.) and to analyze the accordant risk, the authors of [3] utilized STRIDE (Spoofing, Tampering, Repudiation, Information Disclosure, Denial of Service and Elevation of Privilege) threat modeling methodology. For assessing the risk, the authors developed a special risk matrix and proposed threat and likelihood criteria.

To assess the characteristics and motivations of adversarial threats to satellites, the authors of [4] analyzed past satellite security threats and incidents. The authors also presented results of segment and sector analysis of satellite security incidents. According to these results, the greatest number of satellite security incidents were reported for the ground segment (83 incidents) and the government sector (91). The work [5] proposes a flexible satellite network intrusion detection system based on deep learning technology in order to detect unforeseen and unpredictable attacks. This system can use a large number of features to obtain implicit knowledge from the unlabeled data.

For efficiently detecting the malicious threats invading the UAV, an autonomous intrusion detection system utilizing deep convolutional neural networks was presented in [6]. The developed system was evaluated by employing the UAV-IDS-2020 dataset including various attacks on UAV networks in un- and bidirectional communication flow modes. The authors of [7] proposed a learning-driven detection scheme and showed how it can detect deficiency attacks against the satellite systems. They designed a lightweight convolutional neural network (CNN) architecture and compared it with a prevalent ML algorithm.

To identify and mitigate spoofing and jamming attacks a detection method based on principal component analysis and one-class classifiers to use flight logs for training data is proposed in [8]. The method was integrated into a developed IDS operating onboard the UAV within a resource-constrained agent device. To detect and trace cyber-attack activities targeting smart satellite networks, a Deep Learning based network forensic framework was proposed in [9]. To increase intrusion detection performance for satellite systems, an ensemble model RFMLP was proposed [10] that integrates random forest and multilayer perceptron. To analyze the efficiency of the model, KDD-CUP 99, NSL-KDD, and STIN datasets were used for experiments and validation. [11] analyzed the attacks that drones are prone to Wi-Fi Jamming, Three-Way Handshake, Wi-Fi Aircrack, Buffer Overflow, Denial of Service, Injection and Modification, Fabrication, and Civilian GPS Spoofing.

Attack scenarios for autonomous ship cybersecurity risk management were discussed and a secure ship network topology to realize autonomous ship operations was proposed in [12]. Issues of guaranteeing satellite system cybersecurity throughout the system lifecycle and the relevant value chain in light of regulatory requirements were considered in [13]. The authors also explained how space stakeholders should define and implement cyber-compliant security measures. To assess the consequences of unauthorized intrusion into IoD systems, the Intrusion Modes Effects and Criticality Analysis (IMECA) method was utilized in [14]. The authors of [15] presented a solution to automate the FMECA process for complex cyber-physical systems to reduce and mitigate the number of critical faults.

A theoretical and mathematical model and method to analyze the internal components of a security system and access to assets were suggested in [16]. The method allowed analyzing asset security through the use of environment variables and physical security controls of the facility. Principles of AI quality model development, the procedure for the realization of its hierarchical construction considering trustworthiness, explainability, cyber security, and other characteristics are described in [17, 18].

The paper [19] suggested a quality model that allowed specifying and assessing qualities for ML systems objectively based on an industrial use case. An example of a quality model building for a concrete industrial use case was given and lessons learned from applying the construction process were analyzed and discussed. A metric-based assessment technique of AIS quality using radial diagrams is described in [20]. [21] discussed terminology and challenges on quality assurance for AI-based systems and characterize AI-based systems along the three dimensions of artifact type, process, and quality characteristics.

Thus, the cybersecurity domain for ATS encompasses main issues considering the application of AI means which should be analyzed and assessed. The system has vulnerabilities that lead to the risk of being exploited causing operational impacts. In this case, it is needed to systemize and define requirements for AI means, assess the risks of critical failures, and mitigate risks by choice of countermeasures.

3   An Approach to the Analysis of AI Application for ATS Cybersecurity Assurance

The suggested approach to the analysis of AI application for ATS cybersecurity assurance comprises the following principles:

- development of scenarios set describing the operation of ATS in conditions of cyberattacks and actor activities considering AI contribution to system protection for analyzed domains. This principle allows partially formalizing of the structure of different cases and makes the analysis of cyber-attacks more understandable;
- scenario-based development and analysis of user stories describing different cyberattacks, their influence, and ways to protect ATs from them via AI means/platforms. Systemizing user stories according to the scenario set and security assessment procedure provides the making integrated decisions to minimize cyber security risks;
- profiling of AI platform requirements by use of a characteristics-based AI quality model [17, 18]. Model-based formation of characteristics profile supports the development of requirements to the system;
- risk-based assessment of cyberattacks criticality and efficiency of countermeasures which can be implemented by actors. Actor-oriented assessment allows separating the responsibilities and possibilities of participants and getting a synergy effect.

4   Scenarios and Stories of AI Based Cybersecurity Assurance

To provide compact description of scenarios, let us classify their attributes and entities using a theoretical-set presentation.

4.1   Scenarios

To form a set of scenarios, the elements/sets of them should be presented as follows:

1. Kinds of ATS and its attributes that are important for described system (KAS

   a. domains: aviation, space, maritime;
   b. systems: UAVs and UAV fleets, satellites, sea robots (autonomous ships/vessels);
   c. tasks: navigation, communication, monitoring, and so on;
   d. components: HW, SW, FPGA (and subsystems).

   Subset KAS can be presented as KAS = {{domains}, {systems}, {tasks}, {components}}.

2. Goals of application of AI and AI platforms (AIG):

   a. AI for cybersecurity assurance of ATSs (AICA): (1) prediction (threats, vulnerabilities, attacks); (2) prevention (analysis of countermeasures and their initialization); (3) detection (attacks and assessment of their effects); (4) tolerance (choice and implementation of mitigation procedures); (5) recovery (choice and initialization of assets recovery); (6) relearning (analysis of cases, identifying means of relearning, accumulating experience, and enhancing proactive decision-making algorithms);
   b. set of AI algorithms, models, software/hardware platforms (AIware) as an object of attacks (AIOA): (1) AIware components; (2) threats, vulnerabilities, and attacks on different levels of AIware components; (3) metrics of criticality; (4) set of countermeasures; (5) AI-based penetration testing;
   c. AI for generation of so-called artificial intelligence-powered attacks (AIAG): (1) objects and goals of white/ethical hacking; (2) kinds of attacks generated by AI support; (3)means for implementation of AI-powered attacks; (4) metrics of efficiency;
   d. AI-based protection against AI-powered attacks (AIPA). This case of AI application is a part of the goal "a" in recognition of specific features of AI-powered attacks.

   Thus, subset AIG can be presented as AIS = {AICA, AIOA, AIAG, AIPA}.

3. Correlation of cybersecurity with other system properties/characteristics (CSA):

   a. performance, availability, safety, resilience,...;
   b. indicators of dependency and degree of correlation.

   Subset CSA can be presented as CSA = {{properties}, {indicators}}.

4. Consequences of cyberattacks (CCA):

   a.effects (failures, harm, damage);
   b.criticality (probability, severity, risks).

   Subset CCA can be presented as CCA = {{effects}, {criticality}}.

5. Actors: developers, regulators, operators, users (ACT). ACT develops and implements the following activities:

   a. Developers (DEV) should: (1) analyze operation experience and challenges caused by intrusions and cyber-attacks; (2) formulate the problem statement, specify threats, vulnerabilities, and types of attacks, and suggest the countermeasures, including AI-based approaches, to prevent, detect and mitigate cyberattacks; (3) develop /redevelop (modernize) system by use of capabilities of AI and other methods/means; (4) verify design decisions and identify secondary risks, threats, and vulnerabilities within the object operating environment, and risks of insufficient level of AI explainability, trustworthiness, and other quality characteristics; (5) implement new decisions and maintain a developed/modernized system.
   b. Regulators (REG) should: (1) analyze experience in close domains, new risks, cyber accidents, and practical cases related to attacks on systems including AI-powered ones; (2) review standard requirements, and actual accident response plans and identify gaps between actual practices of operation/development and existing regulatory base considering advanced AI-based protection possibilities and AI-powered attacks; (3) develop new requirements, guides, and standards considering identified gaps, and processes of their implementation excluding new cyber risks; (4) upgrade tools to provide processes of audit and reformulate the requirements to tools applied by developers; (5) audit projects against new requirements.
   c. Operators (OPR) should: (1) analyze operation experience/cases caused by cyber-attacks, their effects, the efficiency of applied countermeasures, and assess the damage from attacks; (2) tolerate threats/attacks using possibilities of the operating system (OS), knowledge and skills of personal, and all available countermeasures; (3) carry out maintenance and/or initiate the upgrade of the system to prevent predicted attacks.
   d. Users (USR) should: (1) analyze the user experience and require operator/developer to meet the renewed requirements; (2) assess potential/ actual losses and specify policy of collaboration and choice of operators/developers.

Subset ACT can be presented as ACT = {{actors}, {activities}}.

Activities, in turn, are implemented as a set of countermeasures (CTM). Thus, a set of scenarios can be presented with the Cartesian product of five subsets:

$$SScen = \{KAS \times AIG \times CSA \times CCA \times ACT\} \tag{1}$$

Analysis of the set allows generating different scenarios via a combination of elements of different subsets and partially formalizing processes of the compilation of user stories.

4.2   Epics and User Stories

A scenario determines the structure of the user story. User stories describe different cases characterized by cyber-attacks, their influence on ATS assets, and ways to protect the system via AI means. Due to the number of potential development opportunities and the difference between domains (aviation, space, maritime and other), a set of stories should be divided into sub-sections according to the major technological domains described, called EPICs for the different domains. Those EPICs were further divided into sub-topics called user stories, each describing specific interrelation between actors and use cases, technology drivers and their targets, and technology alternatives and their timelines.

The user story should answer the following questions: (1) To what happened? (2) What happened? (3) How did it happen? (4) Which are the effects? The content of the story can be complemented with recommendations to minimize the risks of attack effects.

Let's consider an example of a user story for space domain [9], which is presented considering scenario structure. Some organization uses a Smart Satellite Network (SSN) that can be defined as a network of satellite systems, the processes of which have been augmented through the inclusion of smart sensors and actuators. Experience with the utilization of the SSN revealed that it is vulnerable to:

- Distributed Denial of Service (DDoS) attacks because of weaknesses in communication protocol or power supply devices (A1);
- Targeted attacks because of weaknesses in power supply devices (A2);
- Tampering attack because of the Operating System (OS)/Firmware weaknesses (A3);
- Man-In-The-Middle (MITM) (A4) attacks;
- Data manipulation attacks (A5) because of weaknesses in channels responsible for transmitting data between satellites and ground stations.

  It is vital to note that:

- A1 resulted in increased network interactions;
- A1 and A2 resulted in power depletion;
- A3 resulted in a non-functional state known as bricks;
- A4 and A5 resulted in the violation of confidentiality/integrity of smart satellites' data.

To detect and investigate the cyber-attacks, the developer proposed a DL-based network forensic framework, consisting of augmented satellites and IoT devices, called INSAT-DLNF (Intelligent Satellite Deep Learning-based Network Forensics). For the development of the proposed INSAT-DLNF framework, the Gated Recursive Unit Recurrent Neural Network (GRU-RNN) was utilized which made it possible to create a model for detecting attacks in collected network traces. Big data collections, such as NSL-KDD, UNSW-NB15, and Bot-IoT were analyzed for investigating attack events and their traces were analyzed for developing reliable network forensics models.

This user story will be analyzed as a case in the next stages of research.

5   AI Quality Model

In the context of the application of AI for ATS cybersecurity assurance, it is important to assess the quality of AI platform. For that assessment, we suggest utilizing characteristics-based AI quality models [17, 18]. So-called basic AIS model quality can be described via a multi-level graph presented in Fig. 1 and combines AI and AIP quality models.

AI quality model includes 4 characteristics of the first level (ethics (ETH), lawfulness (LFL), explainability (EXP), trustworthiness (TST)) and 16 characteristics of the second level (fairness (FRN), greenness (GRS), human agency (HMA), redress (RDR), completeness (CMT), comprehensibility (CMH), transparency (TRP), interpretability (INP), interactivity (INR), verifiability (VFB), diversity (DVS), resiliency (RSL), robustness (RBS), safety (SFT), security (SQR), accuracy ACR).

AIP quality model has only one level of characteristics: auditability (ADT), availability (AVL), controllability (CNT), effectiveness (EFS), reliability (RLB), maintainability (MNT), sustainability (SST), usability (USB), VFB, DVS, RSL, RBS, SFT, SQR, and ACR. Thus, characteristics VFB, DVS, RSL, RBS, SFT, SQR, and ACR (marked with 'AIG') belong to both AI and AIP quality models.

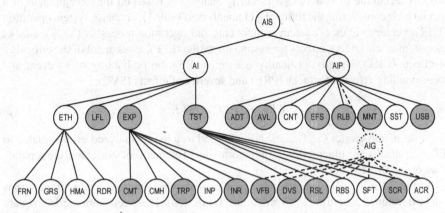

Fig. 1. The graph of a general AIS quality model with marked characteristics for the system (Subsect. 4.2)

In the point of view of subset AIS = {AICA, AIOA, AIAG, AIPA}, this model can be interpreted as a subsystem for implementation of cybersecurity protection functions (AICA) including against AI-powered attacks (AIPA) or as an AI system implementing functions of ATS (AIOA) and system for generation of cyberattacks (AIAG). It is clear that models of AI (AIS) quality for different applications of artificial intelligence and kinds of ATSs can be different.

Let us build a quality model for the AI system described in the user story (Subsect. 4.2, case AICA). The AI quality model is shown as a subgraph with the characteristics of AIS which are important for the analyzed system and marked by grey color. For this system the following characteristics should be taken into consideration:

- for the first level of AI quality: LFL, EXP, and TST (in this case, characteristic ETH is not obvious);
- for the second level of AI quality: CMT, TRP, INR, and VFB for AI explainability; DVS, RSL and SCR for AI trustworthiness;
- for the first level of AIP quality: ADT, AVL, EFS, RLB, MNT, and USB.

Note that characteristics VFB, DVS, RSL, and CSR are general for AI and AIP quality sub-models. Profiled model of quality (Fig. 1) can be applied to assess AIS using metric-based techniques [20]. This technique comprises operations of: assessing metrics values for AI quality characteristics/sub-characteristics; determination of their weights; calculation of integrated quality indicator using additive convolution.

Metrics for cyber security, safety, and other characteristics can be derived using the IMECA technique [14].

6 IMECA for Cyber Security Assessment and Assurance

6.1 IMECA Technique

IMECA technique of system cybersecurity analysis is based on the development of a special table considering the following elements (see Table 1): threats to system operation (THR); vulnerabilities of system components and operation processes (VLN); attacks on system assets (ATA); effects for system operation (EFF); assessment of the criticality of effects (CRT). Usually, criticality is estimated by the probability of an event and corresponding effects of attacks (PRE) and severity of effects (SVE):

$$CRT = PRE \times SVE. \tag{2}$$

A set of sub-stories (SS1,…, SSN) is formed as a list of analyzed events related to different attacks on vulnerabilities. Sub-stories detail elements of stories and are separate rows of the IMECA table.

Using IMECA analysis and Table 1, a matrix of cyber risks of successful intrusions can be developed according to Expression (1) (Fig. 2, a). The green color marks a square of low risk (sub-stories SSi, SSj, SSk), the yellow color marks a square of moderate risks (SSl, SSp, SSq), and the red color marks a square of high or unacceptable risk (SSr, SSs, SSt).

Table 1. IMECA table

Threats, THR	Vulnerabilities, VLN	Attacks, ATA	Effects, EFF	Probability, PRE	Severity, SVE	Criticality, CRT	Sub-stories, SSX
							SS1
							...
							SSN

	Severity		
Probability	L	M	H
L	SSi	SSj	SSq
M	SSk	SSp	SSs
H	SSl	SSr	SSt

a)

	Severity		
Probability	L	M	H
L	SSi	SSj, SSp	SSq, SSs
M	SSk	SSr	
H	SSl		SSt

b)

Fig. 2. Matrixes of cyber risks: initial (a) and after implementing of countermeasure (b)

Besides, criticality can consider a level of system operation maintainability, first of all, the possibility of recovery after the attack on assets [16] evaluated by the indicator REC. The REC value is smaller, the less time and cost of recovery. In this case:

$$CRT = PRE \times SVE \times REC \qquad (3)$$

The IMECA table can be added by columns of recovery (REC) as a metric of criticality, countermeasures (CTM) and actors (ACT) implementing CTMs (Table 2).

Table 2. Extended IMECA table

Threats, THR	Vulnerabilities, VLN	Attacks, ATA	Effects, EFF	Probability, PRE	Severity, SVE	Recovery, REC	Criticality, CRT	Counter-measures, CTM/ actors, ACT	Sub-stories, SSX
									SS1
									...
									SSN

The three-dimension matrix of cyber risks developed according to expression (2) is presented by a cube of risks [16] where spaces are marked according to the function of membership. Besides, the cube of risks can be presented by a set of matrixes of risks for a fixed value of recovery/maintenance. Implementation of countermeasures decreases the risks of successful attacks/intrusions.

In this case, some sub-stories decrease criticality due to decreasing, first of all, probabilities of successful attacks. For example (see Fig. 2, b), after implementing CTMs can be decreased probabilities of sub-stories SSp, SSr, SSs, and the general value of risk.

It should be noted that different countermeasures can be efficient for the different sub-stories. There is a task of choice of optimal CTM set according to criteria risk of security (and safety)/costs. Thus, an algorithm of IMECA-based cyber security assessment and assurance consists of the following operations:

- determination (collection) of stories and sub-stories set for analyzed system considering the domain experience (ATS);
- decomposing and analyzing sub-stories, building an IMECA table and matrix of risks;
- analyzing matrix or cube of criticality and assessing risk value;
- determination of a set of countermeasures considering the responsibility of actors;
- specification of criteria for the choice of countermeasures;
- choice of countermeasures and verification of acceptable risk.

6.2 Case Study for User Story

To demonstrate the utility of the IMECA technique, let's analyze the user story for the SSN, which is defined as a network of satellite systems, the processes of which have been augmented through the inclusion of smart sensors and actuators ([9], see Subsect. 4.2).

Results of the IMECA technique application are presented in Table 3. Criticality level is assessed for two cases: with the application of recovery procedures and without application. Besides, a feature of this table is that the column of countermeasures is divided into four columns which present results of possible decreasing of criticality for the corresponding sub-stories considering CTM implemented by four actors (DEV, REG, OPR, USR).

Developers can decrease only the probability by:

- analyzing operation experience pertaining to intrusions and cyber-attacks and their effects considering the weakness of AI means;
- redeveloping the system by use of capabilities of AI and other methods. Regulators can decrease the probability and improve maintenance by:
- analyzing cyber accidents and updating standard requirements to the system considering advanced AI quality models, possibilities of AI platforms, and maintenance procedures;
- upgrading tools to provide processes of the audit. Operators can decrease probability, improve maintenance and partially decrease severity by:
- analyzing cases and tolerating threats/attacks using possibilities of the OS and decision making about redistribution of responsibility between AI and operator;
- carrying out maintenance to minimize risks of successful attacks.

Users can't decrease risks directly but can analyze the experience and require the operator/developer to consider new challenges and meet the regulatory requirements.

Table 3. IMECA table for smart satellite network

THR	VLN	ATA	EFF	PRE	SVE	REC	CRT	AI-based CTM (Criticality)				SS
								DEV	REG	OPR	USR	
Activities of hacker centers	Communication protocol weaknesses	DDoS attack	Increased network interactions	M	M	L	M/L	L/L	L/L	M/L	M/L	SS1
	Power supply devices	DDoS or targeted attack	Power depletion	L	M	H	L/M	L/M	L/L	L/M	L/M	SS2
	Possibility of tampering with the OS /Firmware	Tampering attack	A non-functional state known as bricks	L	H	M	M/M	M/M	M/M	M/M	M/M	SS3
	Vulnerabilities of transmitting data between satellites and ground station	Man-In-The-Middle (MITM) attack	Violation of confidentiality and integrity of smart satellites data	M	M	L	M/L	L/L	M/L	M/L	M/L	SS4
		Data manipulation attacks		M	H	M	H/H	M/M	M/M	M/M	H/H	SS5

The results of risk analysis are shown in Figs. 3, a–d. The first matrix doesn't consider the application of CTMs by different actors (Fig. 3, a). The matrixes (Figs. 3, b–d) describe a potential decrease of risks after implementing CTMs by developers, regulators, and operators correspondingly.

a) Probability	Severity		
	L	M	H
L		SS2	SS3
M		SS1, SS4	SS5
H			

b) Probability	Severity		
	L	M	H
L		SS1, SS2, SS4	SS3
M		SS5	
H			

c) Probability	Severity		
	L	M	H
L		SS1, SS2	SS3
M		SS4, SS5	
H			

d) Probability	Severity		
	L	M	H
L		SS2	SS3
M		SS1, SS4, SS5	
H			

Fig. 3. Matrixes of risks: initial (a), considering CTMs taken by DEV (b), REG (c) and OPR (d)

7 Conclusion

The methodology of analyzing AIP applied for ATS cybersecurity assurance suggested in the paper is based on the scenario and story-related consideration, AI quality model and IMECA technique of criticality assessment of attack effects and risks.

Application of the scenario model allows structuring presentation of story set and forming epics for different domains and actors. Profiling of the AI quality model for chosen ATS kinds provides the specification of requirements to AI means of system cyber security assurance. The IMECA technique adds to the methodology of AIS assessment due to semi-formal analysis of threats, vulnerabilities, effects of attacks, and their criticality. It is important that the discussed matrixes and cubes of risks are convenient models to analyze and illustrate the choice of countermeasures.

The following directions of research in the context of the AI and AIP application to assure cybersecurity of ATSs and mobile systems as a whole:

- providing scalable and parameterized AI/Edge computing capability embeddable both in already existing legacy kinds of ATSs of all types and into the new autonomous transport systems with included AI algorithms to ensure overall mobility systems cybersecurity (treating safety of people and environment as a top priority);
- development of integrated tools for analysis of AI-based ATSs cyber security using models of AI quality and IMECA techniques, and for choice of countermeasures according to criteria "cyber risk/cost".

Acknowledgments. The authors appreciate the scientific society of the Horizon 2020 project ECHO consortium and the staff of the Department of Computer Systems, Networks and Cybersecurity of the National Aerospace University "KhAI" for invaluable inspiration, hard work, and creative analysis during the preparation of this paper.

Funding. This work was supported by the ECHO project, which has received funding from the European Union's Horizon 2020 research and innovation program under the grant agreement no 830943.

References

1. Autonomous Transportation Will Arrive Faster Than Predicted And Afford Bigger Business Opportunities. https://www.forbes.com/sites/oliverwyman/2018/02/05/autonomous-transp ortation-will-arrive-faster-than-predicted-and-afford-bigger-business-opportunities/?sh=262 f479841e7. Accessed 16 June 2022
2. Yahuza, M., et al.: Internet of drones security and privacy issues: taxonomy and open challenges. IEEE Access **9**, 57243–57270 (2021)
3. Kavallieratos, G., Katsikas, S., Gkioulos, V.: Cyber-attacks against the autonomous ship. In: Katsikas, S.K., et al. (eds.) SECPRE/CyberICPS -2018. LNCS, vol. 11387, pp. 20–36. Springer, Cham (2019). https://doi.org/10.1007/978-3-030-12786-2_2
4. Manulis, M., Bridges, C.P., Harrison, R., Sekar, V., Davis, A.: Cyber security in new space: analysis of threats, key enabling technologies and challenges. Int. J. Inf. Secur. **20**(3), 287–311 (2021)

5. Zhu, J., Wang, C.: Satellite networking intrusion detection system design based on deep learning method. In: Liang, Q., Mu, J., Jia, M., Wang, W., Feng, X., Zhang, B. (eds.) CSPS 2017. LNEE, vol. 463, pp. 2295–2304. Springer, Singapore (2019). https://doi.org/10.1007/978-981-10-6571-2_280
6. Abu Al-Haija, Q., Al Badawi, A.: High-performance intrusion detection system for networked UAVs via deep learning. Neural Comput. Appl. **34**, 10885–10900 (2022)
7. Gecgel, S., Kurt, G. K. Intermittent Jamming against telemetry and telecommand of satellite systems and a learning-driven detection strategy. In: WiseML 2021 - Proceedings of the 3rd ACM Workshop on Wireless Security and Machine Learning, pp. 43–48. Association for Computing Machinery, Inc. (2021)
8. Whelan, J., Almehmadi, A., El-Khatib, K.: Artificial intelligence for intrusion detection systems in Unmanned Aerial Vehicles. Comput. Electr. Eng. **99**, 107784 (2022)
9. Koroniotis, N., Moustafa, N., Slay, J.: A new intelligent satellite deep learning network forensic framework for SSNs. Comput. Electr. Eng. **99**, 107745 (2022)
10. Ashraf, I., et al.: A deep learning-based smart framework for cyber-physical and satellite system security threats detection. Electronics (Switzerland) **11**(4), 667 (2022)
11. Yaacoub, J.P., Noura, H., Salman, O., Chehab, A.: Security analysis of drones systems: Attacks, limitations, and recommendations. Internet of Things (Netherlands). Elsevier B.V. (2020)
12. Furumoto, K., Kolehmainen, A., Silverajan, B., Takahashi, T., Inoue, D., Nakao, K.: Toward automated smart ships: designing effective cyber risk management. In Proceedings - IEEE Congress on Cybermatics: 2020 IEEE International Conferences on Internet of Things, iThings 2020, IEEE Green Computing and Communications, GreenCom 2020, IEEE Cyber, Physical and Social Computing, CPSCom 2020 and IEEE Smart Data, SmartData 2020, pp. 100–105. Institute of Electrical and Electronics Engineers Inc. (2020)
13. Mendonça, H. C., Cocco, M., Miranda, C.M.: Security-compliant cyber measures for satellite systems. In: Proceedings of the International Astronautical Congress, IAC, vol. 2020-October. International Astronautical Federation, IAF (2020)
14. Torianyk, V., Kharchenko, V., Zemlianko, H.: IMECA based assessment of internet of drones systems cyber security considering radio frequency vulnerabilities. In: CEUR Workshop Proceedings, vol. 2853, pp. 460–470. CEUR-WS (2021)
15. Piumatti, D., Sini, J., Borlo, S., Sonza Reorda, M., Bojoi, R., Violante, M.: Multilevel simulation methodology for FMECA study applied to a complex cyber-physical system. Electronics **9**, 1736 (2020)
16. Waleed Al-Khafaji, A., Solovyov, A., Uzun, D., Kharchenko, V.: Asset access risk analysis method in the physical protection systems. Radioelectron. Comput. Syst. **2019**(4), 94–104 (2019)
17. Kharchenko, V., Fesenko, H., Illiashenko, O.: Basic model of non-functional characteristics for assessment of artificial intelligence quality. Radioelectron. Comput. Syst. **2022**(2), 1–14 (2022)
18. Kharchenko, V., Fesenko, H., Illiashenko, O.: Quality models for artificial intelligence systems: characteristic-based approach, development and application. Sensors **22**, 4865 (2022)
19. Siebert, J., et al.: Construction of a quality model for machine learning systems. Softw. Qual. J. **30**, 307–335 (2021). https://doi.org/10.1007/s11219-021-09557-y
20. Vasyliev, I., Kharchenko, V.: A framework for metric evaluation of AI systems based on quality model. Syst. Control Navig. **2**(68), 41–46 (2022)
21. Felderer, M., Ramler, R.: Quality assurance for ai-based systems: overview and challenges (introduction to interactive session). In: Winkler, D., Biffl, S., Mendez, D., Wimmer, M., Bergsmann, J. (eds.) SWQD 2021. LNBIP, vol. 404, pp. 33–42. Springer, Cham (2021). https://doi.org/10.1007/978-3-030-65854-0_3

Integration of Image Analysis Component with Industrial Workflow Management System

Wojciech Chmiel[✉][iD], Stanisław Jędrusik[iD], Piotr Kadłuczka,
Joanna Kwiecień[iD], Zbigniew Mikrut[iD], Dariusz Pałka[iD], and Michał Turek

AGH University of Science and Technology, Krakow, Poland
{wch,stj,pkad,kwiecien,zibi,dpalka,mitu}@agh.edu.pl

Abstract. The paper presents our solution based on the vision analysis and workflow management that can realise automated supervising of the workers, and/or their practical training to make better decisions and avoid various accidents. These tasks are the key objectives of the INRED system (created within R&D project) that integrates innovative solutions, components (e.g. surveillance system, workflow engine, knowledge bases, and so on), and has to improve the quality of complicated repair and service procedures. In general, the management of the sequence of work activities during the valve screwing process has been developed, and the proposed calibration and wrench detection modules are briefly described. Moreover, the workflow system and its constituent components are described, with particular emphasis on the Mobile Devices Communication Subsystem dedicated to organize Bluetooth/WiFi communication. The proposed solution was tested many times. In order to show its applicability, the selected results are presented. This solution met the requirement of maintenance training and monitoring of work activities, and can be readily applicable in many repair and service companies.

Keywords: Workflow · INRED · Vision system · Image recognition · Communication devices

1 Introduction

In repair companies, employee turnover is becoming a growing problem. Newly employed people must be trained relatively quickly, safely and effectively. In good companies, practical training in specially constructed workplaces for this purpose becomes a standard.

The teaching place used by one of the companies that cooperate with AGH-UST (see Fig. 1), is designed to train the employee on the proper maintenance of the valve flange connection. The order of screw tightening plays a crucial role in service management. The wrong order of tightening can cause damage to the device or, in an extreme case, to the risk of life of the employees. Therefore, the

A. Dziech et al. (Eds.): MCSS 2022, CCIS 1689, pp. 80–93, 2022.
https://doi.org/10.1007/978-3-031-20215-5_7

implementation of methods that can supervise this process increases the safety of operations during device service, especially in a power plant. Safety can be increased in two ways: by training employees or using sophisticated software based on image analysis.

The main goal of the INRED system is to improve the quality of services by ensuring their complete execution, continuous monitoring, and reporting of their proper enforcement. The INRED system allows each service procedure to be defined as a workflow process which is stored in the XML document form. Supporting the system relies on providing detailed descriptions of the tasks to be performed and technical documentation which describes these tasks in detail using e.g. augmented reality (AR) and/or technical documentation such as pictures, technical documents, 3D models with animation, movies, and parameter values). In addition, the system automates some actions, such as measuring and decision-making. An employee can be equipped with a mobile terminal or augmented reality (AR) glasses, a camera-equipped helmet, and Bluetooth measurement devices. These tools, after registration in the workflow system, allow the results of the measurements to be sent from the procedure level to the workflow management system. All sent values can be validated in the workflow procedure. Integration of tools with the workflow system is based on the Mobile Devices Communication Subsystem (MDCS).

In Sect. 3, the main modules of the INRED system involved in the screw tightening process are described. The workflow process supporting valve maintenance is presented in Sect. 4. The screw tightening algorithm supported by the vision system is shown in Sect. 5, whereas in Sect. 6 the *Mobile Devices Communication Subsystem* and communication devices are presented.

2   Related Works

Workflow management (WfM) is an emerging technology that is increasingly being used in a wider range of industries. Its main feature is the automation of processes that employ both human and machine activities. The first attempt to standardise workflow systems was made in 1993 by the Workflow Management Coalition (WfMC) [14]. WfMC created the reference model (workflow scheme) which specifies a framework for workflow systems and interfaces between the workflow engine and external cooperating applications and systems. Since then, workflows have been the subject of research both in business and in science. Many articles discuss the limitations of existing workflow systems and outline important research issues [1,15]. There exist several producers of the workflows system for different world markets; one can mention Appian, BP Logix, Creatio, Oracle Workflow, BonitaSoft and Nintex Workflow. However, there are no vendors that allow us to integrate service processes with wireless tools, augmented reality technology, and image recognition algorithms. The proposed system is part of the Industry 4.0 concept, where people and IT systems can be strongly integrated with each other. Very good review of the most important Industry 4.0 technologies can be found in [11–13].

Many researchers have focused on techniques for monitoring structural components, e.g., the tightening force of a bolt [9,10].

a)   b)

Fig. 1. Examples of stands; a) the didactic one in the company, b) borrowed from the company with additional elements, located at AGH-UST

3   INRED System

The INRED system aims to control and record all phases of the repair and maintenance processes. The main modules of the system are, among others, *Platform Process Management Knowledge Base, Communication Management System, Enterprise Process Management, Objects and Threats Recognition, Mobile Devices Communication Subsystem, Competence Centre, Integrated Video and Data Streams Management Platform, Smart Procedures Repository* and *Individual Diagnostic System.*

These modules are responsible for: exchange of information between the Competence Centre and service units, implementation of self-organising communication network, wireless tools management, storing 3D models, storing and processing data from processes and tools, objects recognition, threat detection and prediction using algorithms based on AI methods, and collecting the biometric data of employees. A detailed description of the INRED system can be found in [2].

Smart Procedures are an important element of the INRED system, which can merge services supplied by external applications or modules such as *Objects and Threats Recognition* (for example, using image recognition and machine learning algorithms), *Tools Management* and *Mobile Devices Communication Subsystem.* *Smart Procedures* have standard programming interface which allows them to be integrated (already at the stage of their creation) with workflow procedures.

Figure 2 shows a main part (modules) of the INRED system that is involved in the screw tightening process, as shown in Fig. 3. *Data and Video Streams Management Platform* allows to connect cameras and stream video to eligible recipients. *Communication Management System* delivers reliable communication medium for data transmission between the modules of the INRED system and the devices. *Mobile Devices Communication Subsystem* manages external devices connected to the system, provides authentication methods, and controls the flow of data between the sender and the subscriber. This module supports devices equipped with WiFi, as well as BlueTooth technology. In the process presented in Fig. 3, three devices with BlueTooth technology are used: two iTag clickers that are used to approve or reject the camera position, and the torque wrench that is used to tighten the screws and measure the tightening force.

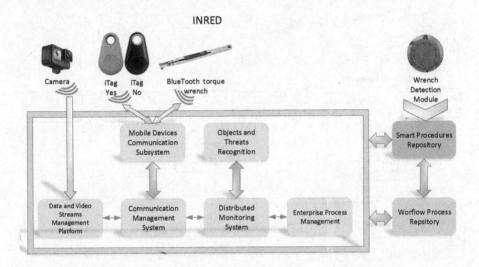

Fig. 2. Modules of the INRED system involved in the screw tightening process with the vision system.

4   Maintenance Process Supported by Workflow Procedure

In Fig. 3, an example of the valve assessment and repair process is presented. At the beginning of the process, the valve is disassembled and its condition is assessed. Depending on the condition of the valve, it can be repaired or replaced with a new one. In both cases, the valve parameters are evaluated. In the repair case, the valve is resubjected to the quality assessment process. If the valve parameters do not meet the assumed values, it is replaced by a new one. The *Screw tightening calibration* subprocess (defined there as the activity of the subprocess) is responsible for camera positioning, and during the *Screw tightening* activity, the screw tightening process is assessed. At the end, the *Valve assessment* activity is executed and then a report is generated from the whole process.

The subprocess *Screw tightening calibration* is detailed described in Sect. 5.1 whereas the internal flow of this subprocess is depicted in Fig. 4. During the *Screw tightening calibration* subprocess, the workflow management system actively cooperates with *Mobile Devices Communication Subsystem* (MDCS) which is responsible for the transmission of data from devices used to confirm actions performed.

Measurement devices are used during *Screw tightening* activity to determine the correctness of the tightening force.

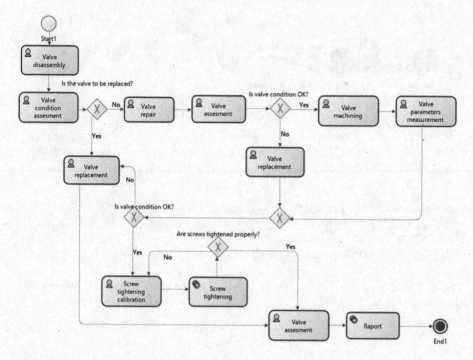

Fig. 3. An example of a valve maintenance workflow process.

The subprocess *Screw Tightening Calibration* (Fig. 4) is responsible for the camera calibration activities. The subprocess consists of 2 user tasks and 2 automated tasks. The first task is performed by the user who manually places the camera between the two calibration circles. After confirming the task, the system goes to the task of automatic detection of the cover. In case the cover cannot be detected, the process returns to the calibration activity. If the cover is correctly identified, the process goes to the activity of automatic bolt detection. The result of this operation is shown to the user. On its basis, the user makes a decision about the acceptability of the matching results. If it determines that the system has correctly detected the bolts, the subprocess ends. Otherwise, it returns to the detection task.

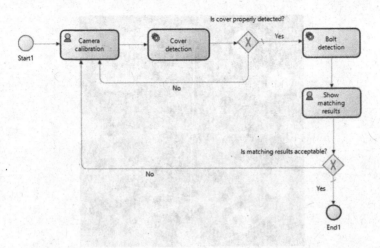

Fig. 4. The subprocess *Screw Tightening Calibration.*

5   Supporting of Valve Assembly with a Vision System

The vision system presented below supports the last stage of maintenance, i.e. the valve screwing process, during which it is important to maintain the correct sequence of tightening the 12 screws (see Fig. 5) with the specified torque.

The system has been divided into 2 modules: calibration and detection of the wrench that tightens the given screw. This calibration may be run several times until the employee confirms that the correct result has been obtained. This result in the form of an affine matrix is passed to the next module.

The wrench detection module is run repeatedly. It is recommended to run in three cycles (with different torques of tightening), where each cycle consists of twelve detections of the wrench that tightens the bolts in the given sequence (Fig. 5).

The procedures described below in Subsect. 5.1 and Subsect. 5.2 are implemented as a part of the process presented in Fig. 3.

5.1   Calibration Module

To simplify the software calibration process, the worker properly sets up the camera (see Fig. 6). The camera should be placed in the front of the screwed surface. The edge of the cover should be between the two calibration circles. Accurate centering of the cover in relation to the 'viewfinder' is not required.

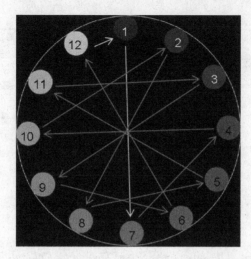

Fig. 5. An exemplary diagram of the bolt tightening sequence.

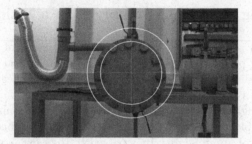

Fig. 6. An example of valve maintenance process.

To locate the bolts, it is necessary to generate a 2D model of the valve cover and correlate it with the current image obtained from a stationary camera. The edge image obtained by the Canny method [3,5] was the source image for the entire algorithm. The algorithm used a version of the Hough transform [4,6], which detected large and small circles. The large circle, with twelve small circles properly spaced out, is a model. Adjusting the model to the current image is carried out in two stages.

The first step consists in selecting the circle corresponding to the edge of the cover. Among the several detected large circles (Fig. 7a), the one is selected, for which the coverage ratio with the real points of the edge image is the greatest. Masks for both calibration circles are generated and it is checked whether the found circle is within them (Fig. 7b).

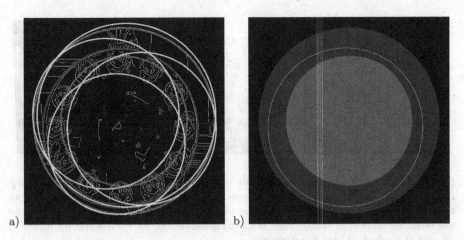

Fig. 7. a) Calibration circles (green), the selected circle (blue) and the remaining circles, detected with the Hough transform, b) checking the position of the selected circle. (Color figure online)

In the next stage, small circles - detected with the Hough transform - are analysed. Ideally, the small circles should correspond to the screws, but, in fact, circles around the screws are also detected. This is due to the heterogeneity of the colour of the cover surface and the shadows.

Due to the type of predicted distortions (slight rotation, magnification, and parallel shift), the fit was performed with the help of an affine transformation. To determine it, at least 4 pairs of model-image points are necessary. The pairs will be created after determining the centres of the model circles and the centres of the small circles, detected by the Hough transform, after analysing their mutual position.

In Fig. 8, red circles mark the model to be fitted to the screw representation (small blue circles). "Blue" circles were selected, the centres of which were closest to the centre of the model circle. The ends of the red sections show the pairs of points on the basis of which the affine transform was calculated.

The blue lines represent the eliminated pairs of points (see Fig. 8a and 8b). The elimination criteria were multiple references of the model points to the bolt representation, detected by the Hough transform (blue circles) or too large a distance (greater than the mean distance increased by standard deviation).

Figure 8c shows the result of the fit after the affine transformation: the real image was slightly enlarged and twisted. In Fig. 8c - apart from the red circles denoting the model - 'areas of interest' surrounding the individual bolts in which the key detection will be carried out (pink colour) are shown.

In the workflow process presented in Fig. 3 these operations are implemented as a subprocedure *Screw tightening calibration*.

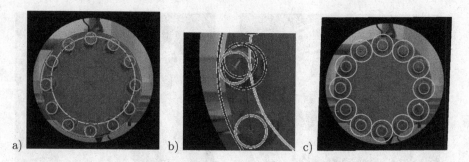

Fig. 8. a) Model of the cover with bolts (red) and small circles, detected with the Hough transform (blue), b) enlarged fragment of Fig. a) - the red segment symbolizes the model-circle pair accepted for further calculations, blue - the pair rejected due to too large a distance, c) image after affine transformation: for each screw its region of interest is marked. (Color figure online)

5.2   Wrench Detection Module

The image after the affine transformation (Fig. 9a) shows the generated message and marks the other screw in red. The worker should start tightening the indicated bolt. Figure 9c shows the result of the wrench detection. The analysis was carried out for the screw no. 6 and its two neighbours. From the two tested methods of wrench detection - subtraction from the background and optical flow (OF), the latter was selected for detection. The Horn-Schunck [7] algorithm was used due to its high efficiency, as demonstrated in the previous work [8].

Figure 9b shows the binarized movement field, which is marked in white. The detected pixels are summarised for the areas limiting the tightened screw and for its both neighbours. These sums are aggregated over time. At the same time, the differences between the aggregate sum corresponding to a tightened screw and the aggregate sums of the adjacent areas are calculated (cf. Fig. 10). After a few seconds, the sign of both differences is checked: if it is positive, the message 'OK screw no x' is generated (see Fig. 9c). If at least one of the differences is negative, the message 'it is NOT screw no x' is generated. If needed, efficiency of an employee may be assessed by the algorithm that counts mistakes made in a given tightening cycle. The outcomes may be subsequently used to evaluate employees' training progress.

The described algorithms of calibration and wrench detection have been tested on several films, which recorded the process of tightening screws with different numbers.

In the workflow process presented in Fig. 3, the operations presented above are implemented as a *Smart Procedure* which is wrapped in *Screw tightening calibration* activity.

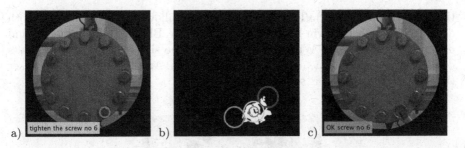

Fig. 9. Messages before a) and after c) the analysis of the results obtained from the optical flow algorithm, b) Movement field binarized with a constant threshold.

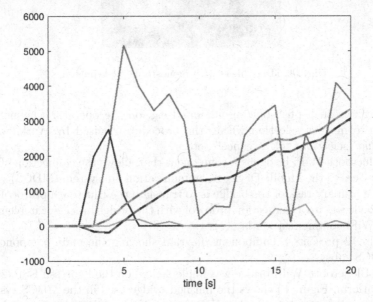

Fig. 10. Temporarily sums of movement field pixels calculated in ROI: red - tightened bolt, blue - previous bolt (no. 5), green - next bolt (no. 7). The red-blue and red-green charts show the differences in aggregate pixel sums for tightened and previous bolts, and tightened and next bolts, respectively. (Color figure online)

6   Mobile Devices Communication Subsystem (MDCS)

The Mobile Communication Subsystem integrates employees with the Enterprise Process Management System. As a result, the work performer may communicate with the Enterprise Process Management System hence control the correct execution of the screw tightening calibration subprocess - both during image calibration and consecutive screws localization.

A wide range of HID devices (Human Interface Device) may be used for validating successive steps of the process performed by Workflow. HID devices can be connected to the INRED system using the Mobile Devices Communication Subsystem (MDCS). The MDCS subsystem allows the connection of both devices communicating via Bluetooth (in particular, Bluetooth Low Energy) and dedicated devices using WiFi communication. The simplest type of HID class device is a clicker with one monostable push-button. An example of such a clicker (in two colour versions) is shown in Fig. 11.

Fig. 11. iTag clikers with monostable push-button.

Using two such push-buttons mounted e.g. on the operator's helmet, it is possible to make a selection within the procedure realised by Workflow (e.g. "yes"/"no" selection, "ok"/"cancel", etc.).

A Bluetooth-WiFi bridge is a component that allows the connection of Bluetooth devices to the Mobile Devices Communication Subsystem (MDCS) subsystem. The primary task of the bridge is to translate the Bluetooth protocol (used by the devices) into a connection protocol with the bridge processor implemented on the WiFi communication layer.

Figure 12 presents a component diagram showing the main components of the MDCS subsystem.

The Blooetooth-WiFi bridge was implemented on the Espressif ESP32 hardware platform. Figure 13 shows the finished bridge used in the MDCS system.

It is possible to support other HID devices in the MDCS system. Adding a new device to the system requires only the preparation of a driver to be used by the bridge processor (Fig. 14).

The INRED system JSON protocol is used, which supports the management of INRED mobile devices. A standard DeviceData will be suitable to transport a 'click' messages as it was transporting many other measuring messages for different previously developed devices:

```
{"Command": "DeviceData",
"DeviceMAC": "f6379e72",
"UnitID": "4",
"State": "Yes"}
```

The device has a built-in charge controller with a battery - a standard set with a 3.7V battery and USB charging was used here. The device will not require any kind of physical interface to provide configuration features. To set a configuration user will press the one and only "maintenance" button on the device

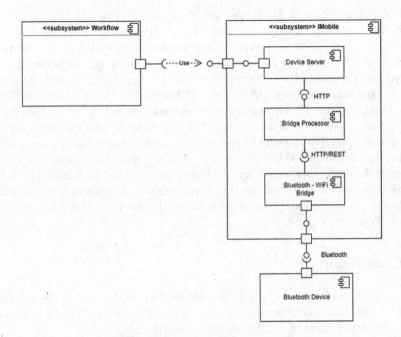

Fig. 12. Component diagram of the MDCS subsystem.

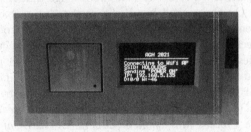

Fig. 13. The BLE-WiFi bridge.

```
23-06-2022 10:23:02.117: INRED Server: New CLIENT with number 0 (IP:/127.0.0.1), unsecured. Currently 2 connections.
23-06-2022 10:23:33.814: CLIENT 0 > SERVER: {"Command": "Login","LoginName": "HID1","Password": "HID1"}
23-06-2022 10:23:33.820: SERVER > CLIENT 0: {"Command":"LoginOK"}
23-06-2022 10:25:45.750: CLIENT 0 > SERVER: }
23-06-2022 10:25:45.770: SERVER > CLIENT 0: {"RSSI":"10","Command":"NewDeviceQuery","DeviceMAC":"A2F79D0872","DeviceName":"MobileSensor-
23-06-2022 10:25:45.773: SERVER > CLIENT 1: {"RSSI":"10","Command":"NewDeviceQuery","DeviceMAC":"A2F79D0872","DeviceName":"MobileSensor-
23-06-2022 10:30:52.539: CLIENT 1 > SERVER: {   "Command": "NewDeviceIdentity",  "DeviceMAC": "A2F79D0872",  "DeviceTypeName": "Virtual d
23-06-2022 10:30:52.549: SERVER > CLIENT 0: {"DeviceType":"Virtual device","Command":"DeviceAccepted","DriverPath":"no driver","DeviceMA
23-06-2022 10:32:13.075: CLIENT 0 > SERVER: }
23-06-2022 10:32:13.078: SERVER > CLIENT 1: {   "Command": "DeviceData",   "DeviceMAC": "A2F79D0872",   "State": "0001"}
23-06-2022 10:33:14.959: CLIENT 0 > SERVER: }
23-06-2022 10:33:45.591: CLIENT 0 > SERVER: }
23-06-2022 10:33:45.593: SERVER > CLIENT 1: {   "Command": "DeviceData",   "DeviceMAC": "A2F79D0872",   "State": "0001"}
26-06-2022 09:29:32.424: CLIENT 1 has dicsonnected.
26-06-2022 09:29:32.427: SERVER > CLIENT 0: {"Command":"DeviceUninstall","DeviceMAC":"A2F79D0872"}
```

Fig. 14. Example of "DeviceData" click message and an INRED protocol session print-out with a clicker device.

housing and will hold it for a specified time. The device will then reload the operating system and switch to a special operating mode, in which, instead of connecting to the INRED server, it will launch its own Wi-Fi Access point. It will then allow logging in from the operator's laptop to the network it has created and then launching the configuration web service. This website will be used to configure the appropriate data of the device (Wi-Fi name and password, INRED server IP address and authentication data). After configuring the device, configuration data will be saved in the clicker's flash memory and used during bootstrap. The concept of autonomous clicker shown above can go in pair with a Bluetooth-enabled one, already used in a system with support a Bridge-processor. In both cases a user (or employee) can be fitted with multiple clickers having either a 'click' or 'yes/no' buttons installed. Triggering another service events the employee can proceed with his work - under a strict control or an INRED Workflow engine.

7   Conclusions

The results reported in the article provide further evidence that the presented solution, based on workflow management system, can be used both in training and in the supervision of employees during work.

The *Smart procedures* proposed in the article can be used for employee training as a separate solution. Therefore, these procedures can be treated as *industry knowledge base* intended to accumulate knowledge that can be easily spread among employees. On the second hand, the same solution based on the image analysis and implemented as an activity of the workflow process provides evidence of the correct execution of the task. The proper execution of the task guarantees that devices that are part of, for example, the power plant, will work properly and will not pose a threat to the health and life of employees. Completion of this task requires cooperation and integration at the data stage of some parts of the INRED system, such as: *Communication Management System*, *Enterprise Process Management*, *Mobile Devices Communication Subsystem*, *Integrated Video and Data Streams Management Platform*, and *Smart Procedures Repository*, which is not a trivial problem. Moreover, proper implementation of the system requires sophisticated methods for image analysis which are fast and reliable.

Acknowledgements. This work was supported by the European Regional Development Fund under the Innovative Economy Operational Programme, POIR.01.01.01-00-0170/17.

References

1. Van der Aalst, W., Weske, M., Wirtz, G.: Advanced topics in workflow management: issues, requirements, and solutions. J. Integr. Des. Process Sci. **7**(3), 49–77 (2003)

2. Chmiel, W.: Workflow management system with smart procedures. Multimedia Tools Appl. **81**, 9505–9526 (2022)
3. Canny, J.: A computational approach to edge detection. IEEE Trans. Pattern Anal. Mach. Intell. **8**(6), 679–698 (1986)
4. Davies, E.R.: Machine Vision: Theory, Algorithms, Practicalities, Chapter 10, 3rd edn. Morgan Kauffman Publishers, Boston (2005)
5. Parker, J.R.: Algorithms for Image Processing and Computer Vision, pp. 23–29. John Wiley & Sons Inc., New York (1997)
6. MATLAB release 2020b. The Math Works Inc., Natick, Massachusetts (2020)
7. Horn, B.K.P., Schunck, B.G.: Determining optical flow: a retrospective. Artif. Intell. **59**, 81–87 (1993)
8. Chmiel, W.: INSIGMA: an intelligent transportation system for urban mobility enhancement. Multimedia Tools Appl. **75**, 10529–10560 (2016)
9. Miao, R., Shen, R., Zhang, S., Xue, S.: A review of bolt tightening force measurement and loosening detection. Sensors **20**(11), 3165 (2020)
10. Zhang, Y., Sun, X., Loh, K.J., Su, W., Xue, Z., Zhao, X.: Autonomous bolt loosening detection using deep learning. Struct. Health Monit. **19**(1), 105–122 (2020)
11. Ahuett, H., Kurfess, T.: A brief discussion on the trends of habilitating technologies for Industry 4.0 and Smart Manufacturing. Manuf. Lett. **15** (2018). https://doi.org/10.1016/j.mfglet.2018.02.011
12. Li, Z., Wang, Y., Wang, K.S.: Intelligent predictive maintenance for fault diagnosis and prognosis in machine centers: Industry 4.0 scenario. Adv. Manuf. **5**, 1–11 (2017). https://doi.org/10.1007/s40436-017-0203-8
13. Fatorachian, H., Kazemi, H.: A critical investigation of Industry 4.0 in manufacturing: theoretical operationalisation framework. Prod. Plan. Control **29**, 1–12 (2018). https://doi.org/10.1080/09537287.2018.1424960
14. Workflow Management Coalition: Workflow Reference Model. Workflow Management Coalition Standards, WfMC-TC-1003 (1994)
15. Elmagarmid, A.; Di, W.: Chapter 1: workflow management: state of the art versus state of the products. In: Dogac, A., Kalinichenko, L., Özsu, T., Sheth, A. (eds.) Workflow Management Systems and Interoperability, pp. 1–17. Springer, Heidelberg (2012). https://doi.org/10.1007/978-3-642-58908-9_1

Impact of Nonbinary Input Vectors on Security of Tree Parity Machine

Miłosz Stypiński[✉] and Marcin Niemiec

AGH University of Science and Technology Institute of Telecommunications,
Mickiewicza 30, 30-059 Krakow, Poland
stypinski@agh.edu.pl

Abstract. Key agreement protocol is an essential step for establishing a secure connection. The inevitable advancements in quantum computing technologies pose a huge threat to the key agreement protocol in use today. Neural cryptography is an alternative key agreement protocol that is not susceptible to any known quantum algorithm. Since the invention of mutual learning of TPM, many improvements have been proposed. One of them was the usage of nonbinary input vectors. This study verifies the impact of nonbinary input vectors on TPM security features. A number of iterations, similarity to intruder's TPM and effective key length were taken into account. The results show that the choice between fast synchronization times and higher security of the final key must be performed with perfect care.

Keywords: Mutual learning · Neural networks · Key agreement · Cybersecurity

1 Introduction

The very first algorithm for key exchange based on asymmetric cryptography was the Diffie-Hellman algorithm [2]. It allows the exchange of cryptographic key over an insecure channel between two parties in network environment. While no eavesdropper can recover the distilled cryptographic key, the entire algorithm is vulnerable to a man-in-the-middle attack. However, we handle this problem in practice by taking advantage of public key cryptography. This allows the parties to authenticate each other, which ensures that only the respective entities cooperate to build the final key. The first proposed algorithm allowing public key cryptography was the RSA algorithm [10].

All asymmetric cryptography algorithms come with one inherent drawback. The security they provide is conditional. The conditional security means there exists well-known ways to break the security of these algorithms, but this is not possible in a time-efficient manner with the current computing power available. The algebraic problem used in the Diffie-Hellman algorithm is the discrete logarithm problem, and the RSA algorithm is based on the factorization problem of large prime numbers.

A. Dziech et al. (Eds.): MCSS 2022, CCIS 1689, pp. 94–103, 2022.
https://doi.org/10.1007/978-3-031-20215-5_8

The inevitable revolution that quantum computers will bring will also have a significant impact on the current state of cryptography. Quantum computers operate on qubits rather than on standard bits. Qubits are a superposition of two quantum states which means that they can be in both states simultaneously. This feature allows implementation of quantum algorithms that are significantly faster compared to the standard algorithm counterpart. This is the case for currently used asymmetric cryptography algorithms. Shor's algorithm is an algorithm that reduces the time needed to find a solution for both of the previously mentioned algebraic problems [14]. Many solutions have been proposed based on problems that currently do not have an effective way of solving them on quantum computer. One of them is Tree Parity Machine (TPM) discussed in this article, in particular its variant with non-binary input vectors.

2   Tree Parity Machine

This section introduces basics of the TPM and describes the current status of this special form of artificial neural networks. Additionally, it covers the security considerations.

2.1   Related Works

Numerous research has been conducted in the field of neural network applications in cybersecurity. The first study showing that two TPMs are able to synchronize in finite time was conducted by Kanter et $al.$ [7] and Rosen-Zvi et $al.$ [11]. The very first application of neural networks on the subject of key agreement was proposed in [5]. This has become the basis for many improvements and applications of TPM. In [13] authors proposed an enhancement to the synchronization process by finding the best-fit weight vector using a genetic algorithm. Alam et $al.$ in [1] proposed an improvement in mutual learning based on sending erroneous output bits during mutual learning. Furthermore, TPM finds applications in error reconciliation. In [9] studies have proven that neural networks successfully find and reconcile errors in quantum key distribution protocols. Other improvements change the value range of the input vectors. In [3,4,15] modifications called Complex-Valued Tree Parity Machine (CVTPM), Vector-Valued Tree Parity Machine (VVTPM) and Nonbinary Tree Parity Machine (NBTPM) were proposed accordingly. The latter variant of TPM is used as reference model in this paper and the names TPM and NBTPM are used interchangeably hereafter. All the concepts presented are the same for both TPM and NBTPM except for random input generation. For TPM all the input values are selected from $-1, 1$ while for NBTPM vector values are selected from $< -M, M >$ range. Details are provided later in this section.

While all CVTPM, its generalization VVTPM and NBTPM change the values the input vectors can take, the difference between the first two and the last one is significant. VVTPM effectively performs mutual learning of multiple TPMs where the number of synchronized TPMs is bound by the length of an exchanged vector. NBTPM synchronizes exactly one TPM but in a faster manner.

2.2   Architecture of Tree Parity Machine

Basically, TPM is just a two-layer perceptron with K neurons in the first layer and only one neuron at the output of the neural network. The inputs are exclusively connected to only one neuron. The weights associated with corresponding inputs are integers varying from $-L$ to L. Each neuron in the first layer has N inputs. In [12] the TPM architecture and all the algorithms allowing for successful key agreement are presented in detail.

In the first design of TPMs, the inputs were binary vectors consisting of $K \times N$ elements. However, in this paper, we only consider TPMs with nonbinary input vectors (NBTPM) presented in [15]. Hence, the input vector elements are integers varying from $-M$ to M. The four parameters K, L, M and N uniquely define NBTPM.

NBTPM output is a binary value. To ensure that the output value is either -1 or 1 custom activation functions are used in the network. The first layer neuron activation function is a modified signum function and is defined in 1.

$$activation(x) = \begin{cases} 1, & x \geq 0 \\ -1, & x < 0 \end{cases} \tag{1}$$

The final output of $k-th$ neuron is defined in (2) where x_{kn} denotes the $n-th$ input of $k-th$ neuron and w_{kn} is its corresponding weight.

$$\sigma_k = activation(\sum_{n=1}^{N} x_{kn} \cdot w_{kn}) \tag{2}$$

The final output of TPM is the product of the first layer output and is presented in (3).

$$O = \prod_{k}^{K} \sigma_k \tag{3}$$

The example TPM with 3 neurons and 5 inputs per neuron is presented in Fig. 1.

2.3   Tree Parity Machine Key Agreement Protocol

To establish a secure key via an insecure channel, the parties must follow a key agreement protocol. This is accomplished by sharing some information publicly between entities performing key agreement. However, the key agreement protocol must ensure that any eavesdropper will not be able to retrieve the key from publicly sent messages.

Let us suppose Alice and Bob want to exchange the secret using TPMs. To achieve this goal by using nonbinary input TPMs they need to perform mutual learning algorithm described below.

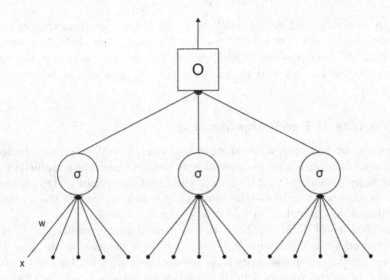

Fig. 1. TPM with $K = 3$ and $N = 5$

1. Both Alice and Bob initialize the weights w_{kn} in their private TPM with random integer within $< -L; L >$ range.
2. Either Alice or Bob generate an input vector X and share it over a public insecure channel. Every vector element x_{kn} is an integer varying from $-M$ to M.
3. After sharing the input vector parties compute the response O of their network using (1)–(3) and share it via public channel.
4. If the responses are the same Alice and Bob will apply one of the learning rules. Otherwise, the input vector is discarded and the process is repeated starting from step 2. The learning rules depend on the chosen algorithm. Examples are presented below.
   (a) *Hebbian learning rule*
   $$w_{kn}^{t+1} = w_{kn}^t + O^t x_{kn}^t \Theta(\sigma_k^t, O^t) \tag{4}$$
   (b) *Anti-Hebbian learning rule*
   $$w_{kn}^{t+1} = w_{kn}^t - O^t x_{kn}^t \Theta(\sigma_k^t, O^t) \tag{5}$$
   (c) *Random walk learning rule,*
   $$w_{kn}^{t+1} = w_{kn}^t + x_{kn}^t \Theta(\sigma_k^t, O^t) \tag{6}$$

   The parameter t denotes the current iteration of the algorithm and Θ is a function which returns 1 if both parameters are the same, and returns 0 otherwise.
5. Steps 2–4 are repeated until the full synchronization is achieved. Fully synchronized TPMs have equal corresponding weights. The vector W consisting of weights w_{kn} might be later used in other security algorithms, e.g. as a shared key in symmetric cryptography.

Both successful and unsuccessful iterations of the algorithm require exactly 3 message exchanges between the parties. Therefore, the algorithm should be finished in the least possible number of steps to prevent eavesdropping parties from recovering the key and to minimize the duration of the key agreement process.

2.4   Security of Tree Parity Machine

Key agreement protocols allow sharing keys over a public insecure channel in such a manner no eavesdroppers are able to recover the cryptographic key from the messages exchanged. Furthermore, the exact algorithm of key agreement protocols are openly available. If no intruder is able to extract the agreed key from information provided, we call it as a secure protocol.

The security of TPM has been the subject of many studies. In [6] Kinzel *et al.* showed that TPM with less than 3 hidden neurons in the first layers provides significantly less security than a neural network with 3 or more neurons. Moreover, in [8] the authors defined the following attacks to which TPM might be susceptible.

- Man-in-the-middle attack – an attack in which an evil party synchronizes one or more TPMs. The evil TPM successfully performs mutual learning in the case when $O_A = O_B = O_E$, where O_E denotes evil TPM output. This attack allows the eavesdropper to synchronize their weight by 60% on average based on research.
- Brute force attack – there have not been proposed any attack that would allow recovering the security key in time-efficient manner.
- Genetic algorithms attack – the attacker utilizes genetic algorithm to predicts weights. Based on conducted research mostly neural networks with only one input neuron are susceptible to this attack.
- Classification-based attack using neural networks attack – studies show that a properly trained Artificial Neural Network (ANN) is able to predict the sign of every weight with approximately 100% accuracy. This means the evil party using this technique with a brute force attack might be able to break the algorithm in half of the time required by just a brute force attack.

To check how changing the parameters affects the security of TPMs, all the simulations presented in Sect. 3 are performed in an insecure environment. All the exchanged messages are eavesdropped on by an intruder carrying out a man-in-the-middle attack.

3   Results

In this section, we check the impact of different parameter values on the TPM security. To check the quality of distilled key the entropy-based measure is presented in Sect. 3.1. The collection of results was performed on a dedicated environment which description is presented in Sect. 3.2. The last Sect. 3.3 contains the analysis of collected results.

3.1   Key Quality Measurement Methodology

After mutual learning is completed both parties have the same TPMs. Weights create a shared key. The length of the key is impacted by the initial parameters of TPM and is presented in (7).

$$Key_{length} = K \cdot N \cdot log_2(2L + 1) \tag{7}$$

However, the key length equation (7) only applies in an ideal scenario where the value distribution of weights is uniform. Studies show that the distribution of weight values in real-world scenario is not consistent with the uniform distribution. The updated key length formula that takes into account the uneven distribution of weights is presented in (8) [15]. In the equation, E denotes the estimated entropy which is calculated based on simulation results and takes into account probability distribution of weights. Additionally, the key length is an integer bounded by (8), therefore the floor is applied to the right side of the equation.

$$Key_{length} = \lfloor K \cdot N \cdot E(W) \rfloor \tag{8}$$

Furthermore, the performed simulations assume that an eavesdropper is trying to synchronize evil TPM. A similarity measure is required to determine how far evil TPM has been from fully synchronizing with the parties performing key agreement. The number of the same corresponding weights suits these requirements later being called the synchronization score. Its formula is presented in (9). In the equation w_{kn}^A denotes the weight vector of the adversarial TPM. The $Sync_{score}$ varies from 0 to 1, where the measure returns 1 for fully synchronized neural networks and 0 for TPMs where any pair of corresponding weight is not equal to.

$$Sync_{score} = \frac{\sum_{k=1}^{K} \sum_{n=1}^{N} \Theta(w_{kn}, w_{kn}^A)}{K \times N} \tag{9}$$

3.2   Simulation Environment

The simulation environment mimics the real-world scenarios where two parties willing to exchange key perform mutual learning. The whole communication is eavesdropped on by the intruder who is trying to retrieve the key by performing a man-in-the-middle attack. The simulation consists of different scenarios in which different sets of parameters are used. The parameters tested are $M \in \{1, 2, 3, 4, 5\}$ and $L \in \{9, 10, 11, 12, 13\}$. The parameters K an N are constant and are set to 3 and 50 accordingly. The results are gathered over 1000 simulations and include a number of iterations required to fully synchronize TPMs, key length calculated by (8) and evil TPM weight vector similarity calculated by (9). All the results are annotated with 95% confidence intervals.

3.3 Simulation Results

The simulation results section is divided into three following parts: analysis of the number of iterations, average evil TPM similarity measurement and comparison of maximum and effective key length.

The average number of iterations, successful iterations and evil TPM iterations are presented in Fig. 2. Increasing the M parameter significantly reduces the required number of iterations required to share the cryptographic key successfully. This results in a faster and more secure key agreement protocol. Noteworthy is the considerable difference in required and successful iterations between the parameters $M = 1$ and $M = 2$. This change of parameters provides the most meaningful improvement. Further changes to the parameter still increase efficiency, however the decrease of required number of iterations is less significant.

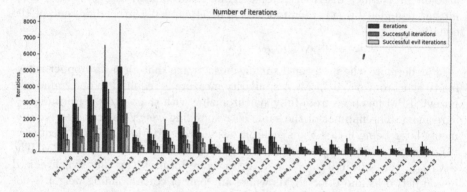

Fig. 2. Average number of iterations, successful iterations and evil iterations

The increase of parameter M also results in faster synchronization of evil TPM. Table 1 presents the average synchronization score for the eavesdropping party, including minimum, maximum and median values. For legitimate parties performing mutual learning, the $Sync_{score}$ will be equal to 1. In the average and median values, only minor growth is noticeable but yet the range of confidence interval increases by a magnitude twenty times. Furthermore, the maximum evil party $Sync_{score}$ more than doubles for parameters $M = 1, L = 9$ and $M = 5, L = 9$. The larger the values of parameter M, the higher the probability of full synchronization of evil NBTPM. This situation would result in cryptographic key compromise and should be avoided at all costs.

Table 1. Evil TPM synchronization score

M	L	Synchronization score $Sync_{score}$			
		Average	Min	Max	Median
1	9	0.12 ± 0.07	0.047	0.24	0.113
1	10	0.12 ± 0.068	0.033	0.26	0.113
1	11	0.11 ± 0.068	0.033	0.227	0.1
1	12	0.1 ± 0.062	0.04	0.22	0.1
1	13	0.1 ± 0.069	0.033	0.227	0.1
2	9	0.12 ± 0.088	0.04	0.32	0.113
2	10	0.11 ± 0.074	0.04	0.24	0.107
2	11	0.11 ± 0.076	0.033	0.253	0.107
2	12	0.1 ± 0.073	0.033	0.227	0.1
2	13	0.1 ± 0.066	0.027	0.213	0.093
3	9	0.13 ± 0.098	0.047	0.387	0.12
3	10	0.12 ± 0.089	0.027	0.333	0.113
3	11	0.12 ± 0.088	0.04	0.3	0.113
3	12	0.1 ± 0.076	0.033	0.233	0.1
3	13	0.1 ± 0.062	0.02	0.2	0.093
4	9	0.14 ± 0.116	0.04	0.467	0.13
4	10	0.12 ± 0.093	0.027	0.447	0.12
4	11	0.12 ± 0.09	0.02	0.267	0.113
4	12	0.11 ± 0.099	0.047	0.313	0.1
4	13	0.11 ± 0.083	0.04	0.253	0.107
5	9	0.16 ± 0.129	0.053	0.593	0.14
5	10	0.14 ± 0.111	0.047	0.393	0.133
5	11	0.13 ± 0.121	0.02	0.36	0.12
5	12	0.12 ± 0.101	0.033	0.407	0.113
5	13	0.12 ± 0.096	0.04	0.34	0.107

Additionally, with the increase of parameter L, the number of required iteration raises to fully synchronize both legitimate NBTPMs. However, simultaneously the growth of parameters L directly extends the cryptographic key. The relationship between parameters of TPM and maximum/effective key length is presented in Fig. 3. Furthermore, with the growth of parameter M, the slight decrease in effective key length is noticeable. This fact is caused by the extrema values effect described in [15].

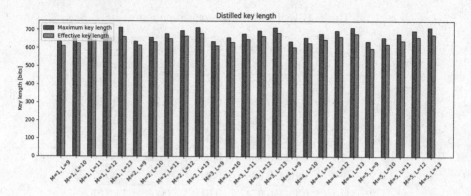

Fig. 3. Maximum and effective key length

4 Conclusion

In this study, the impact of different TPM parameters on security features of mutual learning key agreement protocol has been presented. In the research, required number of algorithm iterations, average eavesdropping party TPM similarity and effective key length were considered.

The studies have shown that cautious selection of parameters is significant while designing cryptosystems using TPMs. Additionally, the parameter M introduced as the part of NBTPM creates another layer of adjustment. With the increase of this parameter, the synchronization time is reduced significantly, however, the security features also start to degrade slightly. It is worth noting this parameter cannot increase infinitely since the trend of the average evil party synchronization score has a growing trend. This means at some point eavesdropping parties would be able to reconstruct the cryptographic key with ease resulting in a compromise of the whole cryptosystem.

As quantum computing advances, more interest may arise in the use of TPMs in the subject of cybersecurity. Hence the choice between fast synchronization times and higher security of the key agreement must be performed with perfect care.

Acknowledgements. This work was supported by the ECHO project which has received funding from the European Union's Horizon 2020 research and innovation programme under the grant agreement no. 830943.

References

1. Allam, A.M., Abbas, H.M.: On the improvement of neural cryptography using erroneous transmitted information with error prediction. IEEE Trans. Neural Netw. **21**(12), 1915–1924 (2010)
2. Whitfield, D., Hellman, M.: New directions in cryptography. IEEE Trans. Inf. Theory **22**(6), 644–654 (1976)

3. Dong, T., Huang, T.: Neural cryptography based on complex-valued neural network. IEEE Trans. Neural Netw. Learn. Syst. **31**(11), 4999–5004 (2020)
4. Jeong, S., Park, C., Hong, D., Seo, C., Jho, N.: Neural cryptography based on generalized tree parity machine for real-life systems. Secur. Commun. Netw. **2021**, 6680782 (2021)
5. Kanter, I., Kinzel, W., Kanter, I.: Secure exchange of information by synchronization of neural networks. Europhys. Lett. (EPL) **57**(1), 141–147 (2002)
6. Kinzel, W., Kanter, I.: Interacting neural networks and cryptography. In: Kramer, B. (ed.) Advances in Solid State Physics. Advances in Solid State Physics, vol. 42 pp. 383–391. Springer, Heidelberg (2002). https://doi.org/10.1007/3-540-45618-X_30
7. Wolfgang, K., Metzler, R., Kanter, I.: Dynamics of interacting neural networks (1999)
8. Klimov, A., Mityagin, A., Shamir, A.: Analysis of neural cryptography. In: Zheng, Y. (ed.) ASIACRYPT 2002. LNCS, vol. 2501, pp. 288–298. Springer, Heidelberg (2002). https://doi.org/10.1007/3-540-36178-2_18
9. Niemiec, M.: Error correction in quantum cryptography based on artificial neural networks. Quant. Inf. Process. **18**(6), 174 (2019)
10. Rivest, R.L., Shamir, A., Adleman, L.: A method for obtaining digital signatures and public-key cryptosystems. Commun. ACM **21**(2), 120–126 (1978)
11. Rosen-Zvi, M., Klein, E., Kanter, I., Kinzel, W.: Mutual learning in a tree parity machine and its application to cryptography. Phys. Rev. E **66**(6), 066135 (2002)
12. Ruttor, A.: Neural Synchronization and Cryptography. PhD thesis, University of Würzburg (2007)
13. Santhanalakshmi, S., Sudarshan, T.S.B., Patra, G.K.: Neural synchronization by mutual learning using genetic approach for secure key generation. In: Thampi, S.M., Zomaya, A.Y., Strufe, T., Alcaraz Calero, J.M., Thomas, T. (eds.) SNDS 2012. CCIS, vol. 335, pp. 422–431. Springer, Heidelberg (2012). https://doi.org/10.1007/978-3-642-34135-9_41
14. Shor, P.W.: Polynomial-time algorithms for prime factorization and discrete logarithms on a quantum computer. SIAM J. Comput. **26**(5), 1484–1509 (1997)
15. Stypiński, M., Niemiec, M.: Synchronization of tree parity machines using nonbinary input vectors. IEEE Trans. Neural Netw. Learn. Syst., 1–7 (2022)

Approach to Sector-Specific Cybersecurity Schemes: Key Elements and Security Problem Definition

Consuelo Colabuono[1]([✉]), Douglas Wiemer[1], Maria Vittoria Marabello[1],
Domenico Lofù[2], Marco Pappalardo[3], Piotr Bogacki[1], Andrzej Dziech[1],
Jan Derkacz[4], Luis Angel Galindo Sanchez[5], Ewa Konieczna[6], Maya Bojilova[7],
Giuseppe Chechile[1], Riccardo Feletto[1], Marco Dri[1], Massimo Zamagni[8],
Emanuele Sansebastiano[9], Grégory Depaix[1], Cyril Ceresola[10], Bernard Opic[11],
Massimo Ravenna[1], Marco Quartullo[1], Andrea Guarino[12], Paolo Modica[1],
Raniero Rapone[13], Massimiliano Tarquini[1], and Stefano Armenia[14]

[1] RHEA Group, Wavre, Belgium
consuelo.colabuono@gmail.com
[2] Exprivia S.p.A., Molfetta, Italy
[3] CIRM, Milan, Italy
[4] AGH, Krakov, Poland
[5] Telefonica, Madrid, Spain
[6] Visionspace, Darmstadt, Germany
[7] Bulgarian Defense Institute, Sofia, Bulgaria
[8] Fincantieri S.p.A.,, Trieste, Italy
[9] Fincantieri NexTech S.p.A., Genoa, Italy
[10] Naval Group, Paris, France
[11] Vitrociset, Libin, Belgium
[12] ACEA S.p.A., Rome, Italy
[13] AON S.p.A., Milan, Italy
[14] LCU, Rome, Italy

Abstract. This paper documents the approach to define cybersecurity certification schemes as candidate methods for sector cybersecurity product certification as part of the EU Cybersecurity Certification Framework being prepared by ENISA. Indeed, it is a very recent area of research within the EU landscape. Our work was undertaken within H2020 ECHO project (www.echonetwork.eu) and it is reported in detail in its deliverables. This document is completing the research reported in our previous publication, which had complete references to the existing state of the art about the certification topic in EU. Our work started with the identification of the sector-specific needs to be addressed for specific critical sectors. The mandatory Key Elements of a certification scheme, as described in the EU Cybersecurity Act, have been customized and the sector specific analysis allowed to define a Security Problem Definition baseline to be used to quickly draft a Protection Profile of an asset category of the considered sectors. Security needs have been identified using also the sectoral risk assessment guidelines provided by ENISA for certification purposes. It has also been developed an inter sector risk scenario to highlight the most important security needs to mitigate cross-sector security

A. Dziech et al. (Eds.): MCSS 2022, CCIS 1689, pp. 104–117, 2022.
https://doi.org/10.1007/978-3-031-20215-5_9

failures. Finally, Cyber Range technologies have been leveraged for the Conformity Assessment activities of two Maritime and a Healthcare product prototypes, for which the substantial assurance level certification has been simulated for the sake of validation of our approach.

Keywords: Certification scheme · Security problem definition · Sectoral risk assessment · Protection profile · Cyber range · Assurance level · Maritime · Healthcare · Energy

1 Introduction

The EU Cybersecurity Act [1] establishes the framework for the cybersecurity certification of ICT products, services, and processes. A Cybersecurity Certification Scheme is defined as *"the comprehensive set of rules, technical requirements, standards and procedures defined at EU level applying to products or services falling under the scope of the specific scheme"*. Afterwards, ENISA applied the Cybersecurity Act to release the first EU scheme specifically for ICT products [2]. Next expected step is to provide sector specific certification scheme for products based on the general EU certification scheme. Following the guidance defined by ENISA with the use of Common Criteria [5–7], our work concentrates on offering an approach for a sector specific certification scheme for some asset categories (products) identified as the most critical according to experts of Healthcare, Maritime and Energy. First, we present in the "Sector specific schemes" chapter how we have qualified the main elements that define a certification scheme by providing the high-level approach to identify such elements [8]. Secondly, it is described the general approach to define a sector specific scheme with respect the general EU scheme. In chapter 4 and 5, we describe how we extended the methodology presented in our previous work [3] to provide a security baseline from which easily draft Protection Profiles for the critical asset categories selected in the subdomains. Indeed, the Security Problem Definition is the core part of a Protection Profile as defined according to the Common Criteria. The sectoral Security Problem Definition has been obtained by integrating the sectoral risk assessment methodology provided by ENISA [4] to merge the traditional risk assessment with cybersecurity certification purposes. Finally, we highlight the innovative use of Cyber Range to execute the conformity assessment of some product prototypes subject to certification according to the proposed sector specific approach. Conclusion and next steps set the possible exploitation of the work performed and the expected evolution within the EU certification landscape.

2 Sector Specific Schemes

To be compliant with the official definition of a Certification Scheme, it is needed to identify rules, requirements and standards for sector specific schemes.

Rules and procedures are the mandatory elements listed in Art. 54 "Elements of European cybersecurity certification schemes" of the Cybersecurity Act [1] that have been already defined by the EU Certification scheme but only for generic ICT products [2].

Technical requirements are security requirements to be identified and we derived them complementing our sector specific analysis with a sectoral assessment carried on following ENISA guidelines [4].

Standards meaningful for specific subdomains are not only identified but we also suggest how to use them, whether to be used as an Organisational Security Policy or to refine Security Functional Requirements.

The following paragraphs describe how we identified and defined the three cornerstones of a scheme [9].

2.1   Rules and Procedures

The following rules and procedures are established in the EU Certification Scheme, and they have been further reviewed by sector experts in Healthcare, Maritime and Energy to identify the need of sector specific customization and in such case a rationale for the customization is explained.

- Subject matter, scope, covered asset categories
- Purpose
- References to standards
- Assurance levels
- Conformity self-assessment
- Evaluation standards, criteria ad methods
- Information to be supplied by an applicant
- Rules related to mark and labels condition of use
- Rules for monitoring compliance
- Rules for issuing, continuing, renewing certificates
- Rules related to consequences of non-conformity
- Rules related to handling vulnerabilities
- Retention period
- Correlation with another national scheme
- Content and format of certificates

It turned out that most of the elements of the list can be directly inherited as already defined by the EU Certification Scheme for ICT products - except for the rules related to the handling of vulnerabilities and to evaluation criteria and methods.

2.2   Technical Requirements

Among all the assets identified and classified in categories and subcategories, sector-experts have identified the most critical ones, to be certified in priority. To build a complete overview of all potential assets, we used ENISA reports and official sector-specific reports to derive a sector-specific Asset Taxonomy. We mark with higher priority such Business Processes that are linked to Services that in turn are supported by the asset categories identified as critical. Security Requirements derivation is based on the sectoral risk assessment that involves a context assessment, Attack Potential (AP) assessment and risk-based Common Security Levels (CSL) for the asset to be certified.

Security Objectives (SO) mitigate the risk and one SO is met by implementing a set of Security Controls, i.e., Security Requirements. A Security Functional Requirement (SFR) [6] is a requirement, stated in a standardized language, which is meant to contribute to achieving the Security Objectives for a Target Of Evaluation (TOE) of the certification.

Security Controls can be technical, operational or organizational. To establish a common set of controls it is suggested [4] to reuse Security Controls from ISO/IEC 27002 [10] or define new control controls which could be employed across sectors.

We provided an initial set of Security Functional Requirements integrating the following catalogues:

- Common Criteria Part 2 [6]
- GDPR [11]
- ISO27001:2022 [10]
- ISA/IEC 62443 [12]
- PIMS specific guidance for ISO 27002 [13]
- The Guidelines on Cyber Security onboard Ships [16]

This should be considered as a baseline to be extended according to other standards and regulation that the Protection Profile writer decide to use to refine Security Controls.

2.3 Sectoral Standards

According to Common Criteria, a standard can be used as an input to build an Organizational Security Policy (OSP) or a refinement of a security requirement. A standard used as an Organisational Security Policy aims to specify some aspects of the implementation of the ICT product or its operational environment, expressing requirements from national or sectoral regulations.

A standard used as a technical refinement of a security requirement aims to force the conformance to the standard as part of the fulfilment of the security requirement including fully or partially part of the text of the standard is.

After mapping the most important standards/guidelines [17–35] to the applicable asset categories, the stakeholders of the sector, according to their experience, have suggested the best option of exploitation for each sector specific identified standard, i.e., standard to be used as a policy or as a refinement of a security requirement.

3 Approach to Sector-Specific Scheme Definition

To provide a sector specific scheme it is worthy to establish a baseline Protection Profiles, that is the Common Criteria document allowing users to express their security needs given the fact that Protection Profiles are an implementation-independent set of security requirements for categories of ICT products that meet specific consumer needs. Consequently, we have provided a baseline for the pieces composing a Protection Profiles: Security Problem Definition, Security Objectives, Security Requirements. In particular, the ENISA guidelines for sectoral risk assessment for certification [4] were integrated to derive the Security Problem Definition. Security Objectives baseline started with the mandatory objectives described in the Cybersecurity Act [1]: they have been declined in lower-level objectives according to sector needs and the ISO27001:2022 Control Objectives. Such Security Objectives are achieved by applying Security Controls, i.e., SFRs, which strength depends on the assurance level established according to the risk level calculated following the ENISA guidelines [4]. In the future, the Security Control catalogue can be extended and deployed in suitable Security Levels according to their implementation strength. The implementation of the SFRs is assessed though the activities defined in the Security Assurance Requirements (SARs) of Common Criteria Part 3 [7] but also leveraging the Cyber Range technology for the Conformity Assessment dealing with the AVA_VAN (Assurance Vulnerability Assessment – Vulnerability Analysis) class of SARs. The below table summarize the main elements needed for a sector specific scheme and our proposition on how to determine them for a specific sector (Table 1).

Table 1. Elements of the sector specific scheme

Element	Proposition for sector definition
TOE categories	Asset Taxonomy of specific sector
Rules and procedures	EU certification scheme, plus sector experts' customization
Security Functional Requirements (SFR) / Technical Requirements	Proposed baseline according to Common Criteria Common Criteria Part 2, proposed integration with ISO27001:2022 and specific standards and regulations. They are mapped in Common Security Levels
Standards	Sector specific, to be used in SFRs or as OSPs
Protection Profile (PP)	To be designed for a TOE category: it is comprehensive of Security Problem Definition, Security Objectives, Security Functional Requirements, Security Assurance Requirements
Security Problem Definition (SPD)	Core of Protection Profile, composed by Organisational Security Policies, assumptions and Threats
Organisational Security Policies (OSP)	Proposed baseline according to the organisational security controls of the ISO27001:2022, sector specific standards, privacy regulations, NIS directive
Assumptions	Proposed baseline according to sector experts

(*continued*)

Table 1. (*continued*)

Element	Proposition for sector definition
Threats	Proposed baseline according to sector experts, ENISA reports, sectoral risk assessment
Security Objectives (SO)	High level baseline from the Cybersecurity Act, proposed lower-level details according to sector experts and ISO27001:2022
Security Assurance Requirements (SAR)	Proposed baseline according to Common Criteria Part 3
Evaluation Methodology	Use of Cyber Range for Conformity Assessment

4 Security Problem Definition

In this chapter, we illustrate how we have defined the core elements of a Protection Profile. Indeed, the usefulness of the results of an evaluation strongly depends on the Protection Profile, whose usefulness strongly depends in turn on the quality of its Security Problem Definition.

4.1 Assumptions, Organisational Security Policy and Threats

A Security problem definition needs to report what are the assumptions that are made on the operational environment (physical, personnel and connectivity) in order to be able to provide security functionality. Secondly, it describes the set of security rules, procedures, or guidelines for an organisation to end up with the identification of threats applicable to the Target Of Evaluation. It turned out [9] that assumptions identified as a baseline are mostly transversal and not sector specific. With respect to policies, they can be defined leveraging a standard as described in paragraph 2.3. Additionally, policies are derived from ISO27001:2022 taking into consideration the Security Controls labeled as "organisational". A baseline is proposed ready to use with the source of controls. Threats are identified after the sectoral risk assessment, which main steps are described in the following paragraph.

4.2 Sectoral Risk Assessment

1. **Context Assessment** – identification of business-critical services, processes and supporting assets according to the sector-specific TOE taxonomy.
2. **Risk Scenarios Assessment** – identification of threats applicable to asset categories through different attack vectors to be exploited by the typical attacker of the sector. For each tuple of asset category-threat it is calculated the Meta Risk Class (MRC) [4] giving a suitable probability and impact for such risk scenario.
3. **Attack Potential Assessment** – calculation according ENISA algorithm [4] of the level of the Attack Potential (AP) of the most dangerous type of attacker in a specific sector.

4. **Assurance Level Assessment** – selection of the suitable Common Assurance Reference (CAR), defined in such a way that the integration of product certification schemes and Information Security Management System certification is possible. CAR concept based on ISO/IEC 15408's AVA_VAN approach to assurance levels and re-use the associated evaluation methodologies (*see* Table 2).
5. **Security Level assessment** - For each Control Objective needed to counteract the risk scenarios, more than one Security Control can be applied. If the MRC is at a lower level than the estimated AP, the AP level should determine the CSL (Common Security Level) that is used for selecting the strength of the controls employed for the treatment of risk.

In the following table, relationships among the key elements of the sectoral risk assessment and the traditional certification assurance levels are displayed.

Table 2. MRC, CAR, AVA VAN and assurance levels

MRC	AP	CAR	AVA_VAN	EU assurance level
MRC1	AP1 Basic	**CAR1**	AVA_VAN.1	**Substantial**
MRC2	AP1 Basic	**CAR2**	AVA_VAN.2	**Substantial**
MRC3	AP2 Enhanced Basic	**CAR3**	AVA_VAN.3	**High**
MRC4	AP3 Moderate	**CAR4**	AVA_VAN.4	**High**
MRC5	AP4 High	**CAR5**	AVA_VAN.5	**High**
NA	AP5 Beyond High	NA	NA	NA

In the following table, the security levels are presented in relation of the risk level determined during the sectoral risk assessment (Table 3).

Table 3. CSL and risk-based approach

CSL	Description	Risk level up to	AP of attacker	Associated EAL	AVA VAN CLASS	CAR
CSL1	CSL 1 provides a basic level of security against unskilled adversaries	MRC1	AP1 - Basic	EAL1	AVA_VAN.1 Vulnerability Survey	CAR1

(continued)

Table 3. (*continued*)

CSL	Description	Risk level up to	AP of attacker	Associated EAL	AVA VAN CLASS	CAR
CSL2	CSL 2 adds requirements to CSL1, providing security against skilled adversaries with limited resources and opportunity to attack a system	MRC2	AP1 - Basic	EAL2	AVA.VAN.2 Vulnerability Analysis	CAR2
CSL3	CSL 3 extends the coverage of the security against skilled adversaries with significant resources and/or significant opportunity to attack a system	MRC3	AP2 - Enhanced-Basic	EAL4	AVA.VAN.3 Focused Vulnerability Analysis	CAR3
CSL4	CSL 4 provides security against a highly skilled adversary with significant resources and opportunity	MRC4	AP3 - Moderate	EAL5	AVA_VAN.4 Methodical Vulnerability Analysis	CAR4
CSL5	CSL 5 provides the highest level of security, capable of protecting against highly sophisticated adversaries with significant resources at their disposal and/or opportunity for an attack	MRC5	AP4 - High	EAL6	AVA_VAN.5 Advanced Methodical Vulnerability Assessment	CAR5
NA	NA	NA	AP5 - Beyond High	NA	NA	NA

In order to ensure that MRC and CSL are commensurate, there shall be by default a one-to-one relationship between MRC and CSL of the same level. During sectoral assessment, the sectoral stakeholders may deviate from this default relationship in specific cases. Such deviations have been justified and documented during sectoral assessment [9].

A special case occurs if AP 5, which matches a 'beyond high' attack potential according to ISO/IEC 18045, was identified for the adversary. Evaluation methodologies for this level are currently not available. In such cases, it is possible to recur to the combined deployment of multiple controls rated at AVA_VAN.5.

5 Security Objectives and Risk-Based Security Controls

The Security Objectives intend to solve security problem, they can be traced to TOE and to the Operational Environment (OE). The Security Objectives have relationship with threats in terms of countering and/or mitigating them; they enforce the Organizational Security Policies and uphold the Assumptions. The following SOs derived from the Cybersecurity Act are the high-level and were tailored in specific ones for the identified TOE categories: this can help in the subsequent selection of Security Controls/SFRs. (Table 4).

Table 4. Detailed SO

CSA objectives (Proposed naming)	Detailed possible SO
O.DATA_AVAILABILITY	O.ATHORIZED_ STORAGE O.ATHORIZED_COMMUNICATIONS O.AUTHORIZED_ACCESS O.SECURE_STORAGE
O.DATA_AVAILABILITY	O.SECURE_ BACKUP O.ACCESSIBLE_DATA
O.DATA_INTEGRITY	O.INTEGRITY_ASSURANCE O.AUTHORIZED_PROCESSING
O.ACCESS_CONTROL	O.ACCESS_RULES O.SECURE_IDENTITY O.TRUSTED_COMPONENTS O.SECURE_SESSION O.STRONG_ROLES_MNG
O.VULNERABILITIES_ANALYSIS	O.VULNERABILITY_GATHERING O.VULNERABILITY_ASSESSMENT
O.EVENT_LOGGING	O.CONTINUOUS_MONITORING O.ACCOUNTABILITY
O.LOG_MANAGEMENT	O.SECURITY_AUDIT O.SECURE_LOGS
O.VULNERABILITY_MANAGEMENT	O.SW_TESTING O.SECURE_SUPPY_CHAIN
O.BUSINESS_CONTINUITY	O.SERVICE_RESILIENCE O.RESOURCES_AVAILABILITY O.SECURE_FAIL
O.SECURITY_BY_DESIGN&DEFAULT	O.SECURE_COMMUNICATION O.SECURE_ARCHITECTURE O.SECURE_INSTALLATION O.PRIVACY_BY_DEFAULT O.PRIVACY_BY_DESIGN O.PHYSICAL_SECURITY
O.SECURE_SW_ DEVELOPMENT_ AND_MAINTENANCE	O.SW_TESTING O.SW_MAINTENANCE

Our work provides for each subdomain a table that highlights the SFRs/SARs proposed by the EU certification scheme to fulfill Cybersecurity Act SOs, mapping them against also to the ones detailed to fulfill sector specific case. It is provided the complete overview on how the threats can be counteracted by Security Objectives and a guidance on which SFRs select to implement the SOs. An added value is provided by detailing which sector-specific standard it is possible to use for the refinement of a SFR Class.

If a sector plans to deploy different variants of the asset category depending on its intended use and Operational Environment, the assignment of security and assurance levels should be carried out for each variant.

Arrived at this point, for each subdomain we have the following analysis flow:

Critical Business Process -> Critical Service -> Critical Asset Category -> applicable threats/attack vector -> MRC based on impact and probability of the identified threats -> applicable AP with respect the most dangerous typical attacker of the sector -> suitable CAR depending on the MRC plus the AP level -> suggested CSL for the identified CAR.

The summary of the analysis was reported for each sector [9] in a table that looks like the following: it reports all the aforementioned steps of the analysis from the beginning (leftmost column) to the end (rightmost column) (Table 5).

Table 5. Summary table used for the outcome of the sectoral risk assessment

Business processes	Services	Asset category	Applicable threat	MRC	AP	CAR	CSL
...	...	...	...	...	...	...	...
...	...	...	...	...	...	...	...

The SO are linked to the MRC: during risk assessment, any identified risk scenario is associated with a MRC. In a second step, the sector expert needs to define Control Objectives/Security Objectives to mitigate such risk.

The SFRs are linked to the CSL: A SO is met by implementing a set of Security Controls (SFRs). For each SO, more than one control can be applied.

The AP is linked to the suitable CSL: if the MRC is at a lower level than the estimated AP, the AP level should determine the CSL, which is used for selecting the strength of the controls employed for the treatment of risk.

CSA requires that certificates should reference technical controls [1, Art. 52.4] and that these should be documented for each assurance level [1, recital 86]. We have seen how a default relationship between the CAR level and CSL can be established by using the MRC and AP as joint reference points. Now, it is needed to think about what Security Controls are used. Security Controls can be technical, operational or organizational. To establish a common set of controls it is suggested [4] to reuse Control Objectives from ISO/IEC 27002 or define new Control Objectives which could be employed across sectors. In the new ISO27001:2022, it is established the use of any kind of "attributes" as a way of creating different views of the controls. The filtering or sorting of the matrix can be achieved by using a tool such as a simple spreadsheet or a database. A possible Security Control "table" has the following columns, which are the ones used in our tool supporting the Protection Profile drafting.

CONTROL TYPE: Organizational, People, Technical
ID: Control ID
*CONTROL (Security) OBJECTIVE: Control Objective originally from ISO27001, but
also from a sector specific standard, regulation or Common Criteria class*
SECURITY CONTROL: Description of the control
CONTROL IMPLEMENTATION: Implementation depending on the strength
*CSL: From 1 to 4, it is possible that for a control there is only a possible level or that
an implementation control is enough for all the levels.*
SECTOR: All, HC, MT, EN
NIS SECURITY DOMAIN: Governance and ecosystem, Protection, Defense, Resilience
NIS SECURITY SUB DOMAIN: 11 sub domains with respect to the 4 domains
*NIS SECURITY MEASURE: 28 categories of security measures, not always enough to
classify all the controls*

In particular, a security control can be implemented in a similar way proposed in the security levels of IEC 62443-3-3–3 [12]. This means that a security control can have different "combinations" of security implementation. It was worthy also make a possible reference to NIS [14] domain in order to demonstrate compliance with it given the fact the considered sector are critical ones according to such directive.

6 Conformity Assessment with Cyber Ranges

The CC has defined in Part 3 [7] the assurance family "Vulnerability Assessment', addressing the possibility of exploiting vulnerabilities introduced in the development or the operation of the TOE. This class has therefore been selected as the most representative class to fulfil the requirements of Article 52.1 of [2]: *"The assurance level shall be commensurate with the level of the risk associated with the intended use of the ICT product, ICT service or ICT process, in terms of the probability and impact of an incident."*

Levelling (from 1 to 5) is based on an increasing rigor of vulnerability analysis by the evaluator and increased levels of attack potential required by an attacker to identify and exploit the potential vulnerabilities.

According to EU Certification scheme [2], *"where no Technical Domain has been defined for a technology of ICT products, associated certificates shall not claim a vulnerability assessment level above the AVA_VAN.3 component. Certification above AVA_VAN.3 for ICT products that are not covered by a Technical Domain shall only be possible based on a specific Protection Profile defined and certified under EUCC scheme that includes mandatory guidance for the specific evaluation methodology and is annexed to the scheme for this purpose."*

Consequently, asset categories for which the suitable MRC, CAR and CSL is above level 3 after the sectoral risk assessment they will need specific evaluation methodology to be accompanied to the PP drafted following the methodology of our work.

The Conformity Assessment is carried on using a Cyber Range, implementing sector-specific scenarios where the product can be tested to define their conformance. The activities were organized as follows:

1. Drafting of the Security Target of a prototype belonging to MT and HC
2. Develop/consolidate the prototype with respect Technological Readiness Level 6 [15]
3. Description of Tests following the suitable AVA_VAN class
4. Creation of a meta narrative for the Demonstration Case
5. Cyber Range scenario development and testing tools deployment
6. Testing of the prototypes using the scenario and the testing tools
7. Creation of the Evaluation Technical Report

With respect the tests, benefits using Cyber Ranges are:

- Ease of design and deployment of realistic test environments
- Ease of backup and restoration of the test environment in case that a test is irreversibly destructive (e.g., ransomware)
- Test environment isolation: with a cyber range no collateral effects on impact on production networks
- Flexibility and adaptability: different test environment setups and configurations
- Access control: with a cyber range it's easy to access to the activities of the range from everywhere, for authorised users
- Orchestration and simulations capabilities: triggering things, generate specific network traffic.
- Content Management System: easy to produce related documentation and reports

The Conformity Assessment is possible only if the Cyber Ranges are accredited environment labs. Not accredited Cyber Ranges can be used before requesting an official certification test from relevant authorities: the product owner may ask simulations in an extended cyber range environment.

7 Conclusion and Next Steps

Our approach to a sector specific scheme is based on the Cybersecurity Act and the EU Certification scheme. Rules, technical requirements, standards and procedures are customized under the scope of the specific sector, after the identification of the sector specific needs and problems. Our scope was including Smart Hospitals in Healtcare, SCADA systems and Smart Meter in Energy and Commercial Ships in Maritime. Sectors Specific asset categories and associated threats have been identified for each sector, ranking the asset categories according to their criticality.

Leveraging sector specific reports and sector analysis, a baseline for the Security Problem Definition has been defined. Some of these documents considered are reported within the references from [10] to [36].

For each subdomain of the sectors, we have the following analysis flow:

Critical Business Process -> Critical Service -> Critical Asset Category -> applicable threats/attack vector -> Meta Risk Class based on impact and probability of the identified threats -> applicable Attack Potential with respect the most dangerous typical attacker of the sector -> suitable Common Assurance Reference depending on the Meta

Risk Class and the Attack Potential level -> suggested Common Security Levels for the identified Commo Assurance Reference.

If a sector plans to deploy different variants of the asset category depending on its intended use and Operational Environment, the assignment of security and assurance levels should be carried out for each variant.

The performed analysis and proposed Security Problem Definition baseline is reported in an excel tool to make it more usable: in the future, the tool can collect all the identified pieces to quickly draft a Protection Profile in a specific sector by guiding the writer through the selection of the main elements of the Security Problem Definition. The Security Controls catalogue will be the most dynamic part of the tool, to be enhanced according the subdomains and sectors desired. The open point is to develop a method to assign Security Controls to a specific Common Security Level and how to estimate the overall CSL resulting from the concatenation of Security Controls. Up to the moment, a ranking of the identified Security Controls has been proposed.

Our work can be also the ground for possible services to be provided in the cybersecurity certification field, such as: support to design Protection Profiles, training on how to build a Protection Profile, simulation tests on cyber ranges, conformity, assessment with accredited cyber ranges.

References

1. Proposal for a Regulation of the European Parliament and of the Council on ENISA (the EU Cybersecurity Agency) and repealing Regulation (EU) 526/2013, and on Information and Communication Technology cybersecurity certification ('Cybersecurity Act'), the European Parliament and the Council. Accessed 13 Sept 2017
2. Cybersecurity Certification: EUCC Candidate Scheme. European Union Agency for Cybersecurity (ENISA). Accessed 02 July 2020
3. Hovhannisyan, K., Bogacki, P., Colabuono, C.A., Lofù, D., Marabello, M.V., Maxwell, B.E.: Towards a healthcare cybersecurity certification scheme. In: Cyber Security (2021)
4. Methodology for Sectoral Cybersecurity Assessments. European Union Agency for Cybersecurity (ENISA). Accessed 13 Sept 2021
5. Common Criteria for Information Technology Security Evaluation: Part 1 - Introduction and general model
6. Common Criteria for Information Technology Security Evaluation: Part 2 - Security functional components
7. Common Criteria for Information Technology Security Evaluation: Part 3 - Security assurance components
8. D2.9 ECHO Cybersecurity Certification Scheme. European Network of Cybersecurity Centres and Competence Hub for Innovation and Operations (2021)
9. D2.14 Update - ECHO Cybersecurity Certification Scheme. European Network of Cybersecurity Centres and Competence Hub for Innovation and Operations (2022)
10. ISO/IEC 27002 - Information technology—Security techniques—Code of practice for information security controls
11. Regulation (EU) 2016/679 of the European Parliament and of the Council of 27 April 2016 on the protection of natural persons with regard to the processing of personal data and on the free movement of such data, and repealing Directive 95/46/EC
12. ISA-62443-3-3 Security for Industrial automation and Control systems Part 3–3: System security requirements and security levels

13. ISO/IEC 27701:2019 Security techniques—Extension to ISO/IEC 27001 and ISO/IEC 27002 for privacy information management—Requirements and guidelines
14. The Directive on security of network and information systems (NIS Directive), the European Parliament and the Council. Accessed 06 July 2016
15. https://it.wikipedia.org/wiki/Technology_Readiness_Level
16. The Guidelines on Cyber Security onboard Ships. IMO
17. Good practices for the maritime sector. ENISA
18. Procurement guidelines for Cybersecurity in Hospitals. ENISA
19. Smart Hospitals - Security and Resilience for Smart Health Service and Infrastructures. ENISA
20. Regulation (EU) 2020/561 for Medical Devices Requirements (MDR)
21. ISO 27799:2008 Health informatics, information security management in health using ISO/IEC 27002
22. Medical Device Directive (MDD)
23. DICOM (Digital Imaging and COmmunications in Medicine)
24. ISO/IEC 27019:2013 Information technology—Security techniques—Information security management guidelines based on ISO/IEC 27002 for process control systems specific to the energy utility industry
25. Port cybersecurity. ENISA
26. Appropriate security measures for Smart Grids. ENISA
27. Smart Grid Threat Landscape and Good Practice Guide. ENISA
28. NIST SP 800–82 Guide to Industrial Control Systems Security
29. ISO/IEC TR 27019 Information security for process control in the energy industry
30. IACS Recommendation on cyber resilience (Rec. 166)
31. SOTA - STATE OF THE ART SYLLABUS Overview of existing Cybersecurity standards and certification schemes
32. Security Measures for Operators of Essential Services
33. Mapping of OES Security Requirements to Specific Sectors. NIS Cooperation Group
34. Guidelines on notification of Operators of Essential Services incidents (formats and procedures). NIS Cooperation Group
35. Guidelines on notification of Digital Service Providers incidents (formats and procedures). NIS Cooperation Group
36. Recommendations for the Implementation of the Industrial Automation & Control Systems Components Cybersecurity Certification Scheme (ICCS)

Technology and Police: A Way to Create Predicting Policing

Abel Gonzalez-Garcia[1]([⊠]) and Luis Angel Galindo Sanchez[2]

[1] MOU (Madrid Open University), Madrid, Spain
abel.gonzalez@udima.es
[2] Telefonica, Madrid, Spain
luisangel.galindosanchez@telefonica.com

Abstract. Technological development is unstoppable. Police forces are no strangers to this development. In this paper we present the advances in this field of different types of technologies applied to the police function (crime mapping, data mining and big data, social media, drones) and also the application of artificial intelligence to policing. Finally, we reflect on the suitability of these applications and the desirable future through recommendations.

1 Introduction

We are currently living in a technological revolution where every aspect of our lives is mediated by some technological innovation. In particular, no work is conceivable in which it is not mediatized by some technological instrument. It is for this reason that police work is not left out of this permanent revolution.

This article aims to explain the main technological changes introduced in the police forces in recent years, especially in terms of the use of data (crime mapping, data mining and big data), technological innovations in criminal investigation or patrolling (body and car cameras or vehicle licence plate readers, UAVs -drones-), to end with a more diffuse technological development such as the application of the misnamed (We say misnamed, because there are multiple types of intelligence and not just one, just as the terminological concreteness leads us to indicate that they are mathematical processes, more or less complex, but still far from human intelligence. We don't know in a few years' time, but at present technological development indicates that this is the case) artificial intelligence to decision-making in the police (predictive policing).

There is no argument in favour of considering that we are in a moment of transition, of change, of development, in short. And this development *is not only a process of capital accumulation and technical progress, but also a process of social change and institutional reorganization* [1].

And here, this development connects with the need to define police models with the use of technology within the criminological specialty of policing, a concept we can define as the activities developed by the police for the preservation of law and order, or the actions, within the scope of policies, of a person or a group with authority to guarantee equity and legality in public life.

A. Dziech et al. (Eds.): MCSS 2022, CCIS 1689, pp. 118–125, 2022.
https://doi.org/10.1007/978-3-031-20215-5_10

Finally, there will be a reflection on all this development and its influence on police models, where, we anticipate, the human factor will be taken into account as the backbone of all this development and as the final "client" of the technology.

The rest of the paper is organised as follows: Sect. 2 presents the literature on the use of technology by police forces, Sect. 3 show technology applications in the role of the police. Section 4 explains how police can predict crimes, protests, etc. Section 5 presents the conclusions of this research.

2 Technical State of the Art

One of the first reviews of the use of technology by police forces was conducted in the United States of America (USA) in 2016 [2], and several key state-of-the-art findings are reproduced here:

- 96% of police agencies have implemented one or more of the 18 technologies analysed in the report.
- The technologies that have been implemented and their percentages are: in-vehicle cameras (70%); information sharing platforms (68%) and social media (68%). Also, but to a lesser extent, cameras on police officers themselves, geographic information systems, phone tracking software, investigation software, number plate readers, and even predictive analytics software have been developed.
- The technologies that were expected to increase the most were: predictive analytics software (15% of police agencies planned to do so); in-vehicle video cameras (15%); in-vehicle electronic ticketing (11%) and drones (7%).

Also interesting in this report is the analysis of the relationship between technology acquisition and policing strategies, for example, police agencies that are closer to community, intelligence-led or hotspot policing models use more technology; conversely, those that use professional, problem-oriented or zero-tolerance policing use less technology.

One study in this regard is Jaime and Torrente's study [3], based on interviews with police officials in Spain, in which they also look at the technological component. In this case, there is growing concern about the technological variable, especially the fear of outdatedness or the perception that the distance to criminals is widening. An indirect problem that is perceived is the relationship with technological operators, mistrust because of the data they handle and because if they were to stop providing their services, they would have multiple problems. Another aspect of the problem with technology that generates tensions with society is the ability of any citizen to record and disseminate police actions with their mobile phone.

Technology is an integral part of police work at the moment, but it is not without controversy. In the next section, we cover which technological developments have been implemented in recent years, and thus we can reach a series of conclusions for the improvement of peaceful coexistence between technology and society.

3 Technological Applications in the Police Role

3.1 Crime Mapping

Crime mapping software is used by police to visualise and analyse, in a geo-referenced manner, crime patterns across space and time. It is also used with socio-demographic data to better understand the contextual characteristics of criminal incidents [4].

There is a wide variation in the techniques, sophistication of methods and frequency of police use of this technology. They range from generating only a visual map, to using geospatial analysis to understand the relationship between different incidents and crimes [5].

In the Strom study, a survey of 1,200 police forces in the USA [6], 31% of all police forces and 81% of the largest police forces use this technology [7].

Buil-Gil, Moretti, and Langton [8] simulate scenarios in the city of Manchester (UK), based on the crimes reported in the Victimisation Survey for England and Wales and the likelihood of them being known to the police. Ultimately, the aim of the study is to find out whether small area data are influenced by the more general mapping data on which policing strategies are based. The result is that aggregated data from small "geographies" cause crimes not known to the police to vary widely and underestimate crime in some places, while overestimating it in others. The conclusion, therefore, is that analyses must be made appropriate to small areas.

3.2 Data Mining and Big Data

The use of large amounts of data and its mining (or classification and analysis) is done by police through software that allows massive data to be analysed in a fraction of the time it would take by manual methods. They are used to analyse texts, visualise criminal networks, identify suspects or recognise criminal patterns and characteristics [9].

A very interesting example in this sense is the study by Aghababaei and Makrehchi [10] in the city of Chicago, in this study the main objective is to try to find out whether the electronic medium (Twitter in this case) is able to provide socio-behavioural signals that can predict crime. The results point in the direction that the model proposed by the researchers - based on content, sentiment and topics as predictive indicators - with the temporal topic predicts better than a static model. In short, and in the words of the authors of the study, it provides an in-depth insight into the correlation between language and crime trends, as well as the impact of social data as an additional resource to provide predictive indicators.

3.3 Social Media

The use of social media by law enforcement agencies can build better relations with the community because it opens a forum for participation.

In this sense, an applied analysis [11] of the use of social networks in the phenomenon of terrorist attacks, specifically the attack on Las Ramblas in Barcelona (Spain) on 17 August 2017, concludes that at first the Mossos d'Esquadra police force was the one guiding all communication of the attacks, which was followed by the media. Insofar as it was initially classified as an incident and not as an attack, the immediacy of the data published and its possible reliability based on the information available at any given time must also be taken into account. This shows the importance of the use of social networks in an initial moment of confusion to better manage these situations in terms of public order.

But on the other side of the coin, beyond the information that can be offered to citizens or the request for information from them, social networks can also be used as an investigative tool. This is evidenced by research cited by Strom [12] in which 80% of the sample of police officers indicated that social networks are a good investigative tool for solving crimes.

3.4 Video Surveillance. Number Plate Readers and Body and Car Cameras

The installation of in-vehicle cameras in police vehicles can document the circumstances of arrests, other police interactions with citizens and can also prevent assaults on police officers. Data from 2015, collected by Storm [13], indicates that 68% of police forces in the United States of America used in-vehicle camera systems.

On the other hand, a 2002 [14] study of 47 state police officers in the US concluded that some officers believed that the cameras were used by their superiors to monitor their on-duty behaviour, and also identified problems with the technology (poor image quality and no sound) or lack of training in their proper use.

Vehicle number plate readers allow character recognition software to read and document thousands of number plates per minute, as well as the location, date and time of the vehicle's location. In 2012, 16% of police forces in the US had such a system in place. Usage, according to a study by Roberts y Casanova [15], is for stolen vehicle recovery (69%), traffic surveillance (28%) and investigative purposes (25%).

And finally, body-worn cameras document evidence, prevent and resolve citizen complaints, and strengthen police accountability and transparency [16].

A 2015 study with the Phoenix Police (Arizona, USA) [16] indicated that police officers who had worn body cameras increased arrests by 17% compared to a 9% increase in arrests for officers who did not wear the cameras. In addition, citizen complaints decreased by 23% compared to police officers wearing cameras, but officers not wearing cameras increased citizen complaints by 10.6%.

3.5 Drones and Police Intelligence (UAVs)

The use of drones can be considered as just another form of video surveillance, but here it is explained their relationship to the use of drones to provide intelligence to the police or as part of the "intelligence-led policing" model of policing.

For example, in Switzerland [17] more than half of the 26 cantonal police forces use drones or UAVs (unmanned aerial vehicles) for aerial photography, observation or surveillance. And it is here that Klauser [18] believes that the air is one more space where the police exercise their power and that the police should have an interest (object of surveillance), a context in which police action can take place and a mediator or perspective of police action.

In another area, an analysis by Rodriguez Herrera [19], focusing on the use of drones as a means of obtaining intelligence data in operations in support of the Panamanian National Police, and through the author's experience, recommends that the Panamanian National Police conduct a study for the acquisition of drones so that they can be used in the strategic planning of National Defence and create courses for training and instruction in the use of this technology (Fig. 1).

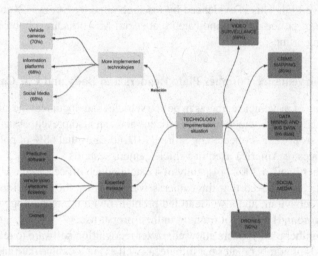

Fig. 1. Implementation of technology

4 Predictive Policing

In the current Artificial Intelligence term, there is an infinite number of mathematical data processing techniques: Data Mining techniques, already discussed in previous sections, and which make it possible to find patterns and summarise large volumes of data to facilitate decision-making; machine learning (One example of the application of this technology is that researchers believe they can use Twitter to find out where protests are going to take place before the police do, as reported in a news report that an analysis of 1.6 million tweets from the 2011 riots in the UK, which resulted in 3,000 arrests, identified the locations before calls to emergency services [20]; natural language processing, so that computer systems can understand language naturally; deep learning or artificial neural networks, based on the known biological structures of the brain [21].

Miro comments that there are two essential aspects to determine the potential of Artificial Intelligence, on the one hand, its capacity to execute instructions and, on the other, the degree of autonomy with which they are executed [22].

It is currently recognised that there are three models of AI, based on the Harbers, Peters and Neerinxc model [23], the first of which is man in the loop, in which human-machine interaction is continuous, human input is needed at intervals; secondly, man on the loop, when the machine is capable of acting by itself based on previous programming;

and thirdly, man out of the loop, in which the machine acts independently based on what it has learned. In this sense, we are evidently taking important steps towards what Miro has called no man on the loop, when machines learn from each other.

Examples of the use of these technologies in law enforcement are as follows [24]:

- Rossmo's Algorithm: to estimate the geographical area where a serial offender may reside based on the location of previous crimes committed.
- The Lethality Screen: to assess domestic violence and provide information for early detection. A similar algorithm is used in Spain in the VIOGEN system.

Prediction of cybercrime: according to the study by BILEN and Bedri Özer [25], the algorithms that perform best in cyberattack detection are, in first place, SVML (95.43% accuracy), followed by RF (94.48%) and LR (94.41%).

Table 1 shows the relation between policing activities and technologies used. As it can be seen, current needs in policing activities are not covered with existing technologies. Only two technologies (Sharing Databases and Social Media) have a significant percentage over 60. All the other technologies used, the matching between needs and technology is in the best situation 39%, which is very low, even in five technologies this percentage is reduced till 10% or lower.

Table 1. Policing activities and Technology (Strom 2017)

Policing activities	Mean (N = 749) (Min = 1/Max. = 5)	Technology	Percentage (N = 749)
Respond to calls for service	4.80	– Sharing Databases – Software to track cell phones – Reverse 9-1-1 emerg – Next generation 9-1-1	68 39 28 12
Conduct follow-up investigations	4.50	– Software investigation case – GPS tracking suspects – Computer forensic techonology – 2D/3D crime-scene imaging – Ballistics /firearm tracing	39 22 19 10 1
Identify and analyze specifics problems	4.06	– Social media – GIS – CCTV with video analysis – Data-mining tools – UAV´s (drones)	68 31 17 10 0
Conduct crime prevention	3.55	– Predictive analytics software	4

5 Conclusions

While technology is a method for more social interaction with citizens, this raises the debate about the power of the police in today's society. This debate stems from the vast amount of data that police forces can collect with the technologies discussed in this preliminary analysis. For this reason, police forces need to be very clear about certain issues, such as: the police model they want to implement (for example: community policing, problem-solving policing, policing oriented hot spots…), an exhaustive analysis of their resources and, above all, whether technology can help in the implementation of this model or, on the contrary, be counterproductive. And to do this I exemplify a case in which the police seek to obtain more information on the needs of the community and are guided only by the demonstrations on social networks, in which case they will only focus on the needs shown by the most active people in this area, thus distancing themselves from other needs of people who do not use social networks. In short, it should be an additional support to meet the objectives proposed in the desired model and not be the end in itself.

Moving on to the conclusions, one of the problems that has already been highlighted in the introduction is the acquisition of technology for the sake of novelty. Ideally, a rational perspective should be used to, first, identify needs, second, implement a strategy based on those needs, and third, answer the question of whether and what kind of technology will help the process. It would be a mistake to follow a model in which one thinks only of giving an image of innovation. This is reflected, as Strom reports, in the research suggesting that police capabilities have increased with technology, but it is less clear that it has made their work more effective.

Related to Artificial Intelligence and considering Miro investigations [28], it must take into account the biases in the algorithms, on the one hand the biases in the training data and, on the other, the biases due to an unequal distribution of the variables. And all of this fits in with not forgetting that it is the human factor that causes biases in the analyses, mainly due to problems in data collection.

And finally, these conclusions also include a series of recommendations; for example, those cited in the report, the first of which is the need for evidence-based research. Nor should it be forgotten, in this regard, that any implementation of technology that is not based on the organisational culture or strategies of the particular police force will not be successful.

And while predictive policing is not a crystal ball for the future, it can be a useful model to provide a framework for the different technological tools that can make policing more effective and, above all, efficient. From this point of view, the future lies in the application of algorithms for the detection and prevention of cybercrime, because, as has been shown in these lines, the technology exists to make it successful.

And all this should not stop here, because in Spain, for example, a facial recognition system is being prepared in which Artificial Intelligence is trained with 5.6 million images, and this implies that there must be a debate on the always problematic decision of more privacy or more security.

References

1. Bernal Calderón, G.: El desarrollo tecnológico, una perspectiva social y humanista. I Congreso Iberoamericano de Ciencia, Tecnología, Sociedad e Innovación CTS+1, México, 19 a 23 de junio de 2006. https://www.oei.es/historico/memoriasctsi/mesa1/m01p02.pdf
2. Strom, K.: Research on the impact of Technology on Policing Strategy in the 21st Century, Final Report. Office of Justice Programs, EEUU, pp. 2–3 (2017)
3. Jaime, O., Torrente, D.: Los desafíos de la Policía como actor político en España. Revista Española de Ciencia Política. España, núm. **45**, 147–172 (2017)
4. Strom, K.: Research on the impact of technology on policing strategy. Op. Cit., 4–5 (2017)
5. Strom, K.: Research on the impact of technology on policing strategy. Op. Cit., 4–6 (2017)
6. Strom, K.: Research on the impact of Technology on Policing Strategy. Op. cit, pp. 1–2 (2017)
7. Strom, K.: Research on the impact of technology on policing strategy. Op. Cit., 6–7 (2017)
8. Buil-Gil, D., Moretti, A., Langton, S.H.: The accuracy of crime statistics: assessing the impact of police data bias on geographic crime analysis. J. Exp. Criminol. **18**, 1–27 (2021). https://doi.org/10.1007/s11292-021-09457-y
9. Strom, K.: Research on the impact of Technology on Policing Strategy. Op. cit, pp. 4–9 (2017)
10. Aghababaedei, S., Makrehchi, M.: Mining Twitter data for crime trend prediction. Intell. Data Anal. **22**, 117–141 (2018)
11. Girao, F.J.: Atentado en Barcelona del 17ª. La calificación institucional y periodística de los hechos en las primeras horas en Twitter. Revista Internacional de Estudios sobre Terrorismo **2**, 18–42 (2021)
12. Strom, K.: research on the impact of technology on policing strategy. Op. Cit., 4–8 (2017)
13. Strom, K.: research on the impact of technology on policing strategy. Op. Cit., 4–10 (2017)
14. Strom, K.: research on the impact of technology on policing strategy. Op. Cit., 4–11 (2017)
15. Strom, K.: research on the impact of technology on policing strategy. Op. Cit., 4–12 (2017)
16. Strom, K.: research on the impact of technology on policing strategy. Op. Cit., 4–13 (2017)
17. Klauser, F.: Police drones and the air: towards a volumetric geopolitics of security. Swiss Polit. Sci. Rev. **27**(1), 158–169 (2021)
18. Klauser, F.: Police drones and the air. Op. Cit., 166–167 (2021)
19. Rodríguez Herrera, J.E.: Uso de drones como medios de obtención de datos de Inteligencia en operaciones de apoyo a la Policía Nacional de Panamá. Repositorio de la Escuela Militar de Chorrillos, Trabajo de Suficiencia Profesional (2021)
20. Fussell, S.: Researchers think they can use twitter to spot riots before police (2017). https://gizmodo.com/researchers-think-they-can-use-twitter-to-spot-riots-be-1796479288
21. Miró, F.: Inteligencia Artificial y Justicia Penal: más allá de los resultados lesivos causados por robots. Revista de Derecho Penal y Criminología **20**, 91 (2018)
22. Miró, F.: Inteligencia Artificial y Justicia Penal: más allá de los resultados lesivos causados por robots. Op. Cit., 92 (2018)
23. Miró, F.: Inteligencia Artificial y Justicia Penal: más allá de los resultados lesivos causados por robots. Op. Cit., 93 (2018)
24. Miró, F.: Inteligencia Artificial y Justicia Penal: más allá de los resultados lesivos causados por robots. op. cit., 102–103 (2018)
25. Bilen, A., Özer, A.B.: Cyber-attack method and perpetrator prediction using machine learning algorithms. Peer J. Comput. Sci. **7**, (2021)

BCI: Technologies and Applications Review and Toolkit Proposal

Tânia Rocha[1,2](✉) , Diana Carvalho[1,2] , Pedro Letra[1], Arsénio Reis[1,2] ,
and João Barroso[1,2]

[1] UTAD - University of Trás-os-Montes e Alto Douro, Quinta de Prados, 5001-801 Vila Real,
Portugal
{trocha,dianac,ars,jbarroso}@utad.pt
[2] INESC TEC, Rua Dr. Roberto Frias, 4200-465 Porto, Portugal

Abstract. A typical example of a Brain-Computer Interface (BCI) is a system that allows a person to move a ball displayed on a computer screen to the left or to the right, simply by imagining the movement of the left or right hand, respectively. Since the term Brain-Computer Interface was coined in 1973, the interest and efforts in this field have grown tremendously and there are now thought to be several hundred laboratories worldwide developing research in this topic. This paper aims at summarizing its resulting knowledge in a way that allows for a quick and clear consultation, highlighting the research lines, technologies and the most relevant cases of applications, so that policy makers, professionals and consumers can make effective use of the findings. With this in mind, a Brain-Computer Interface toolkit is proposed with a focus on different target audiences (e.g., children, seniors, people with intellectual disabilities) that can take advantage of this resource and promote an independent life routine.

Keywords: BCI · BMI · BNCI · Brain-Computer Interface · Brain-machine interface · Brain/Neural - Computer Interface · Interaction design · UX design · Human-computer interaction · Multimedia

1 Introduction

Since the term Brain-Computer Interface (BCI) was first coined in 1973 by Jacques J. Vidal [1], the interest and efforts in this field have grown tremendously and there are now thought to be several hundred laboratories worldwide developing research in this topic. The most typical example of this technology put in practice is the direct control of a graphical element (e.g., a computer cursor) by a person using a BCI based on electrophysiological signals, allowing the user to move it to the left or to the right, simply by imagining the movement of the left or right hand, respectively.

The aim of this research is not only to create an inventory of existing BCI technologies, but also to identify where they can or are applied, analyzing the challenges of implementing such a system to assist in the decision-making process. To that end, a BCI toolkit is presented. This resource is to be used with different target audiences (e.g.,

A. Dziech et al. (Eds.): MCSS 2022, CCIS 1689, pp. 126–143, 2022.
https://doi.org/10.1007/978-3-031-20215-5_11

children, seniors, people with intellectual disabilities), thus enhancing Human abilities and consequently providing independent living.

Indeed, we intend to answer the following questions:

Q1. Which technologies and applications of BCI exist today?

Q2. How can one provide a BCI Toolkit to further test and enhance Human abilities?

To know the current state in terms of existing technologies and applications in BCIs, we followed the methodology of Levac et al. [7] and thus conducted a survey through an exploratory study. After covering the theoretical framework for this study, we share our research methodology and present the results. A toolkit covering the equipment and demonstration programs to be used is also conferred later on.

2 Literature Review

2.1 Brain-Computer Interface (BCI)

Since the term Brain-Computer Interface (BCI) [1] has been first coined, interest and efforts in this field have grown tremendously and there are today, it is believed, several hundred laboratories worldwide conducting research on this topic [2].

The term BCI was also extended to Brain Machine Interface (BMI), which is more comprehensive, since it is not limited only to the indication of a Brain-Computer Interface but also to a Brain-Machine Interface, which means any device other than a computer that can be controlled in any way by commands coming from the brain. BCI can be invasive or non-invasive, depending on whether an implant (placing an electronic device inside the body, usually in the head) or an external device needs to be used.

Indeed, some indicators of this field's rapid growth are the number of research groups around the world doing work in BCI, peer-reviewed journal articles, abstracts and participation in relevant conferences. With dozens of companies and research groups actively participating in the development of this field and its associated technologies, topics such as collaboration, terminology and clear future planning are of great importance. To address these needs, the European Commission funded the coordination action "Future BNCI: A Roadmap for Future Directions in Brain/Neuronal Computer Interaction" in 2010/2011. This project was undoubtedly the first effort to promote collaboration and communication between key stakeholders [3].

BCI systems have been evolving over time in various ways. Some of the identified main trends have explored sensor enhancement, software usability, more natural and sensitive context, hybridization with other communication systems (including Brain/Neural - Computer Interface or BNCIs), new applications such as motor recovery and entertainment, testing and validating target users in home environments, or even using BCI technology for basic scientific and diagnostic research. Moreover, BCIs are gaining increased attention in academia, business, the assistive technology community, the media and the general public [3].

However, despite progress, BCIs remain quite limited in real-world scenarios. They are slow and unreliable, especially over long periods of use by target users. Also, BCIs require expert assistance in many ways: e.g., a typical end-user today needs help identifying, purchasing, installing, configuring, maintaining, repairing and updating the BCI.

Besides, many of these interfaces still use gel-based sensors that require expert help for their setup and cleaning.

Another factor is design, which is often not taken into account considering the end user, but instead is implemented according to the designer's goals and skills. Evidently, the integration of BCI with other systems is still in its infancy, which is the case with assistive technologies, different BNCI systems, head-mounted devices and practical and usable interfaces [3].

It is known that people can communicate only through thought. That is why BCIs, since they do not require movement, may be the only possible communication system for users with severe disabilities who cannot speak or use keyboards, mice or other interfaces [3].

2.2   Implementation of BCI Systems

There are often misunderstandings about what can and cannot be done with BCI systems. To clarify and facilitate deep reflection, this technology does not write information into the brain; it does not alter perception; or implants thoughts or images.

Indeed, BCIs cannot work remotely or without the user's knowledge. To use a BCI, a person must have a sensor of some kind in their head and must voluntarily choose to perform certain mental tasks to achieve the proposed goals [4].

In the most commonly adopted definition, any BCI must meet four criteria [5]:

1. Direct: The system should be based on direct measurements of brain activity.
2. Intentional Control: At least one measurable brain signal, which can be modulated intentionally, must be provided as input to the BCI (electrical potentials, magnetic fields or hemodynamic changes). That is, users must choose to perform a mental task, with the goal of sending a message or command, each time they want to use the BCI.
3. Real Time Processing: The signal processing must take place online and produce a communication or a control signal.
4. Feedback: The user should get feedback on the success or failure of their communication or control efforts. If a BCI does not provide feedback, there is no "interface" and the device or system is simply a monitor of brain activity.

BNCI differs only on the first criterion; the signals can also reflect direct measurements of other nervous system activities, such as eye movement (EOG)[1], muscle activity (EMG)[2] or heart rate (HR)[3]. BNCI systems are also referred to as hybrid BCIs or multimodal BCIs [5].

2.3   BNCI Horizon 2020

The Horizon 2020 BNCI project, as well as its predecessor, the Future BNCI, are important for the area of BCIs and, therefore, are presented and mentioned in this study, not only

---

[1] *Electrooculogram.*

[2] *Electromyogram.*

[3] *Heart rate.*

for the level of information they contain, but also for other relevant aspects. The project "Future in Brain/Neural-Computer Interaction: Horizon 2020" ran from November 2013 to April 2015.

BNCI Horizon 2020 was a Coordination and Support Action (CSA) funded under the European Commission's 7th Framework Programme. Therefore, this project does not cover research, but instead aims to promote collaboration and communication between stakeholders in the field of Brain-Computer Interfaces (including research groups, companies, end users, policy makers and the general public) [6].

Indeed, BNCI Horizon 2020 aims to continue and enhance the efforts initiated by Future BNCI. Its main goal is to provide a global perspective on the field of BCIs now and in the future. The consortium includes eight major European BCI research institutions, three industrial partners and two end-user organizations (one of which is also a research partner) [6].

The applications of BCIs are diverse [6] and can:

- Replace functions that have been lost due to injury or illness (e.g., communication and wheelchair control).
- Restore lost functions (e.g., stimulation of muscles in a paralyzed person and stimulation of nerves to restore bladder function).
- Improve functions (e.g., in stroke rehabilitation[4]).
- Enhance functions (e.g., detecting stress levels or attention lapses during demanding tasks).
- Be used as a Research Tool to study brain functions.

Figure 1 shows some of BCIs' scenarios of use.

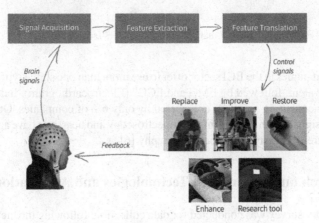

Fig. 1. Usage scenarios (source: [6]).

In terms of BCI Market and Stakeholders, the BNCI Horizon 2020 project has identified 148 related companies:

---

[4] Cerebral Vascular Accident.

1. BCI sector (65 companies).
2. Automotive and Aerospace Sector (7 companies).
3. Medical Technology, Rehabilitation and Robotics Sector (46 companies).
4. Entertainment and Marketing Sector (10 companies).
5. Technology Sector (20 companies).

Figure 2 illustrates the relative proportion of large enterprises, public entities (non-profit organizations), small and medium-sized enterprises (fewer than 250 employees) and startups (founded in 2010 or later) for each sector.

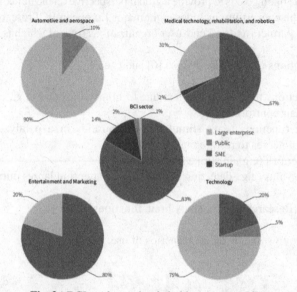

Fig. 2. BCI market and stakeholders (source: [6]).

Many companies in the BCI sector offer to use more than one signal type, but EEG[5] is the most prevalent, followed by EMG and ECG[6] (Electrocardiogram). Indeed, invasive brain signal acquisition solutions are offered by only 6% of companies. Other potential BCI-related signals such as near-infrared spectroscopy and heart rate have approximately the same share as invasive electrocorticography [6].

3   Research on Current BCI Technologies and Applications

An exploratory survey was conducted for data collection, following the methodology of Levac et al. [7] for conducting a survey of current BCI technologies and applications. After outlining the question that motivated the study and the objectives to be achieved, the approach was as follows. Firstly, searches were conducted for papers on Google

---

[5] *Electroencephalogram.*

[6] *Electrocardiogram.*

Scholar platforms [38], IEEE Xplore [39], Science Direct [40] and Frontiers [41]. The first three are the most frequently used in academia and the fourth was founded by a group of neuroscientists. The key words employed in the search were "BCI" or "BMI" or "BNCI" + "Technology" or "Application" and the time range of publications was narrowed from 2015 to 2021. Secondly, the papers obtained through this search were carefully selected, so that similar and incremental publications by the same author were removed, leaving only those whose content is distinct and significant for the survey of BCI technologies and applications. Finally, all the information collected was synthesized and presented clearly and succinctly in order to facilitate the interpretation of the results.

3.1 Results

After the search, from the results obtained, a total of 30 diverse papers were selected. These papers were the ones that best answered the question initially formulated.

Depending on the needs of each case, BCI technologies can be: Invasive (installed inside the body, using surgery to place an implant), Minimally Invasive (making a small superficial incision and placing the implant under the skin) and Non-Invasive (easy to place and use, without the need for any surgical operation).

The non-invasive technology most common and most used in BCIs for brain signal is the EEG (Electroencephalogram, recording the brain's electrical activity), among others such as MEG (Magnetoencephalogram), fNIRS (functional Near-Infrared Spectroscopy), fMRI (functional Magnetic Resonance Imaging) and fTCD (functional Transcranial Doppler).

Table 1 briefly illustrates the BCI technologies and applications currently used and presented in the papers obtained during the research.

Table 1. BCI technologies and applications

References	Brain areas	Technologies	Applications	Accuracy
[8]	Front, centre and rear	[EEG + EOG]-BCI	Control of an auxiliary home robot	93%
[9]	All	EEG-BCI	Control of an exoskeleton	–
[10]	Frontal and prefrontal	[EEG + fNIRS]-BCI	Controlling a *quadcopter* (*drone*)	76,5–86%
[11]	Visual cortex	EEG-SSVEP-BCI + *Eye Tracking*	Mental spelling	90%
[12]	Motor cortex	[EEG + fNIRS]-BMI and EEG-SMR-BMI	Communication with ALS patients and restoration of motor disability after severe stroke	71,76–89%
[13]	Motor cortex	EEG-MI-BCI	*Motor* Rehabilitation through the use of Brain-Computer Interfaces based on *Motor Imagery* (MI)	–

(*continued*)

Table 1. (*continued*)

References	Brain areas	Technologies	Applications	Accuracy
[14]	Prefrontal	EEG-BMI	Prevention of road accidents	–
[15]	Sensory-motor cortex	MEG-BMI	Treatment and reduction of pain in patients with phantom limbs	–
[16]	AFZ, CZ, PZ, PO3, PO4, O1, O2, OZ, O9 and O10	[EEG-SSVEP + EMG]-BNCI	Mental spelling	92,37–100%
[17]	Posterior parietal cortex and motor areas	EEG-MRCP-BCI	Restoring the ability to reach and grasp in people with spinal cord injury	37–73%
[18]	AF3, F7, F3, FC5, T7, P7, O1, O2, P8, T8, FC6, F4, F8, AF4 and CMS(P3)/DRL(P4)	EEG-BCI + *Oculus Rift + Eye Tracking*	Control of 3D objects in Virtual Reality environments	–
[19]	Visual cortex	EEG-cVEP-BCI	Control of computer mouse and keyboard	20 error-free characters per minute
[20]	PZ, PO5, PO3, POZ, PO4, PO6, O1, OZ and O2	EEG-SSVEP-BCI	Reduced training time needed in BCI systems	50–70%
[21]	Temporal, parietal and frontal of the right hemisphere	μECoG-BMI Minimally Invasive	Robotic arm control	–
[22]	AF3, F7, F3, FC5, T7, P7, O1, O2, P8, T8, FC6, F4, F8 and AF4	EEG-BMI	Representation of the user's intended direction	100%
[23]	FP1, FP2, F7, F3, FZ, F4, F8, FC3, FC1, FC2, FC4, C5, C3, C1, CZ, C2, C4, C6, CP5, CP3, CP1, CPZ, CP2, CP4, CP6, P7, P3, PZ, P4, P8, O1 and O2	[EEG + EMG]-hBMI	Motor rehabilitation of stroke patients	–
[24]	Prefrontal and temporal	EEG-VEP-BMI	User authentication in computing devices through EEG	–
[25]	FPZ, OZ and DRL(A2)	EEG-SSVEP-BCI	Integrated *Augmented Reality* (AR) and BCI *Health 4.0* hands-free system for acquiring and viewing remote patient information	70%
[26]	FP1, FP2, F3, FZ, F4, F7, F8, T3, C3, CZ, C4, T4, T5, T6, P3, PZ, P4, O1, O2, A1 and A2	rsEEG-BCI + *Machine Learning*	Obtaining private data	73%
[27]	All	MREG	Technique for future BCI and *Neurofeedback* applications with high temporal resolution	–
[28]	FP1, FP2 and A1	EEG-pBCI	Analysis of the operator's *mental workload* in air traffic management	–

(*continued*)

Table 1. (*continued*)

References	Brain areas	Technologies	Applications	Accuracy
[29]	FY3, FY4, F3, F4, F7, F8, FC5, FC6, T7, T8, P7, P8, O1 and O2	EEG-BCI	Therapy for drug cravings	–
[30]	All	fTCD-BCI	BCI in real time based on fTCD (*Functional Transcranial Doppler*)	65,27–82,35%
[31]	All	BCI2000Web + WebFM	Platform for real-time BCI development and functional brain mapping	–
[32]	All	EEG-BCI	Competitions in computer games through the use of BCIs	–
[33]	FZ, CZ, PZ, OZ, P3, P4, PO7, PO8, TP8 and AFZ	EEG-P300-BCI	Communication (spelling) through brain activity in patients with severe motor disability	62,5%
[34]	All	EEG-BCI + *Deep Neural Network + Sparse Autoencoder*	Classification of emotions based on EEG	89,49–96,77%
[35]	Motor cortex	Invasive ECoG-BMI	Neuroprosthetic control	70–90%
[36]	All	fNIRS-BCI	Stand-alone, multi-channel, open-source fNIRS instrument for mobile NIRS-based neuroimaging, neuroergonomics and BCI/BMI applications	65,14%
[37]	All	[EEG + EOG + EMG]-mHMI	Real-time control of a soft robotic hand	93,83%

From the results obtained, several were the specific EEG signals used, such as: the P300 (Potential 300, event-related potential, elicited in the decision-making process), the ERP (Event Related Potential, an analysis that allows identifying the specific brain activity when the individual is exposed to certain stimuli), the VEP (Visual Evoked Potential, potential caused by a visual stimulus), the SSVEP (Steady State Visual Evoked Potential, signals that are natural responses to visual stimulation at specific frequencies), the SMR (Sensorimotor Rhythm, the sensorimotor rhythm is a brain wave with a frequency in the range of 13 to 15 Hz), the MRCPs (Movement-Related Cortical Potentials, used for the detection of intent to move) and the MI (Motor Imagery, motor imagery is a mental process by which an individual rehearses or simulates a particular action).

The applications of BCIs were the most diverse and go far beyond the simple use in the area of health [15, 29] and rehabilitation [9, 13]. Applications have been found in areas such as security [14, 28], communication [11, 16, 33], control of drones [10], obtaining private data, emotion classification [26], computer games [32, 34], mouse and keyboard control [19], virtual reality [18], authentication [24], augmented reality [25], among others.

4   Kit for Experimentation

A BCI toolkit was developed with different target audiences in mind (children, seniors, people with intellectual disabilities) and its main goal was to provide users a way to promote an independent life routine. This kit for experimentation included specific artifacts: free *software* dedicated to the study of the brain; *dataset* available online for download; *equipment* for experimentation; and *demonstration applications* developed specifically for this study in Python and Unity. Our intention was to understand if this all-in-one solution could be of value regarding BCIs.

4.1   Software Dedicated to the Study of the Brain

On the internet, a simple search on Google makes it possible to find free software dedicated to the study of the brain that can be used in research or in educational activities, such as teaching. Some examples of such software are detailed below.

BCI2000. A software package oriented to the investigation of BCIs. It is usually used for data acquisition, stimulus presentation and brain monitoring applications. BCI2000 supports a variety of data acquisition systems, brain signals and study/feedback paradigms. During operation, data is stored in a common native format or in GDF (General Data Format for Biomedical Signals), along with all relevant event markers and system configuration information. Various tools for data import/conversion are also included, such as the possibility of directly loading data files into MATLAB and exporting resources to ASCII (American Standard Code for Information Interchange). More information and the corresponding download can be found at [42].

BioSig. An open-source software library for biomedical signal processing, featuring, for example, the analysis of biosignals such as electroencephalogram (EEG), electrocorticogram (ECoG), electrocardiogram (ECG), electrooculogram (EOG), electromyogram (EMG), respiration, etc. BioSig's main application areas are: Neuroinformatics, Brain-Computer Interfaces, Neurophysiology, Psychology, Cardiovascular Systems and Sleep Research. It can be obtained from [43].

BrainBay. A bio and neurofeedback application designed to work with various EEG amplifiers, including the open hardware OpenEEG and OpenBCI. It supports Human-Computer Interface functions and the *NeuroServer Software Framework* to transmit live recordings via Internet/LAN. BrainBay can be downloaded from [44].

Brainstorm. An open-source collaborative application dedicated to the analysis of brain recordings: MEG, EEG, fNIRS, ECoG, depth electrodes and multi-unit electrophysiology. The goal is to share a comprehensive set of easy-to-use tools with the scientific community using MEG/EEG as an experimental technique. For clinicians and researchers, the main advantage of Brainstorm is its rich and intuitive graphical interface, which does not require any programming knowledge. The Brainstorm website is [45].

Cartool. The EEG analysis software developed at the Functional Brain Mapping Lab (FBMLab) in Geneva, Switzerland. This project was started in 1996, and is still actively developed to this day. It was fully programmed by Denis Brunet in C++ and has no other dependencies to run. It can be downloaded from [46].

EEGLAB. A MATLAB interactive toolbox for processing EEG, MEG and other continuous and event-related electrophysiological data, incorporating independent component analysis (ICA), time/frequency analysis, artefact rejection, event-related statistics and various useful modes of visualization of averaged and single-trial data. EEGLAB runs on Linux, Unix, Windows and Mac OS X. It can be reached at [47].

FieldTrip. A MATLAB software toolbox for MEG, EEG and iEEG (*intracranial electroencephalography*) analysis. It is developed by members and collaborators of the Donders Institute for Brain, Cognition and Behavior at Radboud University, Nijmegen, The Netherlands. It offers pre-processing and advanced analysis methods, such as time-frequency analysis, source reconstruction using dipoles, distributed sources and beamformers, and non-parametric statistical tests. It supports the data formats of all major MEG systems and the most popular EEG and iEEG systems. New data formats can be added easily. FieldTrip contains high-level functions that the user can use to build their own analysis protocols as a MATLAB *script*. It is freely available as open source *software* under the GNU General Public License and can be obtained from [48].

MNE-Python. An open-source Python module for processing, analysis and visualization of functional neuroimaging data (EEG, MEG, sEEG - *stereoelectroencephalography*, ECoG and fNIRS). There are also several related or interoperable software packages that the user may want to install, depending on the analysis needs they have. MNE-Python is available at [49].

NeuroExperimenter. Allows visualization and monitoring of brain waves while the user tries different "mental states", such as meditation, relaxation, concentration, etc. NeuroExperimenter uses MindWave and MindWave Mobile *headsets* by NeuroSky, thus providing access to and combination of these brain waves, and even, through "formulas", specifying combinations that may characterize a mental state, in order to train the user to generate and achieve that state by means of visual and auditory *feedback*. It can be obtained at [50].

OpenViBE. A software platform that allows designing, testing and using Brain-Computer Interfaces. OpenViBE can also be used as a generic real-time EEG acquisition, processing and visualization system. The software can be downloaded at [51].

4.2 Datasets Available Online

The preparation of an individual and the respective process of recording EEG or other biosignals can be laborious and time consuming. Nowadays, there are freely accessible data that have been recorded in the laboratory and are available to the scientific community and to the general public, which may be used in research, such as in the development of algorithms using machine learning techniques, in the study of diseases like epilepsy, in teaching or in the most varied scenarios. Table 2 shows the links to some of these datasets available online for download.

Table 2. Datasets

Description/Link
Repository of the University of California at Irvine, containing EEG and other datasets for empirical analysis of *machine learning* algorithms
https://archive.ics.uci.edu/ml/index.php
BCI datasets from the BNCI Horizon 2020 project open access for the general public
http://www.bnci-horizon-2020.eu/database
List of publicly available brain signal data
http://www.brainsignals.de
Free and open platform to validate and share MRI, PET, MEG, EEG and iEEG data compatible with BIDS (*Brain Imaging Data Structure*)
https://openneuro.org
Sleep database in EDF (*European Data Format*)
https://www.physionet.org/content/sleep-edf/1.0.0
Sleep-EDF database with 197 sleep recordings of an entire night, containing EEG, EOG, chin EMG and event markers. Some recordings also contain respiration and body temperature
https://www.physionet.org/content/sleep-edfx/1.0.0
Free and publicly downloadable EEG / ERP data (list updated in 2020)
https://sccn.ucsd.edu/~arno/fam2data/publicly_available_EEG_data.html
List with some *links to* free databases of SSVEP biosignals and others
https://sccn.ucsd.edu/pipermail/eeglablist/2013/006187.html
National Sleep Research Resource (NSRR) *Polysomnography Datasets*
https://www.sleepdata.org/datasets
ISRUC-Sleep public dataset of the University of Coimbra, for sleep researchers
https://sleeptight.isr.uc.pt

4.3   Equipment for Experimentation

There are several examples of equipment that can obtain signals from the human body. Nevertheless, there are others that give us the possibility, in a perspective of experimentation and DIY (*Do It Yourself*), to collect biosignals in a more relaxed and educational way.

Arduino. Arduino [52] is a hardware that allows electronic prototyping in a simple way, being easy to learn for anyone, even if they have no knowledge of electronics or microcontroller programming. Arduino is basically a single board with an Atmel AVR microcontroller, with a series of analogue and digital input/output ports to which sensors or other components can be connected and which is programmed using a standard language, with an open-source IDE available for this purpose. There is a documentary film made in 2010 about the platform entitled *Arduino: The Documentary,* which was later made available online [53]. Nowadays there are several existing Arduino boards (https://www.arduino.cc/en/Main/Products), a true panoply of them for the most diverse interests and uses. But Arduino is not only limited to its single board, its capabilities can be expanded according to the needs of each project or application, through the addition of other boards called *shields*. One of these *shields,* named HackEEG [54] was funded in 2020 through *crowdfunding* and allows to carry out neuroscience studies. HackEEG (Fig. 3) is an affordable, open-source high performance shield, ideal for digitising biosignals such as EEG, EKG and EMG; or if the user wishes, establishing a Brain-Computer Interface. A maximum of four HackEEG can be stacked on an Arduino Due (https://docs.arduino.cc/hardware/due) so as to total 32 EEG channels. A rate of 4000 samples per second, or 16000 if only one HackEEG is used (8 EEG channels), can be achieved with this configuration. Data can also be transmitted by Wi-Fi (*Wireless Fidelity*) through the Lab Streaming Layer communication protocol. HackEEG is used by leading research institutions and pharmaceutical companies in the U.S. and Europe (Starcat, 2022).

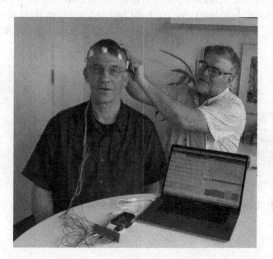

Fig. 3. HackEEG (source: [55]).

BITalino. BITalino is an affordable, open-source biosignal platform that allows anyone, from students to professional developers to create projects and applications using physiological sensors [56]. BITalino (Fig. 4) consists of an electronic *kit* that provides a series of sensors with applications in areas as diverse as electroencephalography, electrocardiography, electromyography, electrodermal activity, electrogastrography (EGG) or sport (Higher Technical Institute, University of Lisbon, 2021). The signals collected can be consulted and stored in an application developed for this purpose, OpenSignals [57]. This software supports multiple channels, thus allowing the collection of data from several sensors simultaneously. Furthermore, OpenSignals has a set of *add-ons* that allow you to perform data analysis, create reports and extract features directly from the recorded signals, without any need for programming by the user. Some creative and interesting projects where BITalino has been employed can be consulted at [58], where it is also possible to view videos of these applications. BITalino was born at the Institute of Telecommunications, Portugal, in 2012 and since then has been conquering the world, having been licensed to Plux in 2013 and placed on the market (Higher Technical Institute, University of Lisbon, 2021). It was one of the 10 projects selected worldwide for the Engadget Insert Coin 2013 semi-final; highlighted by The New Zealand Herald as one of that year's favorite technologies; and elected in 2014 as one of the 14 bets and one of the *top* 10 innovations [59, 60]. There are innumerous fields of interest using it: MIT (Massachusetts Institute of Technology) and Stanford University and Imperial College London, in their Laboratories; Facebook, to study the users' reactions while they surf the Internet; Boeing, to study the reactions of clients to new services. Today, BITalino is already present in more than 30 countries. Moreover, a new version was launched in 2016 and goes by the name of BITalino (r)evolution (Fig. 4), presenting improvements compared to the previous one, such as greater reduction in the size of the sensors. This version has almost twice as many accessories in the same format, without changing the dimensions of the board, with support for *Bluetooth Low Energy* (BLE), whilst maintaining the price point. Interestingly, each BITalino carries in the back a representation of Portugal and the inscription *"Designed in Portugal, built for the World"*.

Fig. 4. BITalino (left) and BITalino (r)evolution (right) (sources: [59, 60]).

4.4 Demonstration Applications

In order to experiment and demonstrate some functionalities and applications that can be used in real life, four applications were developed where the input mode is achieved through the use of brain waves. Three of these programs were implemented using the python programming and the fourth through the 3D/2D game development platform unity. In the first three applications, the NEuroSky's BCI "MindWave Mobile 2" was employed, whereas the unity-based application used the BCI "NextMind". We describe each of the applications' workflow below.

In the first program (Fig. 5) the user can control the whole interface by intentionally varying their attention levels, meditation and blink intensity. The graphical interface is divided into three sections: *"Speech Settings"*, *"Text to Speech"* and *"Feedback"*. When *"Setup"* is selected, it is possible to change the speed (*"Speed"*) of pronouncing words, choose the desired voice ("*Voice*") and increase or decrease its volume ("*Volume*"). When "*Talk*" is selected, it is possible to alternate between the different text options, varying the level of meditation. When the desired text is selected, by the blinking of the eyes, it is converted into voice, enabling the user to communicate if they are unable to do so in any other way or by regular means. To help the users interact with the application, they are given *feedback on* the levels of attention, meditation and intensity of the blink, so that they can have a better perception, in real time, and if necessary, shape their mental state to achieve the desired interaction.

The second program (Fig. 6) allows playing the "Rooster Game" (*Tic Tac Toe*). The mouse cursor is controlled by varying the player's attention level, thus enabling positioning on the desired square (one of nine possible positions); the mouse *click, in* order to execute the move, is achieved by the blinking of the eyes. This way the player can interact without using the usual keyboard and mouse for program control. Whenever the game ends, because the player wins, draws or loses, a new one is automatically started and the result is added to the *score. Feedback* is given to the player, by the mouse cursor jumping from square to square, whenever the player has a certain level of attention.

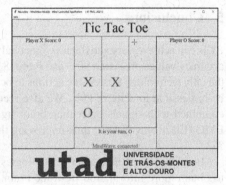

Fig. 5. EEG text to speech   **Fig. 6.** EEG Tic Tac Toe

The third piece of software (Fig. 7) is an example of Physical Computing. Here, the user can control the switching on and off of three LEDs using Raspberry Pi [61], although other electronic components can also be used. The Raspberry Pi is a small and affordable single-board computer that can be used for learning how to code through fun and practical projects. Interaction with the hardware is achieved by using the computer's GPIO (General-Purpose Input/Output). Two distinct operations have been implemented, one when a certain level of attention is reached and another when a blink of an eye is performed with a certain intensity.

Finally, a game resembling the classic game "Pong" was developed through the IDE (*Integrated Development Environment*) Unity. This type of game that was first developed by Atari Inc., and that would eventually be released in the *Arcade Machines,* on 29 November 1972, having obtained enormous success. In this modern version (Fig. 8), the player, resorting to BCI NextMind, can control the up and down movement of the right *paddle,* while the left one being controlled by the computer. Here the control is achieved by means of the player's visual attention, that is, when the player looks at the

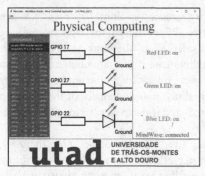

Fig. 7. EEG physical computing   **Fig. 8.** EEG Pong

upper right square on the screen, the *paddle* moves upwards, and the opposite happens when he looks at the lower right square. *Feedback* is given to the player via the "green triangular crosshairs", which indicate their level of visual attention.

5 Conclusions

BCIs can achieve very satisfactory practical results where no other technology can, with accuracy values of around 90% and more [8, 16, 22, 37]. Indeed, in some areas, BCIs are the only technology that enable actions to be carried out by the user that would otherwise be impossible to achieve [12]. We also recognize that some solutions allow BCI to be combined with signals other than brain signals, such as EOG (Electrooculogram) and EMG (Electromyogram), thus improving the effectiveness of the resulting system [16, 37].

In addition to EEG, other technologies have been developed and applied in order to obtain more information from the brain. We are aware that these technologies may lead to the creation of better BCIs, such as MEG, fMRI (measures brain activity through variations in blood flow associated with it) and more recently fNIRS and fTCD (ultrasound technique that uses sound waves to assess blood circulation in and around the brain) [27, 30, 36]. In this regard, we established a BCI toolkit that granted users an all-in-one solution to implement the interaction mode and developed four applications with the focus on the users' interaction. Our intention was to propose a toolkit that grants interaction for different user profiles, such as children, seniors or people with intellectual disabilities, as to provide them with an independent life routine. We are aware of the need to conclude further testing of these applications and understand their performance in a real-life scenario, but acknowledge that this may be a starter point in the creation of user-friendly interaction modes regarding BCI.

To conclude, the future of BCIs is promising and the applications are immense. To be able to gather the literature's resulting knowledge in a way that allows for a quick and clear consultation is extremely relevant, thus highlighting the research lines, technologies and the most relevant cases of applications so that policy makers, professionals and consumers can make effective use of the findings.

Acknowledgments. This work was supported by the RD Project "Continental Factory of Future, (CONTINENTAL FoF) / POCI-01- 0247-FEDER-047512", financed by the European Regional Development Fund (ERDF), through the Program "Programa Operacional Competitividade e Internacionalização (POCI) / PORTUGAL 2020", under the management of AICEP Portugal Global – Trade Investment Agency.

References

1. Vidal, J.J.: Toward direct brain-computer communication. Annu. Rev. Biophys. Bioeng. **2**, 157–180 (1973)
2. Nam, C.S., Nijholt, A., Lotte, F.: Brain-Computer Interfaces Handbook: Technological and Theoretical Advances, pp. 1–8. CRC Press (2018)
3. European Commission: Future BNCI: A Roadmap for Future Directions in Brain/Neuronal Computer Interaction (2012). http://bnci-horizon-2020.eu/images/bncih2020/FBNCI_Roadmap.pdf. Accessed 22 Feb 2021
4. European Commission: BNCI Horizon 2020. http://www.bnci-horizon-2020.eu/about/basics. Accessed 12 Mar 2021
5. Brunner, C., et al.: BNCI horizon 2020: towards a roadmap for the BCI community. BCI J. 1–10 (2015)
6. European Commission: The Future in Brain/Neural-Computer Interaction: Horizon 2020 (2015). http://www.bnci-horizon-2020.eu/images/bncih2020/Roadmap_BNCI_Horizon_2020.pdf. Accessed 24 Feb 2021
7. Levac, D., Colquhoun, H., O'Brien, K.K.: Scoping studies: advancing the methodology. Implement. Sci. **5**(1), 69 (2010)
8. Wang, F., Zhang, X., Fu, R., Sun, G.: Study of the home-auxiliary robot based on BCI. Sens. Biosignal Process. **18**(6), 1779 (2018)
9. Frolov, A.A., et al.: Preliminary results of a controlled study of BCI-exoskeleton technology efficacy in patients with poststroke arm paresis. Bull. RSMU (2) (2016)
10. Khan, M.J., Hong, K.-S.: Hybrid EEG-fNIRS-based eight-command decoding for BCI: application to quadcopter control. Front. Neurorob. **11**(6) (2017)
11. Stawicki, P., Gembler, F., Rezeika, A., Volosyak, I.: A novel hybrid mental spelling application based on eye tracking and SSVEP-based BCI. Brain Sci. **4**(35) (2017)
12. Chaudhary, U., Birbaumer, N., Curado, M.R.: Brain-machine interface (BMI) in paralysis. Ann. Phys. Rehabil. Med. **58**(1), 9–13 (2015)
13. Alonso-Valerdi, L.M., Salido-Ruiz, R.A., Ramirez-Mendoza, R.A.: Motor imagery based brain-computer interfaces: An emerging technology to rehabilitate motor deficits. Neuropsychologia **79**(B), 354–363 (2015)
14. Ghube, C., Kulkarni, A., Bankar, C., Bedekar, M.: BMI Application: accident reduction using drowsiness detection. In: Abraham, A., Gandhi, N., Pant, M. (eds.) IBICA 2018. Advances in Intelligent Systems and Computing, vol. 939, pp. 66–72. Springer, Cham (2019). https://doi.org/10.1007/978-3-030-16681-6_7
15. Yanagisawa, T., et al.: Induced sensorimotor brain plasticity controls pain in phantom limb patients. Nat. Commun. **7**(13209) (2016)
16. Rezeika, A., Benda, M., Stawicki, P., Gembler, F., Saboor, A., Volosyak, I.: 30-Targets Hybrid BNCI Speller Based on SSVEP and EMG. In: 2018 IEEE International Conference on Systems, Man, and Cybernetics (SMC), Miyazaki, Japan (2018)
17. Müller-Putz, G.R., et al.: Towards non-invasive EEG-based arm/hand-control in users with spinal cord injury. In: 2017 5th International Winter Conference on Brain-Computer Interface (BCI), Gangwon, Korea (South) (2017)

18. Chun, J., Bae, B., Jo, S.: BCI based hybrid interface for 3D object control in virtual reality. In: 2016 4th International Winter Conference on Brain-Computer Interface (BCI), Gangwon, Korea (South) (2016)

19. Spüler, M.: A brain-computer interface (BCI) system to use arbitrary Windows applications by directly controlling mouse and keyboard. In: 2015 37th Annual International Conference of the IEEE Engineering in Medicine and Biology Society (EMBC), Milan, Italy (2015)

20. Han, X., Zhang, S., Gao, X.: A study on reducing training time of BCI system based on an SSVEP dynamic model. In: 2019 7th International Winter Conference on Brain-Computer Interface (BCI), Gangwon, Korea (South) (2019)

21. Tahir, M.N.: Wireless brain machine interface (BMI) system (review & concept). In: 2020 International Conference on Computing and Information Technology (ICCIT-1441), Tabuk, Saudi Arabia (2020)

22. Kim, H.-H., Jeong, J.: Representations of directions in EEG-BMI using winner-take-all readouts. In: 2017 5th International Winter Conference on Brain-Computer Interface (BCI), Gangwon, Korea (South) (2017)

23. Sarasola-Sanz, A., et al.: A hybrid brain-machine interface based on EEG and EMG activity for the motor rehabilitation of stroke patients. In: 2017 International Conference on Rehabilitation Robotics (ICORR), London, UK (2017)

24. Rodriguez, R.J.: Electroencephalogram (EEG) based authentication leveraging visual evoked potentials (VEP) resulting from exposure to emotionally significant images. In: 2016 IEEE Symposium on Technologies for Homeland Security (HST), Waltham, MA, USA (2016)

25. Arpaia, P., Benedetto, E.D., Duraccio, L.: Design, implementation, and metrological characterization of a wearable, integrated AR-BCI hands-free system for health 4.0 monitoring. Measurement **177**(109280) (2021)

26. Landau, O., Cohen, A., Gordon, S., Nissim, N.: Mind your privacy: privacy leakage through BCI applications using machine learning methods. Knowl.-Based Syst. **198**(105932) (2020)

27. Lührs, M., et al.: The potential of MR-Encephalography for BCI/Neurofeedback applications with high temporal resolution. NeuroImage **194**, 228–243 (2019)

28. Aricò, P., Borghini, G., Flumeri, G.D., Colosimo, A., Pozzi, S., Babiloni, F.: A passive brain-computer interface application for the mental workload assessment on professional air traffic controllers during realistic air traffic control tasks. Prog. Brain Res. **228**, 295–328 (2016)

29. Mazzoleni, M., Previdi, F.: A comparison of classification algorithms for brain computer interface in drug craving treatment. IFAC-PapersOnLine **48**(20), 487–492 (2015)

30. Khalaf, A., Sybeldon, M., Sejdic, E., Akcakaya, M.: A brain-computer interface based on functional transcranial doppler ultrasound using wavelet transform and support vector machines. J. Neurosci. Methods **293**, 174–182 (2018)

31. Milsap, G., Collard, M., Coogan, C., Crone, N.E.: BCI2000Web and WebFM: browser-based tools for brain computer interfaces and functional brain mapping. Front. Neurosci. **12**, 1030 (2019)

32. Novak, D., et al.: Benchmarking brain-computer interfaces outside the laboratory: the Cybathlon 2016. Front. Neurosci. **11**, 756 (2018)

33. Medina-Juliá, M.T., Fernández-Rodríguez, Á., Velasco-Álvarez, F., Ron-Angevin, R.: P300-based brain-computer interface speller: usability evaluation of three speller sizes by severely motor-disabled patients. Front. Hum. Neurosci. **14**(583358) (2020)

34. Liu, J., et al.: EEG-based emotion classification using a deep neural network and sparse autoencoder. Front. Syst. Neurosci. **14**(43) (2020)

35. Matsushita, K., et al.: A fully implantable wireless ECoG 128-channel recording device for human brain-machine interfaces: W-HERBS. Front. Neurosci. **12**(511) (2018)

36. Lühmann, A.V., Herff, C., Heger, D., Schultz, T.: Toward a wireless open source instrument: functional near-infrared spectroscopy in mobile neuroergonomics and BCI applications. Front. Hum. Neurosci. **9**(617) (2015)

37. Zhang, J., Wang, B., Zhang, C., Xiao, Y., Wang, M.Y.: An EEG/EMG/EOG-based multimodal human-machine interface to real-time control of a soft robot hand. Front. Neurorob. **13**(7) (2019)
38. https://scholar.google.com/. Accessed 26 July 2022
39. https://ieeexplore.ieee.org/Xplore/home.jsp. Accessed 26 July 2022
40. https://www.sciencedirect.com/. Accessed 26 July 2022
41. https://www.frontiersin.org/. Accessed 26 July 2022
42. https://www.bci2000.org. Accessed 26 July 2022
43. http://biosig.sourceforge.net/index.html. Accessed 26 July 2022
44. http://www.shifz.org/brainbay. Accessed 26 July 2022
45. https://neuroimage.usc.edu/brainstorm. Accessed 26 July 2022
46. https://sites.google.com/site/cartoolcommunity. Accessed 26 July 2022
47. https://sccn.ucsd.edu/eeglab/index.php. Accessed 26 July 2022
48. https://www.fieldtriptoolbox.org. Accessed 26 July 2022
49. https://mne.tools/stable/index.html. Accessed 26 July 2022
50. https://sites.google.com/view/fredm/home. Accessed 26 July 2022
51. http://openvibe.inria.fr. Accessed 26 July 2022
52. https://www.arduino.cc. Accessed 26 July 2022
53. https://blog.arduino.cc/2011/01/07/arduino-the-documentary-now-online. Accessed 26 July 2022
54. https://www.starcat.io/products/hackeeg-shield. Accessed 26 July 2022
55. https://www.crowdsupply.com/starcat/hackeeg. Accessed 26 July 2022
56. https://www.pluxbiosignals.com/collections/bitalino. Accessed 26 July 2022
57. https://www.pluxbiosignals.com/collections/opensignals. Accessed 26 July 2022
58. https://www.pluxbiosignals.com/pages/projects. Accessed 26 July 2022
59. https://www.futurebehind.com/bitalino-pelo-mundo-plux-technologies. Accessed 26 July 2022
60. https://tecnico.ulisboa.pt/pt/noticias/bitalino-a-conquista-do-mundo. Accessed 26 July 2022
61. https://www.raspberrypi.com/products. Accessed 26 July 2022

Clustering-Based Filtering of Big Data to Improve Forecasting Effectiveness and Efficiency

Tiago Pinto[1,2]($\boxtimes$), Tânia Rocha[1], Arsénio Reis[1], and Zita Vale[2]

[1] Universidade de Trás-os-Montes e Alto Douro and INESC-TEC, Porto, Portugal
{tiagopinto,trocha,ars}@utad.pt
[2] GECAD, Institute of Engineering – Polytechnic of Porto (ISEP/IPP), Porto, Portugal
{tcp,zav}@isep.ipp.pt

Abstract. New challenges arise with the upsurge of a Big Data era. Huge volumes of data, from the most varied natures, gathered from different sources, collected in different timings, often with high associated uncertainty, make the decision-making process a harsher task. Current methods are not ready to deal with characteristics of the new problems. This paper proposes a novel data selection methodology that filters big volumes of data, so that only the most correlated information is used in the decision-making process in each given context. The proposed methodology uses a clustering algorithm, which creates sub-groups of data according to their correlation. These groups are then used to feed a forecasting process that uses the relevant data for each situation, while discarding data that is not expected to contribute to improving the forecasting results. In this way, a faster, less computationally demanding, and effective forecasting is enabled. A case study is presented, considering the application of the proposed methodology to the filtering of electricity market data used by forecasting approaches. Results show that the data selection increases the forecasting effectiveness of forecasting methods, as well as the computational efficiency of the forecasts, by using less yet more adequate data.

1 Introduction

The 21th century economy produces a constant stream of data that is being monitored and analysed. Social interactions, mobile devices, facilities, equipment, R&D, simulations, and physical infrastructure all contribute to the flow. In aggregate, this is what is called Big Data. Right from its emergence, Big Data technology and services market has grown from $3.2 billion in 2010 to $16.9 billion in 2015. This represents a compound annual growth rate (CAGR) of 39.4% or about seven times that of the overall information and communication technology (ICT) market. By 2020 this market is estimated at $138.62 billion, with an expected CAGR of 10.6% for the period 2020–2025 [1]. Big Data involves new generation technologies and architectures with the aim of extracting value from huge amounts of a wide variety of data, involving data capture, storage, analysis, visualization and knowledge discovery. Nowadays, data sets are growing up in size because they are increasingly being gathered by a several kind of sensors, devices

A. Dziech et al. (Eds.): MCSS 2022, CCIS 1689, pp. 144–152, 2022.
https://doi.org/10.1007/978-3-031-20215-5_12

and applications, such as, software logs, cameras, microphones, radio-frequency identification readers, wireless sensor networks, etc. Such useful information that the data
may disclose, can provide competitive advantages over rival organizations and result in
business benefits, such as more effective marketing and increased revenue. These trends
are also "democratizing" use of data analytics. The type of analytics that used to be
only available to the biggest companies in the world can now be done by smaller companies. In order to mine hidden insights from data, enterprises have started leveraging
these Big Data systems. An important aspect is that the analysis of large amounts of
data may intensify the inferential power of algorithms that have shown to be successful
on modest-sized data sets. The real challenge is to develop and increase the theoretical
principles needed to scale inference and learning algorithms to massive scale [2]. On
the other hand, massive data analysis may amplify the error rates that are part of any
inferential algorithm. Thus, the challenge is to control such errors even in the face of the
heterogeneity and uncontrolled sampling processes underlying in many large data sets
[3].

This paper proposes an innovative data selection methodology that chooses the most
appropriate data to be used by forecasting methods. The data filtering process searches
for correlations in data, so that only the most relevant data is used in each context.
This way the use of data is adapted to each distinct situation, improving the forecasting
process by reducing the variability of the used data. The data filtering process also
provides its contribution by reducing the forecasting execution time by using less, but
more adequate data, in the training process. In this way, efficient contextual services are
enabled. The proposed methodology is based on a clustering process application to data
with an automatic evaluation. With this, training data for forecasting methods can be
chosen automatically according to the relevance and correlation of data for each given
problem, preventing the use of excessive and ambiguous data; and also preventing an
over-filtering of data that often comes from using only small amounts of highly correlated
data while discarding information that could be relevant but whose value is not easily
perceived.

After this introductory section, Sect. 2 presents the factory of the future project,
in which this work is framed. Section 3 presents the proposed methodology, including
the clustering process and the evaluation procedure. Some experimental findings are
presented in Sect. 4, where results from the use of Artificial Neural Networks (ANN)
and Support Vector Machines (SVM) to forecast electricity market prices are compared
when using the proposed methodology and when not using it. Finally, Sect. 5 presents
the conclusions and contributions of the presented work.

2 Continental Factory of the Future

With the advances of worldwide technological infrastructure, both in terms of software
and equipment, it is becoming possible to achieve levels of automation and advanced
decision making that were unthinkable in the past. Project Continental Factory of the
Future [4] is developing new solutions towards the modernization of factories activities. These include relevant aspects that include the operation, maintenance, stock
management, social aspects, and also energy efficiency and management.

Such improvement requires dealing with large amounts of real data from distinct sources and natures, which includes, as depicted by Fig. 1, data from the factory itself (data gathered from sensors, measured data and data from the internal management software systems) but also contextual data (e.g. weather data, electricity prices data among many others). It is, therefore, crucial that advanced models are developed to enable analyzing and processing these different data in a way that the relevant data in each moment can be identified and afterwards used by the diverse contextual services that provide support to the factory activities, e.g. for distributed product testing [5].

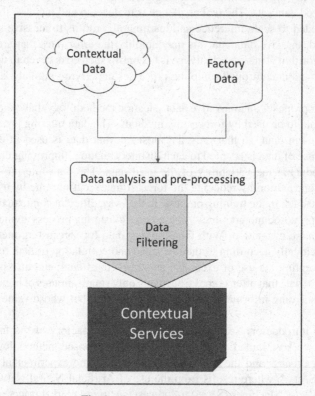

Fig. 1. Contextual data handling

In this specific work we are addressing the filtering of data related to electricity market prices as the way to enable improved forecasting of market prices as a contextual service. This process is described in Sect. 3.

3 Proposed Methodology

Large amounts of data from distinct natures with high associated variety are, nowadays, essential for the decision making process in the most diverse fields. Dealing with the so called Big Data brings an urgent need to manage all these data appropriately [6], in acceptable time frames, depending on each scope of application. Hence, data must be used wisely, since not all available data are necessary (or even useful) for specific decision making tasks. The need to filter and use the most appropriate data (most correlated, which present the bigger potential gain of information for solving each specific problem) becomes, therefore, essential.

Simple yet fast methods, which do not degrade the computational demand of the decision making methods themselves, are most likely to present good results in a Big Data scope. As Big Data is often associated to Big Gaps in Data, complex methods are not able to perform well, nor bring the necessary added value. Moreover, the execution time that is often required by complex methods to treat data before data are used by the decision support methods, is impracticable when dealing with large volumes of data, especially when fast responses are required.

The methodology proposed in this paper enables filtering the available data, with the aim of filtering the most significant data, so that it can be used by forecasting methods. This work accomplishes this goal by applying a clustering approach to divide the available data into different groups according to their similarity and correlation. The data clusters are then assessed, in order to guarantee the achievement of a suitable balance between the number of clusters and the data variability associated to this clustering process. This enables using the smaller possible number of clusters that allows the maximum data separation (least variability of data). When using a large number of clusters, the available data to train the forecasting methods decreases significantly. This causes a decrease in the effectiveness of the forecasting process. Alternatively, a low number of clusters leads to a very small separation of data, and to a consequent increase in the data variability. A suitable balance between the number of clusters and the associated variability is thereby crucial, aiming at reaching the smaller number of data clusters that results in the higher gain in terms of data variability reduction. The proposed methodology process is presented in Fig. 2.

From Fig. 2 it is visible that data that is gathered from multiple sources, and then integrated into a common data base originates a Big Data collection, with high associated variability. This raw data is, therefore, analysed by the proposed methodology, where a clustering process is applied. The clustering results are evaluated so that the balance between the number of data sub-groups and the gain in variability reduction can be optimized. The filtered data resulting from the data sub-group that contains the information most related to each distinct problem is finally used by the forecasting methodologies, so that an adequate forecast, using only the necessary data can be performed.

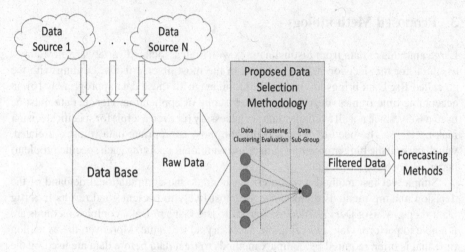

Fig. 2. Overview of the proposed methodology

The clustering model used in this work is the well-known K-Means algorithm [7], which enables separating data into different groups, each one containing samples with high similarity among each other but with big differences between different clusters. K-Means contemplates a set of n observations $(x_1, x_2,..., x_n)$, in which each is a d-dimensional real vector. The clustering process partitions the n observations into k ($\leq n$) clusters $C = \{C_1, C_2,..., C_k\}$ so that the Within-Cluster Sum of Squares (WCSS) is minimized.

In order to assess the quality of the clustering process, the Mean Index Adequacy (MIA) and Clustering Dispersion Indicator (CDI) are used [8].

4 Experimental Findings

The case study presented in this section has the goal of demonstrating the application of the proposed methodology to the problem of electricity market prices forecasting. With this objective, a data base containing real data from the Iberian electricity market operator – MIBEL [9] is used. These data are collected in real time by an automatic data extraction tool, which has been presented in [10]. This tool is connected to the websites of several electricity market operators, and extracts all kinds of data related to electricity markets, as they are made available. This means that data from diverse natures is constantly being gathered, in different timings, and added to the already stored data.

These experiments regard electricity market prices forecast considering both the forecasting accuracy and execution time. The forecasting models that are used are:

The proposed methodology is applied to the log of historic market prices, with the objective of filtering the data that will be used by an ANN – described in [11], and SVM – described in [12] in forecasting process. The used data set contains hourly electricity market prices from MIBEL ranging from January 2008 onwards (until September 2014). Figure 3 shows the clustering evaluation using MIA and CDI.

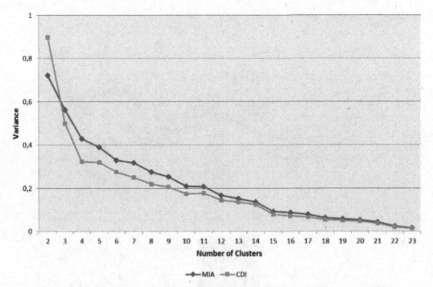

Fig. 3. MIA and CDI clustering evaluation for different numbers of clusters

From Fig. 3 three different "elbows", where data variance stabilizes, are clearly identified: using 4 clusters, 10 clusters, and 15 clusters. These three points present the transition points in which the variance decrease stabilizes; i.e. they represent the alternative ideal numbers of clusters that show the least variance between data, using the least number of data sub-groups.

Figure 4 presents the results of the clustering process using: a) 4 clusters, b) 10 clusters, and c) 15 clusters. These results show visually how data has been grouped, using a small exemplification group of 31 days, each containing 24 hourly periods. These 31 days are referent to the 31 days of January, 2014.

From Fig. 4 it is visible that the clustering process is able to group data according to its similarity. In Fig. 4a) it is visible a clear separation between the peak periods (where the market price is higher, namely hours 20 and 21); off-peak periods, between hours 2 and 7; mid-valued price periods, between hours 8 and 18, and hours 1 and 24; and near-peak periods, namely hours 19, 22 and 23. Using 10 and 15 clusters, as seen in Fig. 4b) and Fig. 4c) a more exhaustive separation is achieved, where the tendency of market prices in all days is captured. As mentioned before, the forecasting methodologies, using the proposed methodology, only consider data of each sub-group when performing a forecast for a corresponding hour. E.g. if performing a forecast for the electricity market price of hour 21, when using 4 clusters, only data referent to the historic market prices in hours 20 and 21 are considered; when considering 10 or 15 clusters, only data from previous days in hour 21 are considered. Table 1 presents a comparison of the average Mean Absolute Percentage Error (MAPE) and the execution time achieved by the forecasting process using the ANN and the SVM with and without the use of the proposed methodology, for a total of 2160 day-ahead forecasts (considering the individual forecast of each of the 24 h of 90 days).

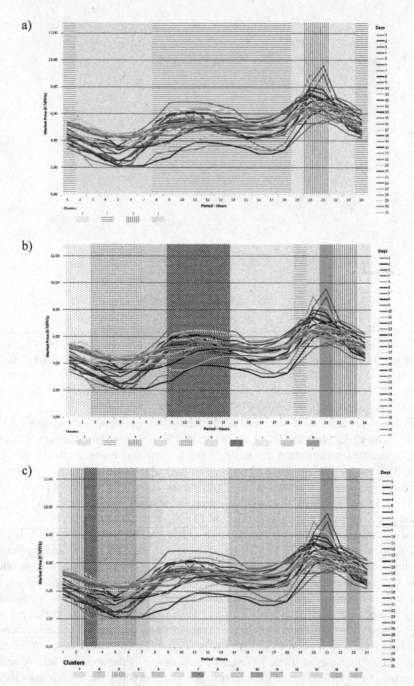

Fig. 4. Data grouping resulting from the clustering process using: a) 4 clusters, b) 10 clusters, c) 15 clusters

Table 1. ANN and SVM MAPE forecast error (%) and execution time (m.s.)

	ANN		SVM	
	MAPE	Time	MAPE	Time
Without proposed model	0,096	18314	0,095	5107
With proposed model (4 clusters)	0,088	13701	0,089	4941

Table 1 shows that the forecast error is smaller when using the proposed methodology for both ANN and SVM. It is also visible that the execution time when using the proposed methodology is lower for both forecasting models, benefiting from the use of less, but more adequate data, in the training process.

5 Conclusions

This paper presents a data selection methodology with the objective of filtering data before its use by complementary forecasting methodologies. The data filtering process aims at searching for correlations in data, so that only the most relevant data is used in each context; this way adapting the use of data to each distinct situation, with the intention of improving the forecasting process by reducing the variability of data. Additionally, the aim is also placed on reducing the forecasting execution time by using less, but more adequate data, in the training process.

Results have shown an increase of the forecasting efficiency through the decrease of the forecasting execution time. Besides resulting in an increase of computational efficiency, the proposed methodology also provides an increase of forecasting effectiveness, as demonstrated in the experimental findings section, showing that an adequate data selection according to the requirements of each distinct situation is able to improve the forecasting quality by reducing the amount of redundant data, hence focusing only on the data that matters the most in each context.

Acknowledgements. This work was supported by the I&D Project "DEoLTA: Digitalisation of end-of-line distributed testers for antennas, operação POCI-01-0247-FEDER-049698", financed by the Fundos Europeus Estruturais e de Investimento (FEEI), through the Program "Programa Operacional Competitividade e Internacionalização(POCI)/PORTUGAL 2020". This work has also received funding from the EU Horizon 2020 research and innovation program under project TradeRES (grant agreement No 864276). The authors acknowledge the work facilities and equipment provided by GECAD research center (UIDB/00760/2020) to the project team.

References

1. Markets and Markets. Big Data Market, report. https://www.marketsandmarkets.com/Top100 UseCases/big_data_and_analytics.html. Accessed August 2022
2. Chen, J., Wu, T.: A computational intelligence optimization algorithm: cloud drops algorithm. Integr. Comput.-Aided Eng. **21**(2), 177–188 (2014)

3. Li, X., Jiao, H., Li, D.: Intelligent medical heterogeneous big data set balanced clustering using deep learning. Pattern Recogn. Lett. **138**, 548–555 (2020)
4. Continental FoF: Continental AA's Factory of the Future, POCI-01-0247-FEDER-047512. https://transparencia.gov.pt/pt/fundos-europeus/beneficiarios-projetos/projeto/POCI-01-0247-FEDER-047512. Accessed August 2022
5. D-EoL-TA: Digitalisation of end-of-line distributed testers for antennas, operação POCI-01-0247-FEDER-049698. https://transparencia.gov.pt/pt/fundos-europeus/beneficiarios-pro jetos/projeto/POCI-01-0247-FEDER-049698. Accessed August 2022
6. Schrage, M.: How is big data transforming your 80/20 analytics? Harv. Bus. Rev. (2013)
7. Jain, A.K.: Data clustering: 50 years beyond K-means. Pattern Recogn. Lett. **31**(8), 651–666 (2010)
8. Ribeiro, C., et al.: Data mining for remuneration of consumers demand response participation. In: De La Prieta, F., et al. (eds.) PAAMS 2020. Communications in Computer and Information Science, vol. 1233, pp. 326–338. Springer, Cham (2020). https://doi.org/10.1007/978-3-030-51999-5_27
9. MIBEL - Iberian Electricity Market Operator. http://www.omie.es. Accessed August 2022
10. Pereira, R., Sousa, T.M., Pinto, T., Praça, I., Vale, Z., Morais, H.: Strategic bidding for electricity markets negotiation using support vector machines. In: Bajo Perez, J., et al. (eds.) Trends in Practical Applications of Heterogeneous Multi-Agent Systems. The PAAMS Collection. AISC, vol. 293, pp. 9–17. Springer, Cham (2014). https://doi.org/10.1007/978-3-319-07476-4_2
11. Pinto, T., et.al.: Dynamic artificial neural network for electricity market prices forecast. In: IEEE 16th International Conference on Intelligent Engineering Systems (INES 2012), Costa de Caparica, Portugal, 13–15 June 2012
12. Pinto, T., et al.: Support vector machines for decision support in electricity markets' strategic bidding. Neurocomputing **172**, 438–445 (2016)

Method for Assessing Objective Video Quality for Automatic License Plate Recognition Tasks

Mikołaj Leszczuk[1]([⊠])(ID), Lucjan Janowski[1](ID), Jakub Nawała[1](ID), and Atanas Boev[2]

[1] AGH University of Science and Technology, Kraków, Poland
{leszczuk,qoe}@agh.edu.pl
[2] Huawei Technologies Dusseldorf GmbH, Düsseldorf, Germany
atanas.boev@huawei.com
https://qoe.agh.edu.pl/

Abstract. In the modern era, there are numerous metrics for overall Quality of Experience (QoE), both those with Full Reference (FR), such as Peak Signal-to-Noise Ratio (PSNR) or Structural Similarity (SSIM), and those with No Reference (NR), such as Video Quality Indicators (VQI), that are successfully used in video processing systems to assess videos whose quality is diminished by various processing scenarios. However, they are not appropriate for video sequences used for jobs that require recognition (Target Recognition Videos, TRV). As a result, a significant research problem remains to accurately assess the performance of the video processing pipeline in both human and Computer Vision (CV) recognition tasks. For recognition tasks, there is a need for objective ways to assess video quality. In this research, we demonstrate that it is feasible to create a novel idea of an objective model to assess video quality for automatic licence plate recognition (ALPR) tasks in response to this demand. A representative set of image sequences is used to train, test, and validate the model. The collection of degradation scenarios is based on a digital camera model and how a scene's luminous flux eventually transforms into a digital image. The generated degraded images are evaluated for ALPR and VQI using a CV library. The value of the F-measure parameter of 0.777 represents the measured accuracy of a model.

Keywords: Video Quality Indicators (VQI) · Target Recognition Video (TRV) · Computer Vision (CV) · Metrics · Evaluation

1 Introduction

The quality of entertainment videos and Target Recognition Videos (TRV) is not the same. Due to the use of TRV, the qualitative evaluation examines how the subject uses TRV to complete specific tasks rather than how satisfied they are with the quality of the video sequence [11]. These jobs could involve things like: video surveillance—identifying licence plates; telemedicine/remote diagnostics—accurate diagnosis; fire safety—fire detection; rear-view cameras—parking the car; gaming—identification and proper retaliation against virtual foe; video messaging and report generation - video summarization [2,4]. Research has been done on the content factors that most affect

© The Author(s), under exclusive license to Springer Nature Switzerland AG 2022
A. Dziech et al. (Eds.): MCSS 2022, CCIS 1689, pp. 153–166, 2022.
https://doi.org/10.1007/978-3-031-20215-5_13

perceived quality in entertainment videos. Through the use of subjective tests and these criteria, predictors can be developed, leading to the development of objective measurements. However, recognition tasks are not suitable for this system. Therefore, we must create new ones. The methods used to gauge a video's quality are just one aspect of the issue. It is also important to consider the circumstances surrounding the video's capture. To conduct a reliable experiment, exposure, ISO, ocular acuity, bit rate, and many other factors must be considered.

In the past, any quality evaluation has been done using subjective techniques, that is, by using human participants in psychophysical studies. The coauthors of this paper have also participated in such work, which has led to, among other things, the particular ITU-T Recommendation [13]. However, such an evaluation takes a lot of time and effort. As a result, quality modelling metrics have a tendency to take the role of psychophysical studies. These days, a variety of metrics for general Quality of Experience (QoE), including those with Full Reference (FR), like Peak Signal-to-Noise Ratio (PSNR) or Structural Similarity (SSIM), and those with No Reference (NR), like Video Quality Indicators (VQI), are successfully used in video processing systems to assess entertainment video quality. However, when dealing with video sequences used for recognition tasks, they are not appropriate (TRV). As a result, both in manual and Computer Vision (CV) recognition tasks, accurately assessing the performance of video processing pipelines remains a major difficulty for academics. An impartial approach is required to assess the quality of the video for recognition tasks.

Applications of such an objective technique to evaluate video quality for recognition tasks can be quite useful. For example, neural network (NN) algorithms used in smart cars are often trained on high-quality data taken in ideal circumstances. It is difficult to foresee how a real car on the road could be required to operate in a wide range of less-than-ideal situations and how that might affect the network's output. When the input quality is insufficient for adequate NN performance, we would like to provide a warning to the driver to avoid catastrophic failures. We create and test a crucial component of a system that can forecast machine vision performance based on the calibre of the input stream in this study to address this demand. The purpose of this work is to demonstrate that it is feasible to develop an accurate model that predicts the efficiency of TRV processing pipelines.

At this point, it is important to emphasise how unique our work is from the most recent efforts of others in the field. Shi et al. [24], suggesting a novel method and data set to evaluate the video quality of damaged recordings. Although this work is related to TRV, the data modality is very different from our case. Shi et al. (this study is a winner of the NIST Enhancing Computer Vision for Public Safety Challenge Prize) focus on public safety, whereas we concentrate on Automatic Number-Plate Recognition (ALPR) jobs. Similarly, Xing et al. [26] address a topic that appears to be related (TRV), but put more emphasis on identifying and categorising specific fusion traces (process windows in selective laser melting). Laparoscopic pictures are another area of TRV quality assessment that is the subject of extensive research. A paper by Khan et al. [9] is a very recent example. Hofbauer et al. [5] published a database of encrypted photos with arbitrary ground truth for recognition. Although the stated study is from a related field to ours, it exclusively addresses distortions in picture encryption. A continuous blind (NR) prediction of image quality using a cascaded deep neural network is what Wu et al. [25] suggests. The deep convolutional neural network (CNN) used to evaluate the quality of picture recognition has had significant success. Wu et al. use the Mean Opinion Score (MOS) to represent quality; however, they do not assess how the individual applies TRV to particular tasks. Both Oszust [22] and Mahankali [17] present NR assessments of video quality using voxel-wise visual cortex fMRI models. Oszust proposes a local feature descriptor and derived filters for NR assessment of image quality. In conclusion, it is important to mention the review of modern techniques for objectively evaluating video quality in recognition tasks that we presented in the paper at [8]. This paper discusses older related solutions created by several research teams.

The remainder of this paper is provided. The necessary experimental study design is presented in Sect. 2. The creation of a corpus of Source Reference Circuits (SRC), which are original video sequences made from previously shot material, is included in Subsect. 2.1. Subsection 2.2 entails creating a collection of Hypothetical Reference Circuits (HRC), which represent various cases of video degradation. The experiments that produce the quality data and the recognition data are included in the Subsects. 2.3 and 2.4, respectively. We can create a model that predicts the recognition outcomes based on video quality indicators, since we have two sets of data (from the quality experiment and the recognition experiment). Section 3 contains a report of the results. The conclusion of this work is found in Sect. 4.

2 Materials and Methods

An overview of the research is given in this section. A source data set (Source Reference Circuits, SRCs, Subsect. 2.1) and a few distortion types (Hypothetical Reference Circuits, HRCs, Subsect. 2.2) are included in the experiment. With each HRC, one degrades each SRC. Both an ALPR computer vision library (Subsect. 2.3) and a VQI (Subsect. 2.4) are used to assess the output sequences.

2.1 Acquisition of the Existing Source Reference Circuits (SRC)

In this subsection, a technical description of the chosen SRCs is provided, which also presents the customised data set used for this investigation. The video that makes up a corpus of original SRC video sequences is already on hand.

The SRC database includes a number of chosen video frames. The creation of a database that covers as many different features as possible was the selection criterion. We have included a description of the data set in the following section.

For the experiment, we used only a portion of the SRC set as a whole. However, figuring out the subset's size is the first step in choosing a subset of SRC. For this purpose, it is assumed that one training experiment, one optional follow-up training experiment, and one testing experiment (model validation) are performed. We arbitrarily decide that the test set has numerous elements that are roughly equivalent to one-fourth of the size of a single training experiment, while the first and second training experiments have sets of equal numbers of elements.

Another presumption is that an experiment iteration cannot take more than a week (due to practical considerations). Since test sets are four times smaller than training sets, this assumption de facto affects how many components there are in the training set.

It is important to note at this point that the number of images used in each experiment is significantly influenced by the processing time of a single image. This period includes the combined image processing results of the Quality Experiment (Subsect. 2.4) and the Recognition Experiment (Subsect. 2.3) of the experiment. We can estimate the number of images that can be processed per week or the number of images that can be used in one experiment iteration, by knowing the average time needed to perform the Quality Experiment for one image and the average time needed to perform the Recognition Experiment for one image.

It is also important to note that the quantity specified by the aforementioned approach refers to the usable Processed Video Sequence (PVS) images rather than the quantity of usable SRC images. We divide the number of viable PVS images by the number of HRCs defined to determine the number of usable SRC images. There are 64 HRCs (plus one SRC).

Moving on to precise values, it is found that the Quality Experiment's average processing time for one image is in the range of hundreds of seconds. The average image processing time of the Recognition Experiment is less than one second, making it comparatively insignificant.

According to the aforementioned, it is possible to process PVS images based on 120 SRC images during the week, which allows the preparation of 80 SRC images for the training experiment, 20 (quarter) additional SRC images for the test experiment, and 20 (quarter) additional SRC images for the validation. Every SRC picture has a single recognisable object (a licence plate). There are 120 objects in total.

A validation set is prepared, as previously indicated, but is left momentarily unprocessed. The size of this set is the same as the corresponding size of the test set.

The source of the complete data set for ALPR is CCTV **Source Reference Circuits (SRC video sequences)** collected at the AGH University of Science and Technology, Krakow, Lesser Poland, by filming parking during high traffic hours [15]. **The data set contains video sequences, containing approximately 15,500 frames in total.** Figure 1 presents the selected SRC frame.

The whole set is subsampled, resulting in 120 images divided into a training set, a test set, and a validation set, in a ratio of 80 vs. 20 vs. 20, respectively. Figure 2 presents the montage of selected SRC frames for ALPR.

2.2   Preparation of Hypothetical Reference Circuits (HRC)

Scenarios for degradation are described in this subsection (i.e., Hypothetical Reference Circuits or HRCs). Various distortions related to the entire digital image capture pipeline are included in the proposed collection of HRCs. The choice of HRC is significant, as it determines whether the quality assessment approach suggested in this paper may be used.

The HRC set is based on how a digital image is ultimately created using a camera's luminous flux that is reflected from the scene. Light may already be reduced before it reaches the lens elements, for example, due to inappropriate exposure to photographic

Fig. 1. Frame of the AGH data set for video quality assessment in plate recognition.

Fig. 2. The montage of selected SRC frames for ALPR.

illumination. The aperture can blur the image and cause the light beam to pass through out-of-focus lens elements (defocus aberration). The light flux then strikes an electronic sensor with a limited amount of resolution. Gaussian noise may once again come from additional analogue-to-digital conversion and signal amplification stages. Additionally, it is possible that a long exposure period will result in the motion blur effect. JPEG compression may produce artefacts in the last stage of processing.

Figure 3 shows the distortion model.

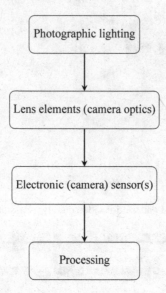

Fig. 3. Model of distortion based on the transformation of the scene's luminous flux into a digital image.

The HRCs that we choose are as follows:

- HRC related to photographic lighting:
    (1) Image under/overexposure
- HRC related to lens elements (camera optics):
    (2) Defocus (blur)
- HRC related to electronic (camera) sensor(s):
    (3) Gaussian noise
    (4) Motion blur
- HRC related to processing:
    (5) JPEG compression

We choose to apply HRC using FFmpeg and ImageMagick, respectively, from the websites [1] and [6]. They already have a selection of pertinent filters. To create all distortions, we use them. The former tool is used to apply Gaussian noise and under-/overexposure to images. The latter tool is used to perform JPEG compression, mimic motion blur degradation, and apply defocus distortion.

When one tests the tools' computation speed using the worst-case scenario (activating all filters), they come up with a result of 439 frames per minute. This test is carried out using a typical laptop (Intel i5 - 3317U and 16 GB of RAM).

The thresholds for various distortions are presented in Table 1 (listed in rows). They are typically calculated to establish the location (HRC value) for which there is zero recognition (this place is the penultimate step; for safety, we include one more step). The progression is linear.

Table 1. Limits for particular hypothetical reference circuits (HRC) - distortions (listed in rows)

HRC	Unit	Min	Max
Under-Exposure	FFmpeg filter parameter	0	−0.6
Over-Exposure	FFmpeg filter parameter	0	0.6
Defocus (Blur)	ImageMagick filter parameter	0	6
Gaussian Noise	FFmpeg filter parameter	0	48
Motion Blur	ImageMagick filter parameter	0	18
JPEG	ImageMagick filter parameter	0	100

The distortions are shown in Table 2. The anticipated number of distortion intensity levels is also provided for each type of distortion. As one can see, most of these distortions have 6 levels. The only exceptions are JPEG and exposure, which need twice as many levels of distortion because of their bidirectional nature. Additionally, there are only 5 levels in the event of a combination of distortions (the last three rows in the table, constituting a separate subsection), since we already produce the extreme levels while generating a single distortion (previous subsection in the table).

Table 2. Distortions caused by Hypothetical Reference Circuits (HRCs)

HRC	#HRC
Over/Under-Exposure (Photography)	12
Defocus (Blur)	6
Gaussian Noise	6
Motion Blur	6
JPEG	19
Motion Blur + Gaussian Noise	5
Over-Exposure + Gaussian Noise	5
Under-Exposure + Motion Blur	5
#PVS	**6720**

The order in which the distortions are applied matters when using a mixture of distortions.

- For Motion Blur + Gaussian Noise, we apply Motion Blur first.
- For Over-Exposure + Gaussian Noise, we apply Over-Exposure first.

– For Under-Exposure + Motion Blur, we apply Motion Blur first (however, the more appropriate order should be: Under-Exposure first, but we reversed the order for technical reasons caused by possible interpolation problems).

Of course, there should be one more "distortion" added to the list, that is, "no distortion" (pure SRC). In conclusion, there are 64 HRC versions (**plus one** SRC).

Real video processing can start once the SRC is ready and the HRC has been established. This creates a corpus of processed video sequences, or PVSs, which are SRC images that have been degraded using HRC degradation scenarios. PVS corpus is what is anticipated to happen.

2.3 Recognition Experiment

Each PVS obtained consists of a single frame. An ALPR system is used for such a frame.

OpenALPR library, written in C++, ensures ALPR. The library analyses pictures and videos to detect and recognise licence plates. The algorithm works with all types of images, but also with videos. Divide a video file into single frames and every frame is subject to detection and recognition. Finally, it returns ten possible licence plates with calculated confidence. Additionally, there is the possibility of saving the JSON file with the coordinates of the detected licence plate. Besides, as is known, licence plates in the world are different, so to increase confidence and efficiency, OpenALPR provides country code option which limits the comparison of plates to region, e.g. EU or US.

We need to know how long it takes for all ALPR processes to compute to determine how many SRCs we can test, as we said earlier. The ALPR computer vision algorithm typically takes 0.21 s to complete one video frame. Importantly, the Intel Core i5-8600K CPU of a computer is used to measure execution times.

2.4 Quality Experiment

With one exception (Temporal Activity VQI), the experiment only applies to individual video frames. A vector of results (one for each VQI) is produced when a set of VQIs is applied. Later, the results will be mixed with those from the recognition test. They will form the modelling input data when combined.

In total, we are using 19 VQIs. Eleven (11) of them come from our AGH Video Quality (VQ) team (Commercial Black, Blockiness [23], Block Loss [12], Blur [21,23], Contrast, Exposure [10], Interlacing [7], Noise [7], Slice [12], Spatial Activity [23], Temporal Activity [23]). Other eight (8) come from external laboratories (LIVE: BIQI [20], BRISQUE [18], NIQE [19], OG-IQA [16], FFRIQUEE [3], IL-NIQE [29]; UMI-ACS: CORNIA [28]; BUPT: HOSA [27]). Depending on VQI, we use the MATLAB or C/C++ code.

3   Results

The results of creating a new objective video quality assessment model for ALPR assignments are presented in this section.

We can build models that predict recognition results based on VQIs due to the two datasets (originating from the quality experiment and the recognition experiment, respectively). The result is a new quality model. Importantly, a model like this can be applied even when there is no target to identify. The information of a recognition algorithm and the model information can both change.

We model data from two groups of VQIs. All VQIs, both our own and those provided by other parties, are included in the first group and are designated as "All metrics". The second category consists entirely of our VQI, which we designate as "only ours".

We assumed classification into two classes (the licence plate was recognised; the licence plate was not recognised). Also, we assumed (much more difficult) classification into five classes (the licence plate was recognised, the licence plate was recognised with one error, the licence plate was identified with two errors, the licence plate was identified with three errors, and the licence plate was not recognised).

We have obtained the following (Table 3) results for 2 classes[1].

Table 3. General results we received for ALPR for 2 classes.

	Precision	Recall	F-measure
All metrics	0.779	0.776	0.777
Only ours	0.758	0.759	0.764

We have obtained the following (Table 4) results for 5 classes.

Table 4. General results we received for ALPR for 5 classes.

	Precision	Recall	F-measure
All metrics	0.415	0.425	0.407
Only ours	0.401	0.405	0.394

The results for the test set are much worse, even when we consider that the results for the validation set are not that good. The main reason is the powerful influence of the source. It seems to be much more critical than the distortion itself. It is cognitive thinking that gives us the opportunity to miss "D" and "O" compared to some other more original letters like "K".

For the model with two classes and all metrics, the results obtained for the test set are not very good. The chance of correctly detecting is around 2/3; see Tables 5 and 6.

For the model with five classes and all metrics, the results obtained for the test are the best for two main classes, which is reasonable, since the largest number of cases represents them. Only for the class, with no plate detected, can we see a reasonable correct classification; see Tables 7 and 8.

---

[1] The meaning of headers in columns is explained in: https://scikit-learn.org/stable/modules/generated/sklearn.metrics.precision_recall_fscore_support.html.

Table 5. Confusion matrix for the test set, ALPR scenario, all metrics, and two classes.

		Algorithm	
		Not more than 2 err.	Other cases
Truth	Not more than 2 err.	292	302
	Other cases	138	628

Table 6. Performance parameters for the test set, ALPR scenario, all metrics, and two classes.

	Precision	Recall	F-measure	Support
Not more than 2 err.	0.679	0.492	0.570	594
Other cases	0.675	0.820	0.741	766
Macro average	0.677	0.656	0.655	1360
Weighted average	0.677	0.676	0.666	1360

Table 7. Confusion matrix for the test set, ALPR scenario, all metrics, and five classes.

		Algorithm				
		Correct rec.	1 err.	2 err.	3+ err.	No detection
Truth	Correct rec.	190	30	21	6	29
	1 err.	109	48	14	11	43
	2 err.	22	24	14	4	29
	3+ err.	25	16	6	6	43
	No detection	101	102	12	23	432

Table 8. Performance parameters for the test set, ALPR scenario, all metrics, and five classes.

	Precision	Recall	F-measure	Support
Correct rec.	0.425	0.688	0.526	276
1 err.	0.218	0.213	0.216	225
2 err.	0.209	0.151	0.175	93
3+ err.	0.120	0.062	0.082	96
No detection	0.750	0.645	0.693	670
Macro average	0.344	0.352	0.338	1360
Weighted average	0.515	0.507	0.502	1360

For the model with two classes and AGH metrics, the results obtained are very similar to the results obtained for all classes; see Tables 9 and 10.

For the model with five classes and AGH metrics, the results are again similar to the one obtained for all metrics, see Tables 11 and 12.

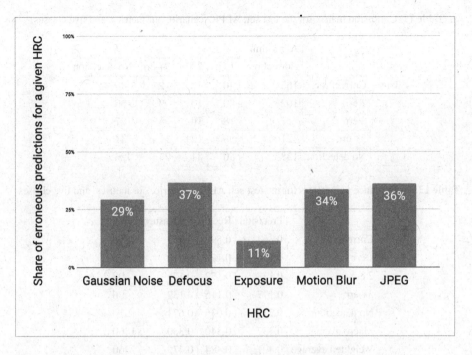

Fig. 4. Share of erroneous predictions for a given HRC in ALPR scenario.

Table 9. Confusion matrix for the test set, ALPR scenario, our metrics, and two classes.

		Algorithm	
		Not more than 2 errors	Other cases
Truth	Not more than 2 errors	232	362
	Other cases	118	648

Table 10. Performance parameters for the test set, ALPR scenario, our metrics, and two classes.

	Precision	Recall	F-measure	Support
Not more than 2 errors	0.663	0.391	0.492	594
Other cases	0.642	0.846	0.730	766
Macro average	0.652	0.618	0.611	1360
Weighted average	0.651	0.647	0.626	1360

Numerical analysis was performed to verify the sensitivity of the model to individual distortions. Figure 4 shows the share of erroneous predictions for a given HRC (the analysis was carried out for the case of using the model of using all metrics; the analysis for a subset of metrics showed practically very similar results).

Table 11. Confusion matrix for the test set, ALPR scenario, our metrics, and five classes.

		Algorithm				
		Correct rec.	1 err.	2 err.	3+ err.	No detection
Truth	Correct rec.	165	40	13	12	46
	1 err.	102	40	18	9	56
	2 err.	27	18	16	5	27
	3+ err.	21	8	12	11	44
	No detection	138	50	31	25	426

Table 12. Performance parameters for the test set, ALPR scenario, our metrics, and five classes.

	Precision	Recall	F-measure	Support
Correct rec.	0.364	0.598	0.453	276
1 err.	0.256	0.178	0.210	225
2 err.	0.178	0.172	0.175	93
3+ err.	0.177	0.115	0.139	96
No detection	0.711	0.636	0.671	670
Macro average	0.337	0.340	0.330	1360
Weighted average	0.491	0.484	0.479	1360

As one can see, for the Gaussian Noise, Defocus, Motion Blur, and JPEG HRCs, the model shows quite similar error sensitivity – it is wrong in about 30% of the cases. The exception is Exposure HRC, for which the model is much less mistaken, only for 11% cases. For JPEG artefacts, the model does not work correctly.

4   Conclusions

In this study, we demonstrate that it is possible to implement the novel idea of an objective model to assess the quality of the video for ALPR tasks. The model accuracy (F-measure parameter) value attained is 0.777.

The best modelling results are achieved when all potential VQIs (VQIs from AGH and other research teams) are used. However, it is important to note that the limitation of AGH VQI does not result in a material reduction in prediction accuracy (F-measure of 0.764).

It is important to note the root of the most frequent issues that the models run into while working. Our findings imply that one significant factor inducing the models' deception is the starting scene's attributes. This component, which has a significant effect on the recognition accuracy, is completely ignored by VQI.

Of course, the limitations of the proposed method must be mentioned. The technique has been tested on a particular dataset, with a particular set of visual distortions, and with a particular ALPR system. Furthermore, although the model is probably generalisable to other sets of licence plates, perhaps to other image distortions, and even to other ALPR systems, it is unquestionably not generalisable to other image recognition systems (such as face recognition systems or object recognition systems), as is clear from other studies (only partially published studies [14]) studies by the authors. The resultant model cannot be easily compared with other approaches for the same reason. Other published approaches, as noted in the Introduction, mainly concentrate on a completely new data modality and various recognition systems.

Acknowledgements. This research received funding from the Huawei Innovation Research Programme (HIRP).

References

1. FFmpeg: FFmpeg (2019). https://ffmpeg.org/. Accessed 04 June 2019
2. Garcia-Zapirain, B., et al.: A proposed methodology for subjective evaluation of video and text summarization. In: Choroś, K., Kopel, M., Kukla, E., Siemiński, A. (eds.) MISSI 2018. AISC, vol. 833, pp. 396–404. Springer, Cham (2019). https://doi.org/10.1007/978-3-319-98678-4_40
3. Ghadiyaram, D., Bovik, A.C.: Perceptual quality prediction on authentically distorted images using a bag of features approach. J. Vis. **17**(1), 32 (2017)
4. Grega, M., et al.: An integrated AMIS prototype for automated summarization and translation of newscasts and reports. In: Choroś, K., Kopel, M., Kukla, E., Siemiński, A. (eds.) MISSI 2018. AISC, vol. 833, pp. 415–423. Springer, Cham (2019). https://doi.org/10.1007/978-3-319-98678-4_42
5. Hofbauer, H., Autrusseau, F., Uhl, A.: To recognize or not to recognize-a database of encrypted images with subjective recognition ground truth. Inf. Sci. **551**, 128–145 (2021)
6. ImageMagick Studio LLC: ImageMagick: Convert, Edit, Or Compose Bitmap Images (2011). https://imagemagick.org/index.php, https://www.imagemagick.org/script/index.php
7. Janowski, L., Papir, Z.: Modeling subjective tests of quality of experience with a generalized linear model. In: 2009 International Workshop on Quality of Multimedia Experience, pp. 35–40. IEEE (2009)
8. Kawa, K., Leszczuk, M., Boev, A.: Survey on the state-of-the-art methods for objective video quality assessment in recognition tasks. In: Dziech, A., Mees, W., Czyżewski, A. (eds.) MCSS 2020. CCIS, vol. 1284, pp. 332–350. Springer, Cham (2020). https://doi.org/10.1007/978-3-030-59000-0_25
9. Khan, Z.A., et al.: Towards a video quality assessment based framework for enhancement of laparoscopic videos. In: Medical Imaging 2020: Image Perception, Observer Performance, and Technology Assessment, vol. 11316, p. 113160P. International Society for Optics and Photonics (2020)
10. Leszczuk, M.: Assessing task-based video quality—a journey from subjective psychophysical experiments to objective quality models. In: Dziech, A., Czyżewski, A. (eds.) MCSS 2011. CCIS, vol. 149, pp. 91–99. Springer, Heidelberg (2011). https://doi.org/10.1007/978-3-642-21512-4_11
11. Leszczuk, M.: Revising and improving the ITU-T recommendation p. 912. J. Telecommun. Inf. Technol. (2015)
12. Leszczuk, M., Hanusiak, M., Farias, M.C., Wyckens, E., Heston, G.: Recent developments in visual quality monitoring by key performance indicators. Multimed. Tools Appl. **75**(17), 10745–10767 (2016)

13. Leszczuk, M., Janowski, L.: Selected aspects of the new recommendation on subjective methods of assessing video quality in recognition tasks. In: Paszkiel, S. (ed.) ICBCI 2021. AISC, vol. 1362, pp. 246–254. Springer, Cham (2021). https://doi.org/10.1007/978-3-030-72254-8_27

14. Leszczuk, M., Janowski, L., Nawała, J., Boev, A.: Objective video quality assessment method for face recognition tasks. Electronics **11**(8), 1167 (2022)

15. Leszczuk, M., Janowski, L., Romaniak, P., Głowacz, A., Mirek, R.: Quality assessment for a licence plate recognition task based on a video streamed in limited networking conditions. In: Dziech, A., Czyżewski, A. (eds.) MCSS 2011. CCIS, vol. 149, pp. 10–18. Springer, Heidelberg (2011). https://doi.org/10.1007/978-3-642-21512-4_2

16. Liu, L., Hua, Y., Zhao, Q., Huang, H., Bovik, A.C.: Blind image quality assessment by relative gradient statistics and adaboosting neural network. Signal Process.: Image Commun. **40**, 1–15 (2016)

17. Mahankali, N.S., Raghavan, M., Channappayya, S.S.: No-reference video quality assessment using voxel-wise fMRI models of the visual cortex. IEEE Signal Process. Lett. **29**, 319–323 (2021)

18. Mittal, A., Moorthy, A.K., Bovik, A.C.: No-reference image quality assessment in the spatial domain. IEEE Trans. Image Process. **21**(12), 4695–4708 (2012)

19. Mittal, A., Soundararajan, R., Bovik, A.C.: Making a "completely blind" image quality analyzer. IEEE Signal Process. Lett. **20**(3), 209–212 (2012)

20. Moorthy, A.K., Bovik, A.C.: A two-step framework for constructing blind image quality indices. IEEE Signal Process. Lett. **17**(5), 513–516 (2010)

21. Mu, M., Romaniak, P., Mauthe, A., Leszczuk, M., Janowski, L., Cerqueira, E.: Framework for the integrated video quality assessment. Multimed. Tools Appl. **61**(3), 787–817 (2012)

22. Oszust, M.: Local feature descriptor and derivative filters for blind image quality assessment. IEEE Signal Process. Lett. **26**(2), 322–326 (2019)

23. Romaniak, P., Janowski, L., Leszczuk, M., Papir, Z.: Perceptual quality assessment for H. 264/AVC compression. In: 2012 IEEE consumer communications and networking conference (CCNC), pp. 597–602. IEEE (2012)

24. Shi, H., Liu, C.: An innovative video quality assessment method and an impairment video dataset. In: 2021 IEEE International Conference on Imaging Systems and Techniques (IST), pp. 1–6. IEEE (2021)

25. Wu, J., Ma, J., Liang, F., Dong, W., Shi, G., Lin, W.: End-to-end blind image quality prediction with cascaded deep neural network. IEEE Trans. Image Process. **29**, 7414–7426 (2020)

26. Xing, W., et al.: Recognition and classification of single melt tracks using deep neural network: a fast and effective method to determine process windows in selective laser melting. J. Manuf. Process. **68**, 1746–1757 (2021)

27. Xu, J., Ye, P., Li, Q., Du, H., Liu, Y., Doermann, D.: Blind image quality assessment based on high order statistics aggregation. IEEE Trans. Image Process. **25**(9), 4444–4457 (2016)

28. Ye, P., Kumar, J., Kang, L., Doermann, D.: Unsupervised feature learning framework for no-reference image quality assessment. In: 2012 IEEE Conference on Computer Vision and Pattern Recognition, pp. 1098–1105. IEEE (2012)

29. Zhang, L., Zhang, L., Bovik, A.C.: A feature-enriched completely blind image quality evaluator. IEEE Trans. Image Process. **24**(8), 2579–2591 (2015)

Author Index

Armenia, Stefano   104

Babeshko, Ievgen   66
Barroso, João   126
Beumier, Charles   11
Boev, Atanas   153
Bogacki, Piotr   104
Bojilova, Maya   104
Bozhilova, Maya   49

Carvalho, Diana   126
Ceresola, Cyril   104
Chechile, Giuseppe   104
Chmiel, Wojciech   80
Colabuono, Consuelo   104

de La Vallée, Paloma   21
Debatty, Thibault   11
Depaix, Grégory   104
Derkacz, Jan   104
Dri, Marco   21, 104
Dziech, Andrzej   49, 104

Feletto, Riccardo   104
Fesenko, Herman   66

Gonzalez-Garcia, Abel   118
Guarino, Andrea   104

Illiashenko, Oleg   66
Iosifidis, Georgios   21

Janowski, Lucjan   153
Jędrusik, Stanisław   80

Kadłuczka, Piotr   80
Kharchenko, Vyacheslav   66
Konieczna, Ewa   104
Kwiecień, Joanna   80

Leszczuk, Mikołaj   153
Letra, Pedro   126
Lofù, Domenico   104

Marabello, Maria Vittoria   104
Mees, Wim   21
Mikrut, Zbigniew   80
Modica, Paolo   104

Nawała, Jakub   153
Nguyen, Hong-Nhu   1
Nguyen, Nhat-Tien   1
Niemiec, Marcin   49, 94

Opic, Bernard   104

Pałka, Dariusz   80
Pappalardo, Marco   104
Pappalardo, Salvatore Marco   49
Pinto, Tiago   144

Quartullo, Marco   104

Rapone, Raniero   104
Ravenna, Massimo   104
Reis, Arsénio   126, 144
Rocha, Tânia   126, 144
Rossi, Andrea   21
Ruoslahti, Harri   36

Sanchez, Luis Angel Galindo   104, 118
Sansebastiano, Emanuele   104
Stiller, Burkhard   49
Stoianov, Nikolai   49
Stypiński, Miłosz   94

Tarquini, Massimiliano   104
Tikanmäki, Ilkka   36
Turek, Michał   80

Vale, Zita   144
Voznak, Miroslav   1

Wiemer, Douglas   104

Zamagni, Massimo   104

Printed in the United States
by Baker & Taylor Publisher Services